D1398107

EXPERIMENTAL
PSYCHOPATHOLOGY

Officers of the
AMERICAN PSYCHOPATHOLOGICAL ASSOCIATION
for 1955

Merrill Moore, M.D., *President*

Oskar Diethelm, M.D., *President-Elect*

Howard S. Liddell, Ph.D., *Vice-President*

Donald M. Hamilton, M.D., *Secretary*

Bernard Glueck, Jr., M.D., *Treasurer*

David McK. Rioch, M.D., *Councillor*

Nathan M. Ackerman, M.D., *Councillor*

Committee on Program

Paul H. Hoch, M.D., *Chairman*

Oskar Diethelm, M.D.

Joseph Zubin, Ph.D.

EXPERIMENTAL PSYCHOPATHOLOGY

Edited by **PAUL H. HOCH, M.D.**
New York State Psychiatric Institute; College of Physicians and Surgeons, Columbia University, New York City

and **JOSEPH ZUBIN, Ph.D.**
New York State Psychiatric Institute; Department of Psychology, Columbia University, New York City

THE PROCEEDINGS OF THE FORTY-FIFTH ANNUAL MEETING OF THE AMERICAN PSYCHOPATHOLOGICAL ASSOCIATION, HELD IN NEW YORK CITY, JUNE 1955

GRUNE & STRATTON

NEW YORK • LONDON • 1957

Library of Congress Catalog Card No. 56-13332

Copyright 1957
Grune & Stratton, Inc.
381 Fourth Avenue
New York City

Printed and Bound in the U.S.A.

CONTENTS

L120849

FONDREN LIBRARY
Southern Methodist University
DALLAS 5, TEXAS

▼

FOREWORD

SINCE THE DAYS of Kraepelin, Bleuler, Jaspers, et al. psychopathology has progressed from description to experiment. The birth pains and labor involved in producing the new experimental psychopathology are doubtless apparent, and some are perhaps of the opinion that the offspring was stillborn. Nevertheless, the present volume attests to the fact that scientific methods are beginning to gain a foothold. As long as phenomenology held sway, cause and etiology were matters for speculation. Much of that speculation invoked pre-scientific models whose hypotheses were not testable. With the advent of the somatotherapies, testable hypotheses began to be presented for verification. Some of these were readily disproved; others, however, took root and are now fully accepted: syphilis as a factor in general paresis, nutritional deprivation as a factor in pellagra with psychosis, and metabolic error as a factor in phenylpyruvic oligophrenia. The success of these somatic models has raised the hope that psychogenic hypotheses can also be subjected to testing. Sociologic factors explaining the differential rates of alcoholism in various ethnic groups, early childhood deprivations as factors in the behavior problems of children, and a host of other variables are now being subjected to scientific scrutiny. It may be that we are about to abandon entirely the realm of phenomenologic description and "brilliant" hunches and enter the domain of experimental manipulation and verification. As Kraepelin said nearly seventy years ago: "It is high time . . . the serious and conscientious investigation of specific problems replaces the clever contentions and profound arguments. With that which is undemonstrable, or irrefutable, we can go no further. We need facts, not theories. To be sure, no science can do without integrative points of view and tentative assumptions; but we must never forget that they have no independent inherent value. They are merely means to an end; their justification can be found only in the fact that they lead to definite questions and thereby to new investigations. Such questions, I think, have been raised in sufficient numbers here. We now ought to proceed to answer them not at the green table (or arm chair) but in the laboratory; not with clever suggestions but with observation and measurement."

In the present volume the main experimental currents in the field of psychopathology are represented. They cover the entire gamut from animal to man, from perception of social attitudes to experimental induction of depersonalization. It is hoped that the collaboration of clinicians and experimentalists in these areas will continue to bear fruit, that the emergence of a common vocabulary for the phenomena with which both now deal will assist integration of the two fields.

THE EDITORS

STANLEY COBB

STANLEY COBB

Samuel W. Hamilton, Memorial Lecturer, 1955

STANLEY COBB, NEUROSYCHIATRIST, was born in Brookline, Massachusetts on December 10, 1887. His father, John Candler Cobb, was a prominent author of a treatise on sociology and economics. The family lived in Milton, a suburb of Boston, where Stanley Cobb's first interest in science grew out of his fascination over watching birds and their habits. To him is attributed a well-known epigram: "The best bird watchers are birds." He attended Milton Academy and Volkmann's School, Harvard College (1910) and received his doctor's degree in medicine from Harvard Medical School in 1914. The next year he married Elizabeth M. Almy of Cambridge, and from this union there came one daughter, Helen, and two sons, Sidney and John. Sidney is Associate Professor of Epidemiology at the Graduate School of Public Health, University of Pittsburgh. John is a Consultant for the Division of Indian Health of the U.S. Public Health Service, Albuquerque, N. M.

From the beginning, Stanley Cobb was strongly interested in human personality and might be regarded as one of the true pioneers who foresaw and fostered what is now called the psychosomatic area of study. He was well grounded in medicine and surgery by his postgraduate training which gradually moved, after he was Surgical House Officer at the Peter Bent Brigham Hospital in Boston, toward the study of the human nervous system. At the Peter Bent Brigham Hospital he was a great favorite of the late Dr. Harvey Cushing. Returning to the Harvard Medical School, he became assistant professor of neuropathology in 1920 and associate professor in 1923. When the Rockefeller Foundation provided him with a two-year fellowship to travel abroad he studied in England and on the Continent, putting more emphasis on neuro-anatomy, neuropathology and clinical neurology. He was Harvard's second Bullard Professor of Neuropathology and held this post from 1926 through 1954, now emeritus. From 1925 to 1934 he was neurologist at the Boston City Hospital and head of the Neurological Laboratories in that institution. In 1934 he was called to the Massachusetts General Hospital as chief psychiatrist, where he extended his interests to include subjects dealing with human personality, placing special emphasis on emotions and states of consciousness.

The list of his publications is extensive and his contributions to the many scientific organizations to which he has belonged is impressive. Because of his studies on cerebral circulation, his name is well known in medical centers from Johns Hopkins to Berlin, Paris and Oxford. He has kept a strong interest in the anatomy of the brain, whether it be human or that of other species. His retirement from his long teaching stint at Harvard has only been a commencement, for now Stanley Cobb is finding time and opportunity to do many other things he always wanted to do, but did not have time to do when he was occupied with teaching and seeing patients for treatment or consultation. He has done much to further the cause of psychoanalysis in America and the cause of dynamic psychology in general.

Always liberal, broad and eclectic in his outlook, friends recognize his remarkable powers as a physician and his fine qualities as a human being. Qualities strengthened by a life-long struggle with a speech difficulty and more recently arthritis. In spite of these handicaps something warm and human emanates from the man that patients are quick to feel and friends are ever ready to appreciate. There is a kindliness, a twinkling, a sense of humor and a rare charm to the man that have made him beloved of all his intimates. One friend said, speaking of him, "He gives a kind of fatherhood and brotherhood along with his other services, whether they be teaching, administrative or therapeutic." Another anecdote concerns a remark he once made to two of his colleagues in his laboratory: "Don't argue, try it."

He served with the U.S.A. General Hospital #11 during World War I and has had many honors and distinctions. Recently he was awarded the Kober Medal, and in April of 1956 received the Albert Einstein Award in New York for outstanding accomplishment. He paints well with water colors, sings well (with a special preference to Gilbert and Sullivan) and has always been interested in nature and the great outdoors. His knowledge of the comparative anatomy of the brain is extensive. According to his present plans, he will spend the rest of his life pursuing these same interests with special emphasis now on the brains and behavior of birds.

MERRILL MOORE, M.D.
25 SEPTEMBER 1956

GENERALIZATION AND EXTINCTION OF EXPERIMENTALLY INDUCED FEAR IN CATS

By NORMA A. SCHEFLEN, Ph.D.*

VARIOUS INVESTIGATORS have studied conflict behavior in animals.[3,4,5,6,12] In most of these studies, conflict is produced by placing the animals in an experimental situation in which incompatible responses are aroused in the presence of differing drives. For instance, Masserman trained cats to press a lever to obtain food. After this training, electric shock was presented to their paws at the time that food was obtained. In this experimental situation the response of pressing the lever was first motivated by hunger and then inhibited by fear. That conflict was produced was evidenced by such behavior as hesitancy, vacillation, and tenseness. Thus, Masserman concludes as his principle of conflict that "two or more motivations come into conflict in the sense that their accustomed consummatory patterns are partially or wholly incompatible."[5]

Dollard and Miller [2,6] carry their analysis of conflict behavior further by considering not only the incompatibility of responses but also the strengths of opposing responses such as approach and avoidance. An important concept in their theoretical development is generalization; that is, when a particular response is learned to one stimulus, similar stimuli tend to evoke the same response. Those stimuli more like the original one elicit a stronger response than those less alike. Empirically it is found that the generalization of avoidance responses results in a steeper gradient than does the generalization of approach responses.[7,10] The stimulus, then, which produces the greatest conflict is the point on the stimulus continuum at which the strengths of the opposing responses are equal. Although the theoretical basis of this

* This study was supported by the Hall-Mercer Hospital, Pennsylvania Hospital Division. The author wishes to acknowledge gratefully the aid of P. O. Therman, M.D., in some of the experimental aspects and of A. E. Scheflen, M.D., in some of the clinical aspects of the paper.

conflict theory is the phenomenon of generalization, the experimental study of fears in new situations needs more attention.

Just as the study of generalization of fear responses is helpful in understanding conflict behavior, it seems that the study of the extinction of fear responses may also have an important bearing upon the problem of reduction of conflict. One question which may be asked is: Can extinction of generalized fear responses reduce the fear of the original stimulus situation or must the fear of the original situation itself be extinguished? The present investigation attempts to study the generalization of fear responses, the extinction of fear both in the original fear-producing situation and in the generalized situation, and performance in the original situation after the generalized fears have been extinguished.

PROCEDURE

The subjects were 10 cats, six females and four males, whose weights ranged from 2.5 kg. to 3.5 kg. These cats were one to two years old and had been raised in the animal laboratory. None of the cats had been used previously for experimental purposes.*

The apparatus consisted of two alley-like boxes, A and B. Box A was 82 in. long, 12 in. wide, 14.5 in. high, and was painted gray inside. Box B was the same length but was 8½ in. wider and six in. higher and was painted white inside. The tops of both boxes were covered with transparent plastic and both alleys had starting boxes with sliding doors. These starting boxes were painted to match the corresponding alley-boxes. The alley-boxes had small openings in the floor at the end opposite the starting box through which a rubber tube eight mm. in diameter and six in. long was inserted. This tube was attached to an air cylinder to deliver an electrically controlled air blast under an initial pressure of 22 lbs. per square inch.

General Experimental Conditions.

The cats were placed in separate cages for a period of 72 hours prior to any experimental training. During the pre-experimental period and throughout the experiment the cats were fed to satiation with

---

* Preliminary investigations with other cats which previously had been used as experimental animals in other studies were also carried out with essentially the same procedure as will be described here. These findings were similar to those reported in this study but are not included in the present material.

commercial cat food every 24 hrs. In order to motivate them, each trial was given after 22 hrs. food deprivation. A trial consisted of placing the cat in the starting box, opening the sliding door, and allowing the cat to run to the opposite end of the alley box to eat a pellet of food. The time from the opening of the door to the eating of the food pellet was recorded with a stop watch. A time limit of 180 sec. was adopted and if the cat did not run the length of the alley and eat the food within this time it was removed from the alley and returned to the home cage until the next trial. For each cat the time between daily trials was approximately 5 min. The 10 cats were divided into two experimental groups, Group I (four cats), and Group II (four cats); and one control group, Group III (two cats).

Approach Training.

Approach training was the same for all animals in the three groups. The cats were trained to run the length of one of the alleys; a food pellet being used as the reward. The alley in which the animal was trained will be referred to as the original situation. In each group, half of the animals had training in Box A and half had training in Box B in order to balance any effects of the particular alley in which the training was given. There were 31 training trials: five on the first experimental day, eight on each of the next three days, and two on the fifth day.

Avoidance.

Immediately following the final approach training trial, the experimental cats in groups I and II received air blast. The air blast was given only in the original situation, in which the animal had been trained to run, and only when the cat started to eat the food pellet. If the cat, having retreated from the food dish after the initial air blast, reapproached it, another air blast was presented. The criterion of avoidance was established as two successive trials of not eating within the 180 sec. time limit. The control animals did not receive air blast nor any additional training during this time.

Extinction.

The experimental cats were given 25 extinction trials where no air blast was presented, but in which the same food reward continued to be available. After a 45 min. interval following the meeting of the avoidance criterion, 10 extinction trials were given. Ten more extinction trials were given on the following day and five on the third day of the extinction procedure. Group I received the extinction trials in the original situation and Group II had extinction trials in an alley different from the one in which the air blast had been presented. Thus, the extinction process was studied both in an original fear-evoking situation and in a new situation with generalization of the original fear. The control group (III) was given the same number of trials in a new situation to show the effects of the new situation per se.

Spread of Extinction.

Following extinction in the new situation, Group II was returned to the original fear-evoking situation and given 13 trials. Group I, which had had extinction in the same alley in which it had received air blast, was given 13 trials in the new situation. Group III was returned to the alley in which it had originally been trained and given 13 trials.

RESULTS

Figure 1 gives group results showing mean running time in seconds for all trials, trials being given in overlapping blocks of three. As can be seen, the approach training showed a regular acquisition of the running response. On the first few trials, the cats demonstrated some exploratory activity which soon diminished. By the end of the 31 training trials the mean running time was almost equal for all groups. The mean running time for Group I was 7.4' and for Group II 5.6'. The difference between these two groups was not statistically significant (p $>$ .05).

The effect of the air blast given to Groups I and II was marked. The cats became hesitant and often approached the food only partway in the alley box, then returned to the starting section. In addition to vacillating the cats trembled, often mewed violently, and after being removed from the alley box resisted being put back for the next trial. From one to three air blasts were required to reach the criterion of two successive trials of not eating within the 180 sec. time limit. The two experimental groups did not differ in the number of air blasts needed to reach the criterion.

Following the air blast, the running time of the experimental groups diverged greatly from that of the control group. And though the control group showed some increase in running time when placed in the new situation, this effect was small compared to the increases in running time observed in Groups I and II, which had received air blast. The running time for Group II in the new situation after air blast was 152.2 sec. while that for the control group was 20.9 sec. The difference between these two means is significant (p < .05). The fact that the running time for Group II, which received air blast, was longer than that for the control group indicates that the fear of Group II in the new situation was due primarily to a generalized fear aroused by air blast situation rather than to a new situation.

There also appears to have been a difference between the two experimental groups after air blast. The mean running time for the cats in Group I, those continued in the original alley-box, was 180.0 sec. In fact none of these cats have any running response at all during five subsequent trials. The cats in Group II, those transferred to a new situation, did run but the running time was significantly prolonged, the mean being 152.2 sec. The difference between groups I and II is significant (p < .05).* An even larger difference might be expected if there were no arbitrary time limit.

The running times for Group II, for which the fear was extinguished in the new situation, were throughout the extinction process somewhat shorter than those of Group I, which remained in the original situation. Toward the end of the series of extinction trials the two curves converge; both groups regaining their former running times. The running time for the control group increased slightly when placed in the new situation, but the cats in this group quickly resumed and maintained their former running speed.

Figure 1 also shows that extinction in a new situation does spread to the original fear-evoking situation, since Group II, upon being returned to the original situation after extinction in the new situation, had a mean running time of 52.5 sec. When compared with the running time of 7.5 sec. for the control group, the results of Group II indicate that there still remained some effect of the air blast. However, extinction in the original situation was more effective in reducing fear of the original situation than was extinction in a new situation. This can be seen by the longer running times for Group II upon return

* Wilcoxon's suggestions for approximate statistics were applied here and at other places in the results where statistical significance is mentioned.

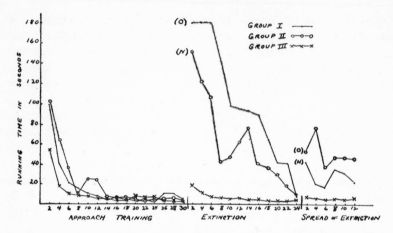

Fig. 1. Group Results Showing Mean Running Time for all Trials (Trials in
Overlapping Blocks of Three).

to the original situation (52.5 sec.) as compared with the final extinction trials of Group I (6.3 sec.). Final extinction trials were used as test trials for Group I since preliminary investigations had shown that after extinction and when the running response reaches its former level, this level is maintained if the animal is continued in the same alley.

Another incidental finding concerned the fact that the amount of fear shown in a new situation seems to be dependent upon prior experience in the training alley. Group II, which was placed in the new situation immediately after having received air blast, had a running time of 152.2 sec. Group I, which was placed in the new situation after having had air blast plus 25 extinction trials, had a running time of 43.4 sec. Group III, which had not received air blast, had a running time of 20.9 sec.

The results when either alley box A or B was used in the original situation were similar, indicating that there were no differential effects due to the particular alley used.

DISCUSSION

In the present study conflict behavior was produced in cats by evoking opposing response tendencies, namely approach under hunger motivation and avoidance under fear motivation. After establishing an approach-avoidance conflict by giving the cats food when they ran to the end of the alley-box and then introducing air blast when they began to eat the food, the cats were placed in a new situation in which fear and conflict were observed but to a lesser extent than in the original situation. In other words, fear aroused in one situation generalized to another similar situation. In addition to the process of generalization of fear, extinction of fear was studied both in the original situation and generalized situation. This study of extinction suggests six inferences concerning the nature of the process: (1) extinction requires repeated trials or exposures in which the fear-evoking stimuli are present but the punishment is not; (2) extinction of fear can occur in either the original fear-evoking situation or in one similar to it; (3) extinction seems to take place a little more rapidly in the new situation; (4) extinction of fear in the new but similar situation reduces the fear of the original situation, i.e., extinction is generalized; (5) extinction of fear of the original situation seems to require fewer trials when this extinction is carried out in the original situation than when it is first carried out in the new situation; and (6) even after extinction is apparently complete there appears to be a residual effect of the original fear in new but similar situations.

Possible Clinical Implications.

In considering the clinical implications let us see how the concepts of generalization and extinction may possibly be related to clinical concepts. Possibly generalization is analogous to one aspect of the genesis of psychiatric disorders and extinction to an aspect of their resolution. The motivations of the child often bring him into conflict with society. Fearing punishment and disapproval, a child learns to fear his own drives and to repress them. From this point on, the fear response comes not from external objective reality but from the danger that these repressed motivations will break forth. What originally was fear has now become anxiety. When the conflict and fear are excessive, the child generalizes in conceiving of many people as the disapproving parents and many situations as the anxiety-producing stimuli. In fact, any expression of these motivations becomes frightening. In the neurotic, for example, the anxiety produced by aggression may generalize to any situation, including normal competition, so that appropriate behavior is then inhibited. The development of a phobia perhaps affords a clearer illustration of generalization. Here people or objects which are related to the original anxiety-producing stimuli become sources of anxiety. For example a phobia of cows may spread successively to other farm animals, to rural countrysides, to landscapes, to paintings of landscapes, and finally to all paintings.

There are perhaps three ways by which people try to handle these fears and anxieties: avoidance, return to the original fear-evoking situation to become accustomed to it, or reconstruction of similar situations. One kind of avoidance is seen in psychological defense mechanisms such as repression and denial, which attempt to negate that which is frightening. Another is regression to infantile patterns of behavior to avoid the conflict. The use of these methods is quite characteristic of neuroses and psychoses. Avoidance may be merely a refusal to participate in situations which provoke the anxiety. In this study avoidance was seen in the refusal of the cats to run in the alleys. Where anxiety or fear is marked avoidance may be the only possible way to deal with the fear-evoking situation. Clinical observations suggest that even after long periods of time the anxiety tends to remain intense if avoidance is the only method employed.

A second method of diminishing fear or anxiety is to return to the original situation and re-experience it. Here clinical observations indicate that this may be an effective method, but its success depends upon two conditions; that the trauma does not recur and that the fear is not so great that it is impossible for the person to place himself in the dangerous situation. Therefore, despite some evidence that extinction in the original situation is most effective, it may not form the basis of a practical way of extinguishing fear. The anxiety may be so intense that it prevents the repeated occurrence of the situation and leads only to avoidance whether real or symbolic. It must also be remembered that in life situations, unlike laboratory conditions, the original situation may not be possible to re-create. There are also indications that even following extinction in the original situation residual effects of the trauma in new situations remain. Thus the oft repeated advice that, after a frightening experience, one should plunge again into this frightening situation may be detrimental rather than therapeutic.

A third way of reducing fear, the reconstruction of situations similar to the original fear-evoking situation, was noted in this study by creating a new but similar situation in which the cats had no trauma. This method has many analogies to life situations and is seen in the normal growth process of childhood. The child, fearful after a visit to the dentist's office, play-acts the situation and becomes familiar with it, thus reducing his fear. Another example is seen in the traumatic neuroses. After a frightening combat experience the soldier repeatedly re-creates imaginatively the battle situation in an attempt to master the anxiety and experience the situation without trauma. An effective therapeutic method for traumatic neuroses is to encourage deliberately these re-living activities in fantasy, dreams, and discussions.

Another important clinical application appears to be psychotherapy and psychoanalysis. In psychotherapy an attempt is made to correct the faulty generalization. The taboo mechanisms which cause anxiety can be recognized without punishment or disapproval from the psychotherapist and after repeated exposures the anxiety is diminished. The new emotional experience is in turn generalized so that, for example, the patient may feel aggression in some socially approved situation without accompanying anxiety. The correction of faulty generalization permits realistic learning. This psychoanalysts have called "corrective emotional experience."[1] The corrective experience may be slowed down by too great a similarity of the psychotherapist and his attitudes to those of the people who originally evoked the fear. Conversely, the corrective experience may be facilitated by a therapist who is somewhat different from the fear-evoking parental figure. The patient views the therapist as a parental figure in the phenomenon called transference. He finds that in the new but similar situation, i.e., the therapy, he does not need to be frightened and has an opportunity to learn that all interaction with people need not be traumatic.

Having gone through the "corrective emotional experience," the individual can return to the original fear-producing situation with much less anxiety. For instance a woman patient had in childhood experienced an extremely frightening situation in a certain city. Soon after this she left the area but for thirty years she had a strong wish to return to this city to visit many of her family and childhood friends. However, every time she planned to do so she became overwhelmed with anxiety and never managed to get there. In psychotherapy the frightening experiences were recalled and discussed enough to allow her to return. After several anxious visits she was able to work through her anxiety in the original fear-evoking situation and was able to find these trips quite enjoyable.

It may be that the fear following a trauma can best be reduced by a combination of these three methods. In psychotherapy the skilled psychotherapist seems to do this. He permits the patient to avoid talking about the frightening experiences when the anxiety is too intense, encourages the re-creation of similar situations until the anxiety is diminished, and as a final step may encourage the approaching and handling of the original fear-evoking situation. A combination of these three procedures is often thought to be an effective way of preventing permanent neurosis in the frightened soldier. The soldier is first removed from the source of the fear to allow him an opportunity to review the frightening experiences and then is returned to the battlefield to face the original situation.

Others have pointed to the need to consider the relationship of experimental concepts to psychiatric ideas.[2,8,9] In discussing the relationships of this experimental study to psychiatric concepts there has been much oversimplification. The analogies are admittedly speculative and incomplete. However, it is felt that further information concerning generalization and extinction of fear can be gained, and an approach to the problem of resolving traumatic experiences and to certain aspects of psychotherapy can be made within this kind of experimental framework. Certainly one advantage of having such an experimental situation is that the effects of other conditions on these processes can be studied. Also one may find clues as to which variables may be important to study further at the clinical level.

REFERENCES

1. ALEXANDER, F., AND FRENCH, T. M.: Psychoanalytic Therapy. New York, Ronald Press, 1946.
2. DOLLARD, J., AND MILLER, N. E.: Personality and Psychotherapy: An Analysis in Terms of Learning, Thinking, and Culture. New York, McGraw-Hill, 1950.
3. LIDDELL, H. S.: Conditioned Reflex Method and Experimental Neurosis. In J. McV. Hunt, ed.: Personality and the Behavior Disorders. New York, Ronald Press, 1944, chap. 12.
4. MASSERMAN, J. H.: Behavior and Neurosis. Chicago, Univ. of Chicago Press, 1943.
5. ———: Principles of Dynamic Psychiatry. Philadelphia, Saunders, 1946, p. 122.
6. MILLER, N. E.: Experimental Studies of Conflict. In J. McV. Hunt, ed.: Personality and the Behavior Disorders. New York, Ronald Press, 1944, chap. 14.
7. ——— AND KRAELING, D.: Displacement: greater generalization of approach than avoidance in a generalized approach-avoidance conflict. J. Exp. Psychol. 43: 217-221, 1952.

8. MOWRER, O. H.: Learning Theory and Personality Dynamics. New York, Ronald Press, 1950.
9. ——: Psychotherapy: Theory and Research. New York, Ronald Press, 1953.
10. MURRAY, E. J. AND MILLER, N. E.: Displacement: steeper gradient of generalization of avoidance than of approach with age of habit controlled. J. Exp. Psychol. *43:* 221-226, 1952.
11. RUSSELL, R.: The Comparative Study of Conflict and Experimental Neurosis. In J. M. Tanner, ed.: Prospects in Psychiatric Research. Oxford, Blackwell, 1953.
12. WATSON, R.: Experimentally produced conflict in cats. Psychosom. Med. *16:* 340-347, 1954.
13. WILCOXON, F.: Some Rapid Approximate Statistical Procedures. New York, American Cyanamid Co., 1949.

2

EXPERIMENTAL PSYCHOGENIC TACHYCARDIA

By W. HORSLEY GANTT, M.D. *and* ROSS A. DYKMAN, M.D.*

THAT CHANGES IN HEART RATE (HR) occur with various emotional and physical states is one of the most ancient bits of physiological knowledge. The heart, an organ whose function can at any moment be brought into consciousness, has been accorded the highest prestige of perhaps any organ or viscus, having been considered by Aristotle as the seat of the intellect. Despite this and the enormous advances made by physiologists and cardiac specialists in the modern era, almost nothing has been done on the question of its participation in the individually acquired habits or conditional reflexes. This lack of specific knowledge was strikingly evident at the beginning of our work when I† posed the question to ten eminent physiologists and cardiologists of whether there would be a change in the HR accompanying the 5- or 10-second action of the conditional stimulus that signalized the giving of food. Seven replied that there would not, and three that there might be. The answer obviously was not known to me (W. H. G.); if it had been, the investigations probably would not have been undertaken.

The questions which we set out to answer were: Would changes in the heart rate occur with the presentation of the *signal* for the food even when the food were only a pellet of 1 or 2 grams? Would the change in HR be different for the conditioned excitation and conditioned inhibition? If there were a change in HR with the conditional reflex, would this be the same for all amounts of food or specifically for the quantitative value of the signal, i.e., larger with the signal which was customarily followed by the greater amount of food, or would it be in the nature of an all or none reaction?

* Pavlovian Laboratory, Johns Hopkins University. The authors desire to thank the American Heart Association for their help in supporting this research.

† When "we" or "I" is used referring to work done before 1950 it refers to the senior author (W.H.G.)

In 1939, with Dr. W. C. Hoffmann of Oslo, we began the systematic solution of these problems. The initial problem was, Would there be any change in the circulatory system measured by HR resulting from action of the conditional stimulus? In 1934 E. Cowles Andrus and I had approached a solution by using as an unconditional stimulus the stimulation of the vagus nerve through implanted electrodes leading from a buried induction coil, a technic which was elaborated with Dr. R. B. Loucks. Owing to technical difficulties this work was abandoned.

In 1939-1940 Hoffmann and I, using food as the unconditional stimulus, demonstrated that there was not only a specific cardiac conditional reflex for conditioned excitation and inhibition but that the change in HR was in proportion to the amount of the unconditional stimulus (food), viz., that there was a quantitative relationship.[5]

Previous evidence indicated that HR fluctuations accompanied certain "anticipations": Liddell referred to Sherrington's observation of such a change in 1900 and Liddell himself was measuring HRs with the conditional reflexes in the early thirties. (We are indebted to Dr. Parmenter of Liddell's laboratory for building our first cardiotachometer). Pavlov was aware perhaps of a cardiac conditional reflex, but he chose the salivary gland instead of the heart because of the very fact that the salivary gland unlike the heart had few connections with activities other than food, whereas the connections of the heart are multitudinous. Lashley told us in 1953 that he had noted an increase in HR in himself (by feeling his pulse) with the signal for a shock as far back as 1912. Watson, in his presidential address to the Psychological Association in 1916 reporting his new experiments on the conditional reflex, discussed the possibility of a cardiac conditional reflex but said that he had been unable to obtain proof of it through measurements on the human subject. In none of these observations were there systematic measurements as there have been with the salivary conditional reflex. Indeed the manifold connections of the heart with nearly all other activities of the body often mask its participation in the conditional reflex unless specific measures are taken to exclude these influences. The greatest interference is that occasioned by the presence of the experimenter, who is a potent accelerator, and under certain circumstances a decelerator of HR. Another interference is the cardiac fluctuation accompanying the orienting reflex, which has to be eliminated before the initiation of conditioning.[6]

Owing to the sensitivity of the HR—its function as the chief nourisher of all the tissues, the commissary as it were of the whole body as well as its participation in the dynamic emotional life of the individual —special precautions are required to get satisfactory controls. If it is necessary to separate the dog from the experimenter in the ordinary salivary and motor conditional reflexes, it is vastly more important to separate the dog in the study of the cardiac conditional reflex.

For the purpose of our experiments it is fortunate that the dog has a labile HR because we are thus able to see the adaptations of the cardiac conditional reflex that otherwise we would miss. But it is only by taking continuous records and counting the HR in 5″ periods that we can see these changes; for the elevation of HR may occur within a few seconds and return to normal within 10″. Thus in the eating of 10 gms. food, the HR can rise from control of 70 to a peak of 120 in 5″ and in 30″ drop to its control level.

There is in general a parallel between the HR and other components of the conditional reflex, for example salivation and movement, but this is only approximate and there are important and fundamental exceptions. Like the salivary conditional reflex, the cardiac conditional reflex varies according to which analyzer is used for the signal, being larger with auditory signals than with visual. The cardiac conditional reflex also varies with the intensity of the unconditional stimulus (US); thus to the signals for 10 gm. food the HR change is greater than to the signal for 2 gm. food. And as is true with most other functions, the change in HR is highly characteristic of the given individual.

The emotional state of the animal relevant to the physiological function being studied is a determining factor. In a hungry dog we get a pronounced HR conditional reflex, perhaps a rise of 40 beats in the 5″ action of the conditional stimulus, but if the same dog is satiated and we measure the HR conditional reflex 5 minutes later, there may be scarcely any change in the HR to the signal.

The course of events during the routine experiments is as follows: there is at first an orienting response (OR) to the new signal which after some 10 to 100 repetitions disappears. At this time reenforcement of the signal with the food or shock is begun. With one or more shock reenforcements the whole level of HR is raised, for example from 50 to 80, and now with the giving of each signal the HR is seen to rise still further. Here we see not only the specific cardiac conditional reflex but also a general one in the rise in level of HR.

Various interpretations and names can be given to this rise in HR to the whole procedure—emotional, anticipation, etc., terms which describe the phenomenon from different conceptual points of view. However, since the same external environment which at first had no influence on the dog has, through virtue of that dog's individual experience, acquired a new potency for that animal we preserve the designation of conditioning in contrast to unconditioning for this new response of the heart.

The development of the HR conditional reflex passes through several stages. With the first reenforcement there is (1) an increase of the HR to high levels; (2) the HR becomes irregular, and irregularity is a sign of stress, whether we see it in the salivation, motor activity, blood sugar, or HR. As conditioning proceeds, another stage follows in which the level of HR drops and the rise to the conditional stimulus is less; somewhere in between these stages differentiation of the excitatory from the inhibitory stimulus is attained.

These stages can be illustrated from the protocols of the dogs *Crazy* and *Pedro* (experiments of Doctors Pinto and Newton). On 18 March 1947, the HR of Crazy on being placed in the camera was 72; during the OR training there was a rise to 138 with the HR fluctuating considerably; when the conditional stimuli were reenforced on the same day for six times at four-minute intervals, the HR fluctuated from 70 to 160 (if the rate to the faradic shock was omitted, from 70 to 122), and although there was no motor conditional reflex, viz., lifting of the leg, there was a cardiac conditional reflex after the second reenforcement, i.e., a rise of HR to each conditional stimulus (duration of conditional stimulus = 5″) besides the general increase of level. Seven months later, on the 16 October, the fluctuation was less (55 to 100 including rise to shock), and the median HR was lower (Fig. 1). In Pedro, before any training but after habituation to the camera, the HR was 40 to 50; on the first day after *one* reenforcement there was a regular rise in HR to each conditional stimulus, and the level of HR rose from 45 to 110 *median* (Fig. 2).

The above cases illustrate the development of the cardiac conditional reflex from the very start. There is also a chronic tachycardia in

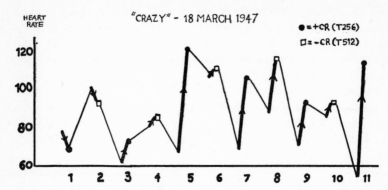

Fig. 1.—Formation of cardiac CRs heart rate, first day. No motor CRs (schizokinesis). Two minute intervals between stimuli.

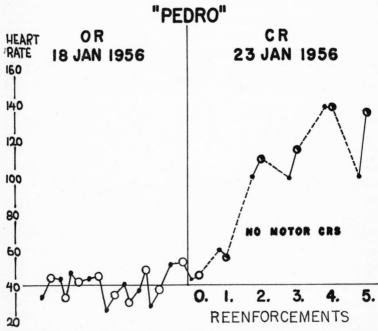

Fig. 2.—Early formation of cardiac conditioned responses. Note elevation of heart
rate and CR after one reenforcement.

these dogs, as well as in many others with whom we have worked, situationally determined; a tachycardia which appears whenever the dog is brought into the environment where it was produced, more pronounced with the specific signals for the stress but present to the room, person, and other elements.

Pathological tachycardia can develop on this basis. We have had a number of dogs in whom tachycardia has persisted for many years. Some examples will be cited. In two dogs trained in 1951 whose HR (as well as blood pressure) was measured 13 months later, the rise developed during the conditioning was found to persist after a year's rest and freedom from experimentation immediately on returning the dog to the environment, to the camera where he had been worked with. The HR rose to the *signals* for stress, 20 to 50 beats during the conditional stimulus, although the stressful stimulus (shock) was not presented.[1]

These animals did not show marked behavior disturbances, although several of our animals have become extremely upset, ranging in their symptomatology from the picture of violent anxiety ("Nick") to typical catatonia ("V3").

Nick showed a train of symptoms soon after work was begun with him in 1932 and continuing with some intermissions until he was killed in 1941. These consisted of asthmatic-like breathing, extreme pollakiuria, ejaculatio praecox, gastric hyperacidity; also visceral perturbations, great restlessness, agitation, negativism toward people he knew who brought out the above train of symptoms, plus sexual erections and often ejaculation. Furthermore there was, paradoxically, impotence in the presence of an adequate stimulus. Upon this background a marked tachycardia developed ranging up to a HR of 250 accompanied by a respiratory rate of 150-300. The tachycardia was evoked by the elements of the milieu in which the breakdown was produced. The specific stimuli used were two tones close together, one representing food and the other no food. The *person*, especially, was found to be a major element in this galaxy, and his mere presence would bring out most of the symptoms. While Nick would have a HR of only about 140 to a cat clawing his back, the HR to the person was often much higher. This tachycardia was somewhat alleviated by removing the dog completely from the Baltimore environment to that of a farm in Virginia for several months to a year, but it returned when Nick was brought back into the laboratory—without repeating the original stress.[3]

It is noteworthy here that once the "process" of deterioration begins it continues and progresses, increasing rather than decreasing in susceptible subjects. Even new developments occur, new symptoms outside the neurotic environment, and without the presence of the original stress. This has led us to postulate a development on the basis of internal factors, proceeding over a long time, to which we have given the name of *autokinesis*.

The same autokinesis was seen in the dog V3, who is now a resident of the laboratory. Born about seven years ago and raised in the laboratory, he was always shy and unfriendly with people. After a few months of experimental work he had psychogenic (?), epileptiform convulsions in the experimental stand and became unfit for the planned experiments. He also developed new symptoms outside the experimental environment and after the experiments were discontinued, the picture of classical catatonia, cerea flexibilitas, insensitivity to pain, immobility, and "freezing," reminiscent of the dogs in Pavlov's laboratory that I saw in 1929 who "stood like marble statues." The dog's HR was also elevated, rising to 190 in the presence of those who worked with him, but dropping rapidly during petting by the same persons.[2] This animal, like Nick, was ambivalent in his behavior, coming out of the paddock with the experimenter but then showing great fear, running away and "freezing" in a corner.

Several important principles are evident in the study of the HR in our dogs. First is the early appearance of the increased HR to the general procedure of conditioning, long before the motor conditional reflex is evident, and the persistence of the cardiac conditional reflex often after the motor has disappeared or been actively extinguished, for perhaps a number of years. This split between the somatic motor and the visceral cardiac responses is what we have given the name of *schizokinesis*.[4,7] Thus, tachycardia can be produced after one or two exposures to a stress situation and can continue sometime for years *in the susceptible individual* without external symptoms or evidence. A second factor in the elaboration of cardiac disorders is the principle of *autokinesis:* the growth of pathological symptoms on the basis of individual past experience plus the qualities (constitution?) of the particular individual *without* the presence of any of the external elements of the original stress, but due perhaps to the internal traces of this stress by which the nervous system has been charged like a Leyden jar or storage battery.* In our experimental set-up we can see the origin of the neurotic disturbance and *trace the tachycardia from the very second* when it began. A great advantage in the study of cardiac disorders!

* There is also a positive side of autokinesis making toward healing and therapy whereby the individual may develop and improve to the traces of a therapeutic agent, but this will be dealt with in another article.

REFERENCES

1. DYKMAN, ROSS A. AND GANTT, W. HORSLEY: Relation of experimental tachycardia to amplitude of motor activity and intensity of the motivating stimulus. Am. J. Physiol., *185:* 495, 1956.
2. GANTT, W. HORSLEY: Effect of alcohol on the sexual reflexes of normal and neurotic male dogs. Psychosom. Med., *14:* 174-181, 1952.
3. ———: Experimental Basis for neurotic behavior. New York, Hoeber & Co., 1944, p. 212.
4. ———: Principles of nervous breakdown: schizokinesis and autokinesis. Ann. New York Acad. Sc., *56:* 143-163, 1953.
5. ———AND W. CHRISTIE HOFFMANN: Conditioned cardio-respiratory changes accompanying conditioned food reflexes. Am. J. Physiol., *129:* 360-361, 1940.
6. ROBINSON, JANICE AND GANTT, W. HORSLEY: The orienting reflex (questioning reaction): cardiac, respiratory, salivary and motor components. Bull, Johns Hopkins Hosp., *80:* 231-253, 1947.
7. STEPHENS, JOSEPH H. AND GANTT, W. HORSLEY: Differential effect of morphine on cardiac and motor conditional reflexes: schizokinesis. Bull. Johns Hopkins Hosp., *98:* 245-254, 1956.

3

A COMPARATIVE APPROACH TO THE EXPERIMENTAL ANALYSIS OF EMOTIONAL BEHAVIOR

By JOSEPH V. BRADY, Ph.D.*

A S THE POINT OF DEPARTURE for the experiments to be described in the following pages, one might begin with the rather common clinical and experimental observation that emotional disturbance can, as one of several possible effects, disrupt or interfere with an organism's ongoing behavior. Of course emotion, broadly defined, is but one of several classes of events which have this property. But with the proper controls it is possible to reproduce dependably the basic features of such emotional disruption in the comparative laboratory and to isolate experimentally important variables of which it is a function. The conceptual framework within which an animal experimental approach to this problem has been conceived is basically uncomplicated, and derives in large part from Schoenfeld's formulation of anxiety, escape, and avoidance behavior presented as part of a similar symposium sponsored by this same organization some six years ago.[27] This paper represents an extension and application of this descriptive behavioristic treatment of emotion to the experimental analysis of such psychopathological phenomena.

The fundamental empirical fact which provides the cornerstone for much of this work is the experimentally demonstrable suppression of some stable aspects of an animal's ongoing behavior under conditions of emotional disturbance. Specifically, these studies have focused upon what Schoenfeld described as the "experimental paradigm for anxiety," defined by the suppressing effect of anticipated pain upon a stable lever pressing habit in trained experimental animals. Estes and Skinner[15] first reported the techniques involved in superimposing such a conditioned "anxiety" response upon the lever pressing behavior of albino rats, although some modifications in the procedure have been developed more recently.[7,18] Briefly, thirsty animals initially are

* Walter Reed Army Institute of Research, Washington.

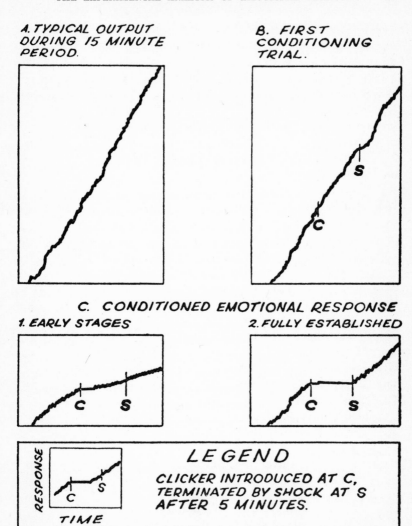

A. TYPICAL OUTPUT DURING 15 MINUTE PERIOD.

B. FIRST CONDITIONING TRIAL.

C. CONDITIONED EMOTIONAL RESPONSE

1. EARLY STAGES

2. FULLY ESTABLISHED

LEGEND
CLICKER INTRODUCED AT C, TERMINATED BY SHOCK AT S AFTER 5 MINUTES.

Fig. 1. The conditioned "anxiety" response as it appears typically in the cumulative response curve. (Hunt and Brady.[13])

trained in lever pressing for a continuous and then a periodic water reward. When their lever pressing output has stabilized they receive a series of conditioning trials, each consisting of the presentation of a clicking noise (the conditioned stimulus) followed by a pain shock to the feet (the unconditioned stimulus). Figure 1 illustrates the basic conditioning procedure and the typical appearance of the "anxiety" response in the lever pressing curve. The clicking noise continues for three minutes and is terminated contiguously with the shock. Within a few trials, the anticipatory response to the clicker begins to appear as a perturbation in the lever pressing curve, accompanied by crouching, immobility and, usually, defecation. Of course, experimental extinction of this response (with progressive recovery of the lever pressing rate in the presence of the conditioned stimulus) follows successive unreinforced presentations of the clicker alone without shock during daily lever pressing trials.

This emphasis upon a rather primitive and in some respects, at least, unlearned reaction pattern as the starting point for an experimental analysis of more fundamental aspects of emotional behavior has several clearcut advantages. First, focus directly upon the conditioned "anxiety" response as such eliminates a major source of error attributable to variables that affect instrumental behavior in more conventional learning experiments approaching the problem of emotion through escape or avoidance techniques. Secondly, this simple, relatively uncomplicated response is elicitable under a wide range of conditions and appears in quite consistent form or topography in all animals. Thirdly, this response is remarkably stable over time, surviving without apparent diminution in the absence of exercise or further reinforcement throughout the entire life of the organism. And finally, the technique of superimposing the emotional response upon a well-established and stable lever pressing habit makes it possible to approximate a quantification of the strength or magnitude of the response in terms of changes in output during various segments of the lever pressing curve. Such conditioned "anxiety" behavior would appear to be prototypical of the most primitive aspects of an organism's emotional repertoire, and the study of the vicissitudes of such a stable response—the conditions which determine its increases and decreases in strength, etc.—could be expected to provide an opportunity for the differential experimental analysis of both the physiological and the psychological variables upon which the organization of emotional behavior depends.

EARLY EXPERIMENTAL FINDINGS

The initial experimental application of this technique in a series of studies on the effects of electroconvulsive shock (ECS) some years ago provided the first indications that such a comparative laboratory approach to psychopathology might yield potentially valuable information. The results of these early experiments demonstrated quite clearly that a series of 21 ECS treatments, administered three times per day for seven days, could virtually eliminate the conditioned "anxiety" response without any apparent adverse effects upon retention of the lever pressing behavior, as illustrated in Fig. 2.[7,18] Follow-

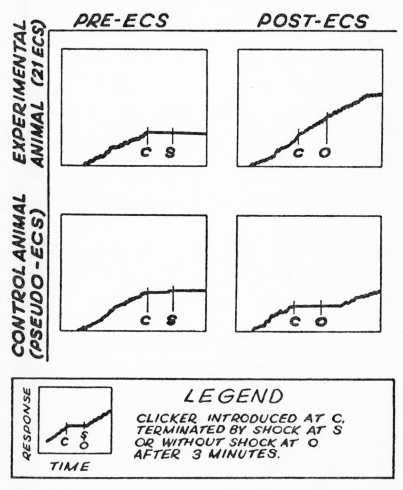

FIG. 2. The effect of electroconvulsive shock (ECS) on the conditioned "anxiety" response—typical illustrative cumulative curves for two animals. (Hunt and Brady.[18])

ing up this finding, it was possible to show that the differential effect of ECS upon the "anxiety" response and upon the lever pressing habit could not be attributable to either the temporal order in which the two behaviors had been conditioned,[16] impairment of auditory function,[8] or the painful characteristics of the ECS treatments.[17] Furthermore, these changes in the conditioned "anxiety" response as a function of ECS were found to have some interesting temporal and quantitative properties, and the relationship of this effect to some of the more important "anxiety" conditioning parameters has been carefully worked out. For example, both the number of conditioning trials and the intensity of the unconditioned grid shock stimulus during establishment of the "anxiety" response have been found to influence the attenuating effects of the ECS treatments.[17] In addition, both the number and temporal distribution of the ECS treatments bear rather important relationships to attenuation of the "anxiety" response.[9]

The results of these early ECS experiments also provided some additional insights into the functional and temporal properties of this conditioned "anxiety" paradigm. First, the attenuating effect of ECS upon the "anxiety" response was found to be transient; the emotional response reappearing within 30 days after the treatments.[4] But even more important, perhaps, was the observation that if the ECS treatments were delayed for as long as 30 days after conditioning of the "anxiety" response, no changes in the emotional response could be demonstrated following the same series of 21 electrically produced convulsions.[5] Of some interest also would seem to be the observation that "prophylactic" ECS convulsions, administered on a periodic basis after the intensive series of 21 ECS, could prevent the reappearance of the "anxiety" response, and when similar periodic prophylactic ECS treatments were administered prior to delayed intensive ECS, the "anxiety" response appeared less resistant to attenuation.[14] Such systematic and orderly response to experimental controls seemed to hold considerable promise for a more detailed analysis of this apparently fundamental aspect of emotional behavior, and much of our more recent work in this area represents an attempt to delimit the critical determinants of this anxiety response at both a behavioral and a neurological level.[1,12,13,19]

SOME RECENT EXPERIMENTS

One of the more provocative observations to emerge from later experiments on this conditioned anxiety response and the parameters of its attenuation by ECS developed from exploring the effects of post-ECS extinction of the response upon its subsequent reappearance.[20] When, for example, a series of experimental extinction trials (clicker alone without shock) is administered immediately following attenuation of the response by the 21 intensive ECS treatments, the "anxiety" response fails to reappear 30 days later, *even though* the cessation of lever pressing, crouching, and defecation do not appear at any time during the course of extinction. This apparently paradoxical finding calls attention to theoretical distinctions between the "sensory-discriminative" and "motor-expressive" aspects of anticipatory behavior, and appears quite consistent with neurological views held by Rioch and others[26] relative to the independence of the anticipatory functions of the brain and overt behavorial expression. Of even more practical significance would seem to be the implication from these results that the availability of such pathological phenomena to psychotherapeutic manipulation, along with the more or less transient effects known to characterize physiological treatment methods, may actually provide an opportunity for significantly increasing the durability of such therapeutic behavioral changes.

Recently some of the functional behavioral properties of this conditioned "anxiety" response and its relationship to variables affecting the maintenance of the lever pressing habit upon which it is superimposed, have been investigated. Specifically, it has now been possible to show that the rate of both acquisition and extinction of the "anxiety" response depends significantly upon the schedule of positive reinforcement used to maintain lever pressing behavior. Stable response rates can be established in thirsty animals by continuous bar press rewards (every response produces water), aperiodically (a response produces water only at variable intervals), or on a ratio basis (a number of responses—e.g., 10—are required to produce water). Distinguishable behavioral properties characterize the reaction patterns generated by each of these reinforcement contingencies. When the emotional response is superimposed upon stable lever-pressing behavior maintained by these different reinforcement schedules, the rate of both acquisition and extinction of the conditioned "anxiety" varies as a function of the water reward contingencies. With animals working on continuous and ratio reinforcement schedules, acquisition of the "anxiety" response was found to proceed significantly more slowly than in the animals on variable interval or aperiodic schedules. Extinction of the "anxiety" response also was significantly more rapid in these continuous and ratio schedule groups than in the interval schedule animals.[2] Figure 3 illustrates typical ratio and interval schedule performance and the characteristic differences in rate of extinction of the "anxiety" response in two representative animals. These results would seem to point up

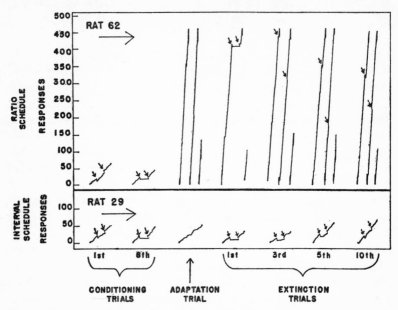

Fig. 3. Extinction of the conditioned "anxiety" response as it appears in sample cumulative response records for two animals showing typical ratio and interval schedule performance. (Brady.[2])

sharply the relevance of a parameter seldom considered in psychopathological studies dealing with "fear" or "anxiety" either in the laboratory or the clinic. Although primary emphasis often focuses upon behavioral effects of such disturbing emotions, surprisingly little attention is given to the characteristics of competing or interacting response systems as important determinants of psychopathology. Indeed, the implications of a careful analysis of such interaction effects for problems related to stress and even psychotherapy do not appear unduly remote.

Of course, such a comparative laboratory approach to the problem of emotional behavior is particularly well suited to the exploration of neural mechanisms in psychopathology, and several recent experiments have been concerned with the functional properties of rather specific neuroanatomic entities and their relationship to the conditioned "anxiety" response. It has been possible to show, for example, that the elaboration of even such basic aspects of affective expression depends heavily upon the integrity of quite specific portions of the central nervous system, notably that group of "limbic system" structures currently receiving considerable multidisciplinary attention.[6,22,25] Although large cortical lesions have been found to produce little or no effect upon either the acquisition, retention, or extinction of the conditioned "anxiety" response, involvement of the more deep-lying subcortical components of the limbic system clearly results in significant changes. Specifically, lesions in the septal region and hippocampus have been found to produce significant decrements in retention of the "anxiety" response, and even more dramatic changes in gross affective expression.[10] Resistance to extinction of the conditioned "anxiety" response also appears to be reduced following lesions of the habenular complex of the thalamus, although cingulate lesions have no apparent effect on such behavior.[11]

Of most recent interest has been the application of this comparative approach to the experimental analysis of emotional behavior in exploring the reinforcing effects of intra-cranial electrical stimulation involving the limbic system. Within the past year Olds and Milner from the McGill University laboratories in Montreal have reported that rats electrically stimulating themselves in various portions of this limbic system by pressing a bar were able to maintain high lever-pressing rates without any other reward.[24] It has now been possible to produce this same phenomenon in the cat, and further to delimit some of the variables of which it is a function, including specific anatomical locus of the stimulating electrodes, schedules of intra-cranial electrical stimulation reinforcement, food deprivation, electrical stimulus intensity, and the like.[3] But of primary interest from the standpoint of our present concern with experimental psychopathology would seem to be the interaction effects between the conditioned "anxiety" response and this intra-cranial self-stimulation phenomenon.

Using a pulse-pair generator, recently described by Lilly and his co-workers,[21] to provide an electrical stimulus reward through chronically implanted electrodes, stable lever-pressing rates have been maintained on several different reinforcement schedules over relatively long periods of time in both cats and rats.[28] Figure 4 shows some typical cumulative response curves obtained from a cat with an electrode in the caudate nucleus, illustrating characteristically stable lever-pressing rates for electrical stimulation, first on a variable interval reinforcement schedule (average 16 sec. interval between rewards), and then on a fixed ratio reinforcement schedule (one reward for every seven lever

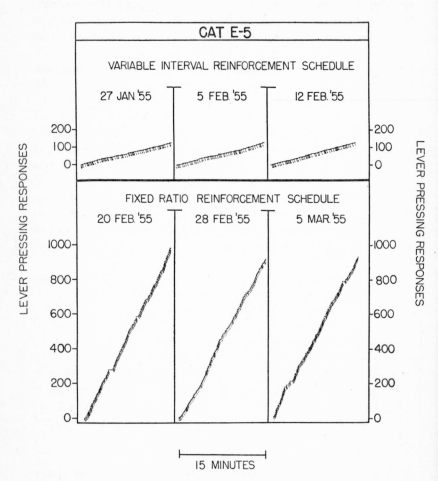

Fig. 4. Sample cumulative response curves showing stable lever pressing behavior for variable interval and fixed ratio intracranial electrical stimulation reward. (Sidman, Brady, Boren, Conrad.[28])

responses). The effects of the conditioned "anxiety" procedure upon such stable lever-pressing habits for intra-cranial electrical stimulation have, however, been found to differ markedly from those observed when the bar pressing response is maintained on a water reward schedule. For example, a conditioned "anxiety" response which has been previously superimposed upon a stable lever-pressing habit for aperiodic (variable interval) water reward, fails to appear when the same animal is lever pressing for an intra-cranial electrical stimulus reward on exactly the same variable interval reinforcement schedule. Presentation of conditioned clicker stimulus fails to suppress the lever-pressing rate or produce the characteristic crouching and defecation, although when the animals are returned to lever-pressing for water the conditioned "anxiety" reappears with all its multiple manifestations in response to the clicker. Figure 5 shows a cumulative response curve obtained from one rat with an electrode in the septal region during a two-hour lever-pressing session with alternating 30-minute periods for water reward and intra-cranial electrical stimulation reward. Although presentation of the clicker (indicated by the first arrow in each segment of the curve) clearly suppresses the lever-pressing rate (and also produces crouching and defecation) during the water reward periods, no such effect is apparent during the electrical stimu-

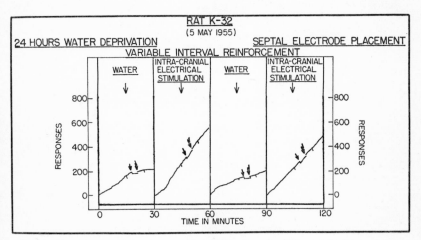

Fig. 5. Sample cumulative response curve showing the differential effects of conditioned "anxiety" procedure upon lever pressing for water and for intracranial electrical stimulation. (Brady.[3])

lation reward periods *even though* termination of the clicker is accompanied on each occasion by shock to the feet (indicated by the second arrow in each segment of the curve). Furthermore, it is now quite clear that a remarkable resistance to acquisition of the conditioned "anxiety" response can be observed when the animal is concurrently provided with the opportunity for intra-cranial self-stimulation of at least these rather restricted portions of the limbic system. Figure 6 shows several cumulative response curves for this same rat, first, during superimposition of the "anxiety" response upon lever pressing for water reward, and then upon lever-pressing for electrical stimulation reward. By the third conditioning trial, presentation of the clicker during the water reward lever-pressing sessions produces the characteristic rate suppression, crouching, and defecation, although no such "anxiety" indicators appear after as many as 16 pairings of clicker and grid shock during lever-pressing sessions for electrical stimulation reward. Again, the small arrows indicate onset of the clicker and its termination with grid shock during each lever-pressing session.

It seems hardly necessary to point out that interpretation of these findings within the descriptive-behavioristic framework represented by the present approach to psychopathology, must await the answers to many experimental questions still under investigation. Of course, the several research studies reported in this paper can be seen to

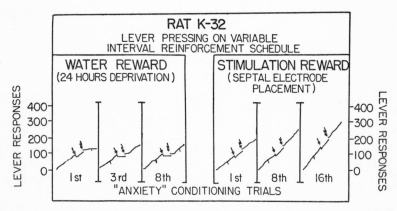

FIG. 6. Sample cumulative response curves showing acquisition of the conditioned "anxiety" response as a function of water and intracranial electrical stimulation reinforcement. (Brady.[3])

share a common emphasis upon the detailed experimental analysis of a somewhat restricted class of behaviors presumed to bear fundamental relationships to at least some forms of psychopathology and their critical determinants—various combinations of stimuli which serve as cues in one form or another, and an unavoidable aversive or unpleasant event of some kind. It is clear, though, that a variety of behavioral and physiological contingencies contribute in most subtle but significant ways to both the topography and dynamic functional properties of such affective phenomena. Many attempts have been made to order these psychopathological diversities to unitary theoretical principles, i.e., emphasis upon the role of "anxiety reduction" as a motivational construct.[23] Indeed, contemporary preoccupation with acquired drives and similar intervening variables would seem to provide ample opportunity for avoiding the conceptual poverty which might be said to characterize the present experimental approach. This more empirical analysis clearly reflects some concern that such monolithic ordering, prematurely embraced, might serve to obscure important behavioral and physiological relationships among psychopathological phenomena presumed to have some crucial dependence on what we conventionally regard as "emotion".

REFERENCES

1. BRADY, J. V.: Does tetraethylammonium reduce fear? J. Comp. & Physiol. Psychol., *46:* 307-310, 1953.

2. ———: Extinction of a conditioned "fear" response as a function of reinforcement schedules for competing behavior. J. Psychol., *40:* 25-34, 1955.

3. ———: Motivational-emotional factors and intra-cranial self-stimulation. Houston Symposium on Brain Stimulation. University of Texas Press, (In Press).

4. ———: The effect of electro-convulsive shock on a conditioned emotional response: the permanence of the effect. J. Comp. & Physiol. Psychol.,*44:* 507-511, 1951.

5. ———: The effect of electro-convulsive shock on a conditioned emotional response: the significance of the interval between the emotional conditioning and the electro-convulsive shock. J. Comp. & Physiol. Psychol., *45:* 9-13, 1952.

6. ———: The paleocortex and behavioral motivation. In Harlow, H. and C. Woolsey, ed.: Interdisciplinary Research in the Behavioral, Biological, and Biochemical Sciences. Univ. of Wisconsin Press, (In Press).

7. ——— AND HUNT, H. F.: A further demonstration of the effects of electro-convulsive shock on a conditioned emotional response. J. Comp. & Physiol. Psychol., *44:* 204-209, 1951.

8. —— AND ——: The effect of electro-convulsive shock on a conditioned emotional response: a control for impaired hearing. J. Comp. & Physiol. Psychol., 45: 180-182, 1952.

9. ——, —— AND GELLER, I.: The effect of electro-convulsive shock on a conditioned emotional response as a function of the temporal distribution of the treatments. J. Comp. & Physiol. Psychol., 47: 454-457, 1954.

10. ——AND NAUTA, W. J. H.: Subcortical mechanisms in emotional behavior: affective changes following septal forebrain lesions in the albino rat. J. Comp. & Physiol. Psychol., 46: 339-346, 1953.

11. —— AND ——: Subcortical mechanisms in emotional behavior: the duration of affective changes following septal and habenular lesions in the albino rat. J. Comp. & Physiol. Psychol. 48: 412-420, 1955.

12. ——, SCHREINER, L., GELLER, I. AND KLING, A.: Subcortical mechanisms in emotional behavior: the effect of rhinencephalic injury upon the acquisition and retention of a conditioned avoidance response in cats. J. Comp. & Physiol. Psychol., 47: 179-186, 1954.

13. ——, STEBBINS, W. C. AND GALAMBOS, R.: The effect of audiogenic convulsions on a conditioned emotional response. J. Comp. & Physiol. Psychol., 46: 363-367, 1953.

14. ——, AND HUNT, H. F.: The effect of electro-convulsive shock (ECS) on a conditioned emotional response: the effect of additional ECS convulsions. J. Comp. & Physiol. Psychol., 46: 368-372, 1953.

15. ESTES, W. K. AND SKINNER, B. F.: Some quantitative properties of anxiety. J. Exper. Psychol., 29: 390-400, 1941.

16. GELLER, I., SIDMAN, M. AND BRADY, J. V.: The effect of electro-convulsive shock on a conditioned emotional response: a control for acquisition recency. J. Comp. & Physiol. Psychol., 48: 130-131, 1955.

17. GOY, R. W.: The effect of electro-convulsive shock on a conditioned emotional response: the relation between the amount of attenuation and the strength of the conditioned emotional response. Unpublished Ph.D. Dissertation, University of Chicago, 1953.

18. HUNT, H. F. AND BRADY, J. V.: Some effects of electro-convulsive shock on a conditioned emotional response ("anxiety"). J. Comp. & Physiol. Psychol., 44: 88-98, 1951.

19. —— AND ——: Some effects of punishment and intercurrent "anxiety" on simple operant. J. Comp. Physiol. Psychol., 48: 305-310, 1955.

20. ——, JERNBERG, P. AND BRADY, J. V.: The effect of electro-convulsive shock (ECS) on a conditioned emotional response: the effect of post-ECS extinction on the reappearance of the response. J. Comp. & Physiol. Psychol., 45: 589-599, 1952.

21. LILLY, J. C., HUGHES, J. R., ALVORD, E. C., AND GALKIN, T. W.: Brief non-injurious electric waveform for stimulation of the brain. Science, 121: 468-499, 1955.

22. MACLEAN, P. D.: The limbic system and its hippocampal formation. Studies in animals and their possible application to man. J. Neurosurg., 11: 29-44, 1954.

23. MILLER, N. E.: Learnable drives and rewards. In Stevens, S. S., ed.: Handbook of Experimental Psychology, New York, Wiley, 1951, pp. 435-472.
24. OLDS, J. AND MILNER, P.: Positive reinforcement produced by electrical stimulation of the septal area and other regions of the rat brain. J. Comp. & Physiol. Psychol., 6: 419-427, 1954.
25. PRIBRAM, K. H. AND KRUGER, L.: Functions of the "olfactory brain." Ann. New York Acad. Sc., 38: 109-138, 1954.
26. RIOCH, D. McK.: Certain aspects of "conscious" phenomena and their neural correlates. Am. J. Psychiat., 3: 810-817, 1955.
27. SCHOENFELD, W. N.: An experimental approach to anxiety, escape, and avoidance behavior. In Hoch, P. H., and J. Zubin, eds.: Anxiety. New York, Grune & Stratton, 1950.
28. SIDMAN, M., BRADY, J. V., BOREN, J. AND CONRAD, D.: The use of reward schedules for investigating behavior maintained by self-administered brain stimulation. Science 122: 830-831, 1955.

4

BEHAVIOR AND METABOLIC CYCLES IN ANIMALS AND MAN

By CURT P. RICHTER, Ph.D.*

IN THIS PAPER I propose to discuss a phenomenon that seems relatively ignored by present-day psychiatrists and psychologists—the phenomenon of cycles in mood and behavior. In the last century many psychiatrists concerned themselves with this phenomenon either directly or indirectly. In this century it is chiefly biochemists who have shown interest in it. Psychiatrists do concern themselves with fluctuations in mood and behavior, but usually for descriptive or diagnostic purposes. And it seems generally accepted that these fluctuations are too irregular to be thought of as true cycles and can best be understood simply as emotional reactions to special events or experiences.

I bring up these considerations because in the course of studies made during the past 35 years on patients and animals our group has arrived at the conclusion that these cycles have a definite biological significance which may throw light on the etiology of the various psychotic conditions. This is but a brief account of the main results of these studies; a more complete account is in preparation.

First of all, to illustrate the genuine regularity of fluctuations in mood and behavior, I shall present a few examples of cycles from over 250 patients with regular cycles in the Phipps Clinic and from patients with regular cycles observed in other clinics and reported in the literature. These patients showed regular cycles at various frequencies from 48 hours to one and a half years; one record will be given for each of a number of frequencies within this range. Equally regular cycles occur in medical patients suffering from so-called "periodic disease" and Reimann[1] has collected histories of over 200 such patients. To our mind the only difference between these patients with periodic disease and those seen in psychiatric clinics is the predominance of physical symptoms in the one, and of mental or

* Henry Phipps Psychiatric Clinic, Johns Hopkins Hospital, Baltimore, Maryland.

34

emotional symptoms in the other. So together we have a large group of individuals with various physical and mental symptoms that show regular cycles of one kind or another. Little is known about the origin or the underlying mechanisms of any of these cycles and this lack of knowledge undoubtedly accounts for the lack of much medical and psychiatric interest in these phenomena.

Finally, a new approach to this problem of cycles will be presented. It depends on observations of animals, in which extraordinary regular cycles of behavior and metabolism— in some instances closely resembling those seen in patients, have been produced experimentally by interfering with the function of the endocrine glands, by brain lesions, or by severe stress.

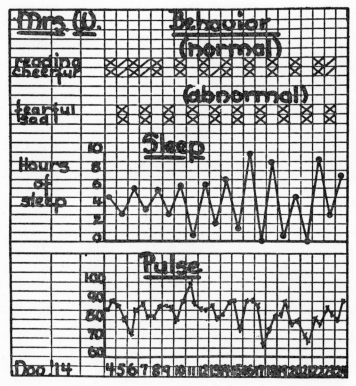

Fig. 1. Part of "Behavior" chart for Mrs. W., a patient showing alternate day cycles of good and bad behavior and mood. The chart shows behavior, hours of sleep and pulse rate.

The first cycle is the shortest, most regular, and most unusual of all. This is the alternate day cycle of good and bad behavior and mood, 48 hours in length. The patient is normal on one day and very sick on the next—in a stupor, manic excitement, or depression. The transition from one phase to the other may be very sharp, lasting only a few minutes. Such cycles may persist without exception for months, years, or even a lifetime. We have had four patients with this cycle in the Phipps Clinic,[2] and Menninger-Lerchenthal has collected records of over 70 patients from all parts of the world, dating as far back as 1798.[3]

Figure 1 shows part of a behavior chart from one of the Phipps patients.[2] It gives markings for normal behavior, abnormal behavior, hours of sleep, and pulse rate. On one day this patient was cheerful and spent her time reading and working; on the next she was sad, wept a good deal, and lacked any interest in work. The hours of sleep ranged from 0 to 10 with a strikingly regular alternate night cycle, being lowest on the nights before the bad days; the pulse rate varied similarly, but not with the same regularity; and usually was lowest on the bad days.

A slightly longer but equally regular cycle was observed in another group of patients. The length of the cycles ranged from 5 to 6 days and is most apparent in the total hours of sleep. Figure 2 shows the sleep record of one of these patients observed in the Phipps Clinic.[4] The hours of sleep ranged from 0 to 10 and showed a very regular 5-day cycle. In each cycle this patient was excited for 3 to 4 days and sluggish for 1 to 2 days. Stiefler[5] and Campbell[6] have described similar cases.

Another Phipps patient showed cycles of still longer duration—

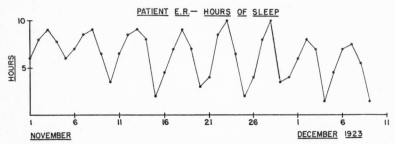

FIG. 2. Sleep chart for psychiatric patient showing regular 5-day cycles.

averaging 10 days.[7] This patient suffered from periodic attacks of depression with severe gastric pains, lasting usually only one or two days, and was completely normal in the interim. The electrical resistance of the skin on the palmar surfaces of the hands showed a sharp increase during the attacks. Figure 3 shows a record of the electrical skin resistance and of the attacks.

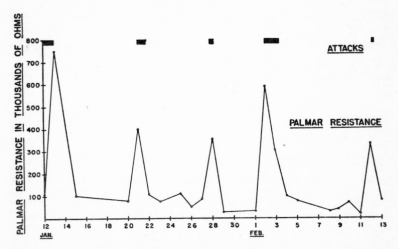

Fig. 3. Graph showing electrical resistance of the skin on palms of hands in thousands of ohms; and occurrence and duration of gastric attacks (solid black shading) in psychiatric patient.

A regular cycle twice as long (20 days) was shown by one of Gjessing's catatonic-schizophrenic patients[8] who was excited for 10 to 15 days and comparatively quiet in the intervals. Figure 4 shows part of the record of this patient; (S) represents mood; (C) ability

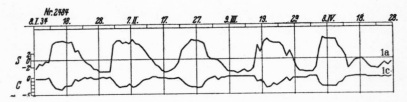

Fig. 4. Part of record from catatonic-schizophrenic showing (S) mood and (C) ability to concentrate at different phases of cycles in excitement. (Gjessing 1936)

to concentrate. During the excited phase of each cycle the patient was unable to concentrate.

A very regular 40-day cycle was shown by a Phipps patient who had a demonstrated parathyroid deficiency.[9] Figure 5 shows part of her behavior chart. Markings above the center line show normal mood

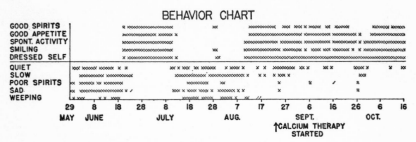

FIG. 5. Part of "behavior" chart of patient with parathyroid deficiency showing normal behavior and mood above line; depressed mood below.

and behavior; those below, abnormal mood and behavior. For 20 days this patient was quiet, sad, and showed little or no spontaneous activity, then suddenly, almost over night, she became active, had a good appetite and a normal interest in her appearance. Twenty days later, equally abruptly, she became sad, slowed, and inactive again. Twenty-five days later her mood and behavior suddenly changed again. When the metabolic deficiency was controlled by calcium and ATIO the patient's mood remained essentially within normal limits.

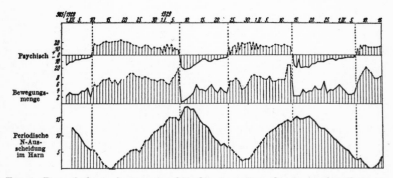

FIG. 6. Part of chart of catatonic-schizophrenic patient showing cycles of stupor. (Gjessing 1932)

A slightly longer but equally regular cycle, 46 days in length on the average, was shown by another of Gjessing's catatonic-schizophrenic patients.[10] This patient was stuporous for 16 to 20 days and fairly normal in the intervals. Figure 6 shows part of his record; the mental state (*psychisch*), spontaneous activity (*bewegungsmenge*), and excretion of urinary nitrogen. Noteworthy here is that the mental and activity curves closely parallel one another, showing very sharp transitions from normal to stupor and again from stupor to normal. In contrast the nitrogen curve swings from retention to excretion and back in even waves. The shift from retention to excretion occurs shortly after the sharp onset of the stupor.

A cycle averaging 56 days in length was reported by Rice in a 14-year-old boy, a patient in the Phipps Clinic.[11] Figure 7 shows part of

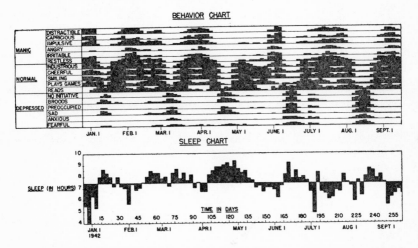

FIG. 7. Part of "behavior" chart showing manic, normal, and depressed moods of 14-year-old boy; also hours of sleep above and below an average of 7.4 hours. (Rice 1944)

the behavior and sleep charts. Markings for manic behavior are shown at the top of the behavior chart, those for normal behavior in the middle, and for depressed behavior at the bottom. As can be seen this boy's behavior ranged from manic through normal to depression and back through normal to manic. The cycles recurred with great regularity in a period of over a year. The chart for the hours of sleep

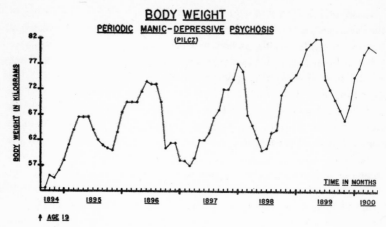

Fig. 8. Body weight curves of patient in Vienna Municipal Hospital. (Pilcz 1901)

shows similar but less regular cycles. Black shading shows hours of sleep above and below the average 7.4 hours. The patient slept longest during the depressed phases, and least during the manic phases.

An example of a much longer but equally regular cycle is shown in Figure 8. This is a portion of the record of a manic-depressive patient in the Municipal Hospital in Vienna and shows very regular cycles in body weight, 15 to 18 months in length, over a period of six years accompanying emotional changes.[12]

The shorter cycles, up to 70 days in length, can be detected in the markings on the behavior charts of the patient's histories, while most of the longer cycles can be detected best from the records of readmission. Some of the Phipps patients with cycles of several years in length have had as many as 14 readmissions.

In some patients the duration of the cycles remained very constant in length, while in some it increased and in others decreased. Typically, each cycle shows two phases—one may be normal or both may consist of abnormal behavior. Most often there is a sharp transition from the one phase to the other. Some patients also showed accompanying cycles of physical symptoms such as fever, tachycardia, headaches, changes in weight, vomiting, and arthralgia.

The study of these cycles leaves little doubt as to the spontaneity of these phenomena, their regularity, and their almost complete independence of any outside influence.

At this point I want to call your attention also to the existence of the aforementioned equally regular cycles that manifest themselves in medical rather than psychiatric patients, and in physical more than emotional symptoms in patients suffering from "periodic disease." They may show periodic fever, vomiting, arthralgia, abdominalgia, headaches either singly or in various combinations as their chief symptoms. Reimann,[1] who has made the largest collection of records from patients with "periodic disease," states that the length of the cycles ranges from two days to six months and may remain very constant or become longer or shorter with time. Such cycles also consist of two phases, normal and abnormal. The cycles may recur for only a short time, months, years, or for an entire lifetime. A patient of Osler's showed periodic edema for 74 years.[13] One of Reimann's patients suffered from periodic arthralgia for 86 years.[1] The regularity of the attacks may be almost incredible: One patient showed neutropenia with fever every 21 days for many years.[14]

Figure 9 shows part of a record of one of Reimann's patients with an 18- to 22-day cycle of body temperature and pulse rate associated with episodes of fever, tachycardia, arthralgia, and visceral pain which recurred regularly for 15 years.[1] The episodes lasted 5 to 7 days and were unrelated to menstrual periods. Figure 10 shows a record of another of Reimann's patients who suffered ulcers, headaches, malaise, and showed neutropenia for 8 to 10 days regularly in cycles of 23 to 26 days.

It must be mentioned here that the histories of patients with "periodic disease" show that in many instances there have been accom-

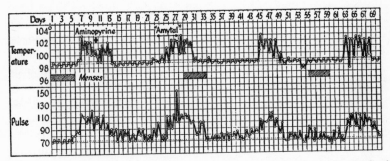

FIG. 9. Chart showing body temperature, pulse rate, and menstrual period of patient with periodic disease. (Reimann 1951)

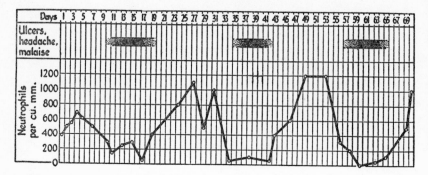

FIG. 10. Chart showing presence of ulcers, headaches, malaise, and neutropenia in patient with periodic disease. (Reimann 1951)

panying emotional disturbances characterized by such symptoms as depression, excitement, or stupor. Thus it is not surprising, after comparing the records of patients with "periodic disease" with those of psychiatric patients with cyclical disturbances, that we have come to feel that there cannot be any fundamental differences between the two types of cycles; that they differ only in predominance of one or the other group of symptoms.

An attempt to find a chemical explanation of cycles was made by Gjessing, who pioneered maintaining patients under constant conditions in bed on a constant fluid diet and made certain that they did not have any infectious disease.[8,10,15] Stokes[16] has given an excellent summary of Gjessing's studies. In periodic catatonic-schizophrenics Gjessing found that the sudden changes in behavior and mood occurred nearly simultaneously with shifts in nitrogen balance in either direction from retention to excretion. He concluded that a toxin is formed at the transition point that is responsible for the mental and other changes. In the belief that these shifts of nitrogen metabolism were of primary importance he administered thyroxine and thyroid extract to eliminate the shifts and the consequent production of toxin. Good results were obtained in a number of his patients, and other workers have also reported clinical improvement of such patients with administration of thyroid.[17,18,19,20,21,22,23,24] Figure 11 shows the record of a periodic cata-tonic-schizophrenic treated with thyroxine and dessicated thyroid gland.[21] Thirteen cycles occurred at very regular intervals over a 21-month period. Six months after thyroxine was started the cycles had completely disappeared and the patient had recovered. The observation of Hardwick and Stokes that changes in nitrogen excretion do not always parallel the behavior and mood cycles has cast some doubt on the validity of Gjessing's thesis. At best, Gjessing's conclusions do not throw any light on the origin of the cycles; as, for instance, what produces the reported shifts in nitrogen excretion.

Menninger-Lerchenthal,[3] who also considers all cyclical variations as manifestations of a single nosological entity, thinks that they result from pathology in the brainstem, chiefly in the hypothalamus. Lindsay,[23] on the basis of observations of two patients, also came to this conclusion. Reimann[1] implies that the cycles occurring in the various forms of "Periodic Disease" must have a common origin. Since in a number of instances these cycles were either seven days in length or a multiple of seven, he speculated that they might depend on the 6.6-day cycle of solar radiation reported by Abbott.[25] Despite these speculations we know very little about the origin of any of the cycles of behavior, mood, or metabolism as seen either in psychiatric patients or in patients with "periodic disease".

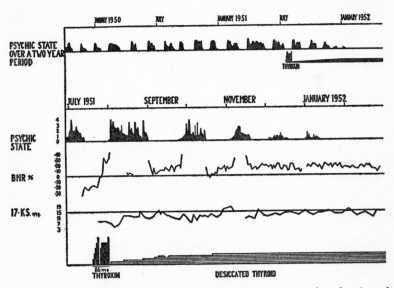

FIG. 11. Chart showing mood and behavior cycles of catatonic-schizophrenic and effect of treatment with thyroxine and dessicated thyroid extract. (Gornall, et al. 1953)

As has been done in other instances when the cause of a given disease could not be determined in man himself, understanding may be sought by the experimental production of similar conditions in animals.

We have attempted to reproduce cycles in behavior and metabolism in one species of animal, the common Norway rat, which lends itself well to this purpose. Its metabolic processes are remarkably similar to those of man and quantitative observations are easily made on significant facts such as its daily spontaneous running activity, food and water intake, and body weight, as well as of the condition of the reproductive tract in females. Furthermore, we have records on thousands of normal rats to serve as control data for observations on rats in which abnormal cycles have been produced experimentally.

We have succeeded in producing abnormal cycles in behavior and metabolism in several different ways: (1) by interfering with the function of the thyroid gland (of special interest in relation to Gjessing's studies), (2) by section of the pituitary stalk or removal of the posterior lobe (of interest in relation to some cases of "periodic disease", and (3) by parathyroidectomy (of interest in relation to the case reported from the Phipps Clinic mentioned above).

First, cycles in behavior and metabolism were produced by interfering with the function of the thyroid gland by partial thyroidectomy,[26] permanent injury to the gland through feeding of a sulfa drug,[27] and partial destruction of the gland by feeding I^{131}.[28]

Sub-total thyroidectomy, i.e., removal of all except very small fragments of the gland, produced abnormal and regular cycles starting with a duration of 40 days and gradually becoming shorter with a duration of 18 days. Three out of 14 thyroidectomized rats showed cycles.

Figures 12 and 13 show a record of extraordinarily regular cycles in running activity and food intake produced in a rat by feeding sulfamerazine (0.5 per cent of diet) over a period of 110 days. The ordinates show daily running activity in number of revolutions of the drum and food intake in grams. Figure 12 covers the period from 587 to 777 days; Fig. 13 from 777 to 947 days, a total of 360 days. Sulfamerazine was discontinued a short time before the start of the record in Fig. 12. During the 360-day period there were 12 regular cycles, each consisting of an active and an inactive phase. The first cycle was 48 days in length; the next 46 days. Each successive cycle became progressively shorter until they were finally only about 20 days in

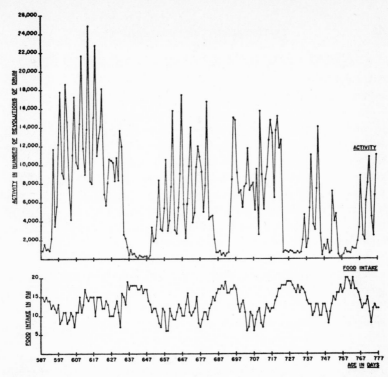

FIG. 12. Graph showing cycles in spontaneous running activity (revolutions of drum) and food intake produced by feeding sulfamerazine (0.5%) for 110 days before start of above record.

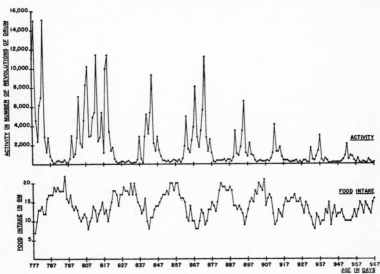

FIG. 13. Continuation of chart in Fig. 12.

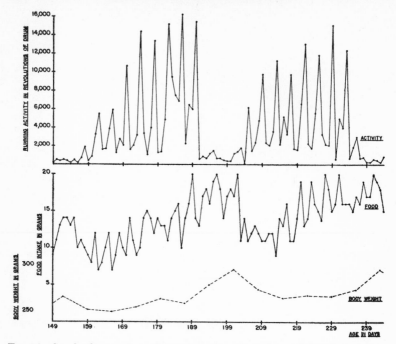

FIG. 14. Graph showing two abnormal cycles of running activity, body weight, and food intake produced by tube feeding with I[131].

length. Food intake was consistently lower in the active phase and higher in the inactive phase and body weight was higher during the inactive phase. The rat showed diestrous smears during the inactive phase and the regular 4- to 5-day estrous cycles during the active phase.

Incomplete destruction of the thyroid gland by feeding I[131] produced equally regular cycles in activity as well as in body weight, food intake, and reproductive cycles. Two cycles from a rat that had been treated with I[131] are shown in Fig. 14. These cycles were both 45 days in length and the record shows clearly the suddennness of the transition from one phase to the other. As with the other two methods, successive cycles became shorter and shorter, finally leveling off in about 20 days.

These abnormal cycles produced by various forms of thyroid deficiency were eliminated and activity was increased to its normal level by treatment with dessicated thyroid powder in each case in which it was used.

It is important to mention at this point that only about three out

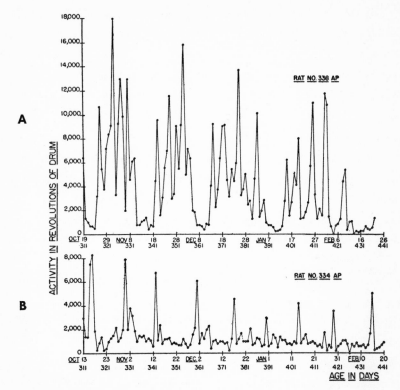

FIG. 15. Graphs showing two types of cycles in spontaneous running activity produced by removal of posterior lobe of pituitary.

of 10 rats showed the abnormal metabolic cycles, regardless of whether they were thyroidectomized or treated with sulfamerazine or with I^{131}. This means that we are not as yet able to produce these thyroid cycles at will, and will be reconsidered in the discussion of the results.

Another type of cycle was produced both by section of the pituitary "stalk" and by posterior lobectomy. After section of the "stalk" the rats became inactive except for sharp bursts of activity that usually lasted one or two days at intervals of 14 to 18 days.[28] In most instances posterior lobectomy produced very similar cycles (*See* Fig. 15B). The bursts of activity occurred at 14-day intervals at the start, then at slightly longer intervals. Figure 15A shows a less frequent type of cycle which was longer than the more common type, but also tended to become slightly longer with time, rather than shorter as in the case of the thyroid cycles.

Parathyroidectomy in rats also produced equally regular cycles in activity, food and water intake, and in the voluntary intake of a solution of calcium lactate.[29] These cycles were 20 days in length for the rat; 40 days for the monkey.

Behavior and metabolic cycles, some with low or high frequency, have been produced by interference with the function of other organs; by lesions of different parts of the brain.

At this point I should like to mention the mechanisms that may possibly be involved in the production of these cycles. In the thyroid cycle the presence of a small fragment of active thyroid tissue seems to be necessary for cycles to appear. A totally thyroidectomized rat does not show cycles, nor indeed does it show more than absolutely minimal activity. The appearance of the cycles presumably depends on interaction between the thyroid fragments and the cells of the anterior lobe that produce thyroid-stimulating hormone and the cells that produce gonadatropin.[30] The operation of a feed-back mechanism seems to play an important part here.

At present we do not have an explanation of the origin of the pituitary and parathyroid cycles produced by stalk section or posterior lobectomy. It is probable that here, too, a small fragment of functioning tissue may be necessary for the appearance of the cycles. It is also possible that this operation may have some direct or indirect influence on the cells of the adjoining hypothalamus. Nor do we have an explanation for the origin of cycles produced by parathyroidectomy.

We must also consider the possibility that various organs of the body have their own cycles, and that in a well-integrated organism the different cycles mesh together in an even, non-cyclical operation. A disturbance of any one organ may thus allow a cycle from one or more of the other organs to appear.[31,32]

What light, if any, do the results of these animal studies throw on the origin of cycles seen in man? To start with, the cycles produced in the rat by incomplete thyroidectomy or by some form of thyroid destruction have much in common with those found by Gjessing and others in the catatonic schizophrenics. They are of the same length and show similar clear-cut phases, with sharp transitions. A comparison of the curves of Gjessing's patient in Fig. 6 with those from one of our rats in Figs. 12 and 13 brings out the close relationship, on the one hand between mood and activity, and on the other between nitrogen metabolism and food intake; all are abolished by thyroid treatment. It would thus appear that Gjessing's patients may have been suffering from a primary thyroid deficiency rather than from a primary disturbance in nitrogen metabolism.

A fairly close similarity exists between the activity cycles produced by stalk section or posterior lobectomy and the metabolic cycles of some patients with "periodic disease." It will be recalled that some of the patients showed neutropenia and fever every 21 days for only a day, at the most two or three, almost over a lifetime. Many of the rats with stalk section and posterior lobectomy also showed bursts of activity every 18 days for only one or two days, over many months.

It is possible that this particular group of patients with "periodic disease" may suffer from some destruction in this region of the

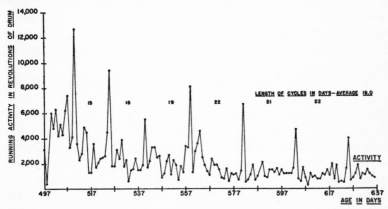

FIG. 16. Graph showing cycles in spontaneous running activity produced apparently by tumor in region of pituitary.

pituitary, a defect of the posterior lobe or of the adjoining brain tissue. It may thus be more than a coincidence that the patient with the extraordinarily regular 3-week cycles of neutropenia described by Rutledge et al,.[14] later developed diabetes insipidus.[33]

It is of interest here that one of our supposedly normal rats showed regular bursts of spontaneous activity every 14 to 18 days; the same reaction found only after stalk section or posterior lobectomy. The cycles were present for about six months, disappearing when the animal became very sluggish and inactive. Autopsy was performed several months after the disappearance of the cycles and an enormous tumor was found at the base of the brain, presumably of pituitary origin. (See Fig. 16.) It is likely that at the time the cycles were present the tumor had grown just large enough to damage the stalk, posterior lobe, or adjacent circulation, but not large enough to interfere with other functions.

It is noteworthy that parathyroidectomy produced 20-day cycles in rats and 40-day cycles in monkeys, and that a patient with a parathyroid deficiency had a 40-day cycle.[7] Treatment of this patient with ATIO and one liter of a two per cent solution of calcium lactate daily restored her to normal behavior and mood, eliminating the cyclical variations.

That faulty function of the adrenal glands may also give rise to cycles was brought out by a case record reported by Rowntree and Ray.[24] The very regular changes in behavior and mood of their patient were accompanied by symptoms of adrenal malfunction. Of special interest from the point of view of dietary self-selection studies is that during remissions the patient ate large amounts of salt and drank large amounts of fluids ravenously.

Cycles may originate because of varied factors: inherited defects of glands, excessive and prolonged treatment with hormones or antihormones, removal of all except a small fragment of the glands, or severe stress.

That behavior and metabolic cycles can actually be produced by stress we were able to demonstrate by two sets of experiments on rats. Several wild rats that had been made to fight each other almost to death over a 20-minute period showed very regular abnormal cycles of running activity; that is, cycles that were not present before fighting or in other normal rats. Figure 17 shows that although no cycles were present before fighting, regular cycles, averaging 43.7 days in length, appeared afterwards and remained unchanged for over 200 days until the animal was killed.

Several laboratory rats that had been forced to swim for 40 to 60 hours also showed cycles. This swimming performance involves the effects not only of fatigue but also of starvation and the loss of sleep. Figure 18 shows the record of one of the rats after swimming 49 hours and 11 minutes. It showed two regular cycles lasting 33 and 36 days respectively, and then a number of shorter cycles with small excursions. In general this type of cycle resembles that obtained by inter-

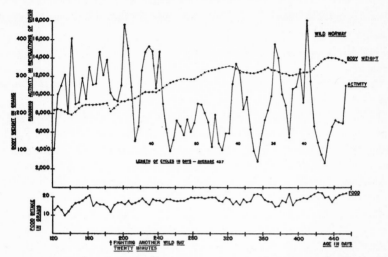

Fig. 17. Graph showing cycles in spontaneous running activity produced in wild Norway rat by severe stress (fighting another wild rat for 20 minutes). Daily running activity and food intake are given in four-day averages.

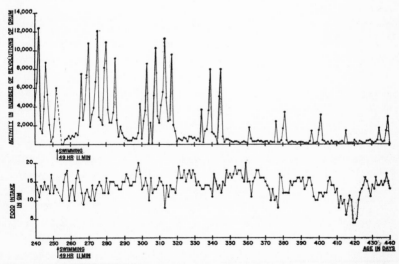

Fig. 18. Graph showing cycles in spontaneous running activity and food intake produced in rat by forced swimming in water (95 F) for 49 hours, 11 minutes.

ference with the thyroid gland. We do not know yet whether the stress changed the thyroid or some other organ, although there is some indication that the pancreas and the hypothalamus may have been damaged.

At this stage we have no idea of how the length of cycles produced experimentally in animals by interference with any one organ will compare with the length of the abnormal cycles seen in man and presumably produced by interference with the same organ. In some instances the rat and human cycles may have nearly the same length, as would appear to be true in the case of the thyroid deficiency and stalk section, or they may be quite different. It must be recalled that the sex cycle in rats is only 4 to 5 days in length, while in human beings it is 28 days; and the life spans are roughly in the ratio of 1 to 20. At present we have no explanation for any of the similarities or differences.

I should like at this point to call attention to the great opportunity offered by the study of patients with cycles, especially patients with short cycles of a few days in length, for the understanding of the parts played by physiological processes in influencing mental processes. For years on end these patients may be normal one day and paranoid, hallucinated, or depressed the next. A comparison of the two phases— the abnormal day with the normal baseline—should throw light on the mechanisms, whether peripheral or central, that are responsible for the great changes seen in behavior, mood, and thinking.

SUMMARY

Human beings that ordinarily do not show cycles in behavior, mood, or metabolism—except those of the menstruating female—may under pathological conditions show extraordinarily regular cycles.

Cycles may manifest themselves chiefly in changes of emotion and mood, in thinking, or in general energy, thus becoming of psychiatric interest; in changes in body temperature, pulse rate, basal metabolism, nitrogen metabolism, the appearance of disturbances in the gastro-intestinal tract, edema, skin eruptions, pain in joints and in other parts of the body, thus becoming of medical concern.

Except for the dominant manifestation, no inherent difference seems to exist between the cycles shown by the patients with primarily emotional complaints and those with primarily physical complaints.

The incidence of patients showing cycles may be higher than would appear from the number of published records. More than 250 patients with regular cycles have been found in one psychiatric clinic. Records of over 200 patients with physical diseases—"periodic disease"—have been published from various medical centers.

Length of the cycles may range from one day to 11 years in different types of patients, but be *quite* constant for any one individual. The origin of the cycles, either physical or emotional, or of the underlying mechanisms involved in their production has long remained a mystery. Explanations have often been sought in external events or experiences.

This mystery has now been attacked by the *finding* that equally regular cycles in behavior and metabolism can be produced experimentally in animals by interfering with (1) the endocrine glands, (2) the brain; and (3) by subjecting animals to very severe stress.

Experimental removal of all except a small functional part of thyroid tissue produces cycles that closely resemble those found in periodic catatonic-schizophrenic patients. Cycles produced by section of the pituitary stalk or by removal of the posterior lobe resemble those found in patients with periodic agranulocytosis; and those produced by parathyroidectomy resemble others produced by parathyroid deficiency in a psychiatric patient.

It is hoped that the information obtained from studies on the experimental production of cycles in animals will help place the studies of cycles in man—whether in psychiatric patients or patients with "periodic disease"—on a firm objective basis.

REFERENCES

1. REIMANN, H. A.: Periodic disease. Medicine *30:* 219-245, 1951.
2. RICHTER, C. P.: Two-day cycles of alternating good and bad behavior in psychotic patients. Arch. Neurol. & Psychiat. *39:* 587-598, 1938.
3. MENNINGER-LERCHENTHAL, E.: Rhythmik und periodik in der psychopathologie. Wien. Zschr. Nervenh. *3:* 261-294, 1950.
4. RICHTER, C. P.: Cyclic manifestations in the sleep curves of psychotic patients. Arch. Neurol. & Psychiat. *31:* 149-151, 1934.
5. STIEFLER, G.: Circular disturbances of sleep after lethargic encephalitis. München. med. Wchnschr. *73:* 981, 1926.
6. CAMPBELL, D.: Periodische Schlafzustände nach Encephalitis Epidemica. Monatsschr. Psychiat. u. Neurol. *65:* 58, 1927.
7. LEVINE, M. AND RICHTER, C. P.: Periodic attacks of gastric pain accompanied with marked changes in the electrical resistance of the skin. Arch. Neurol. & Psychiat. *33:* 1078-1080, 1935.
8. GJESSING, R.: Beitäge zur kenntnis der pathophysiologie der katatonen erregung. Arch Psychiat. *104:* 355-416, 1936.
9. RICHTER, C. P. HONEYMAN, W. M. AND HUNTER, H.: Behavior and mood cycles apparently related to parathyroid deficiency. J. Neurol. Neurosurg. & Psychiat. *3:* 19-26, 1940.

10. GJESSING, R.: Beiträge zur kenntnis der pathophysiologie des katatonen stupors. Arch. Psychiat. *96:* 319-392, 1932.
11. RICE, K. K.: Regular forty to fifty-day cycles of psychotic behavior in a 14-year-old Boy. Arch. Neurol. & Psychiat. *51:* 478-480, 1944.
12. PILCZ, A.: Die periodischen geistersstörungen. Jena, Gustav Fischer, 1901.
13. OSLER, W.: Hereditary angio-neurotic edema. Am. J. M. Sci. *95:* 362-367, 1888.
14. RUTLEDGE, B. H., HANSEN-PRÜSS, O. C. AND THAYER, W. S.: Recurrent agranulocytosis. Bull. Johns Hopkins Hosp. *46:* 369-389, 1930.
15. GJESSING, R.: Disturbances of somatic functions in catatonia with a periodic course and their compensations. J. Ment. Sc., *84:* 608-621, 1938.
16. STOKES, A. B.: Somatic research in periodic catatonia. J. Neurol. Neurosurg. & Psychiat. *2:* 243-258, 1939.
17. HARDWICK, S. W. AND STOKES, A. B.: Metabolic investigations in periodic catatonia. Proc. Roy. Soc. Med., *34:* 733-756, 1941.
18. DANZIGER, L. AND KINDWALL, J. A.: Thyroid therapy in some mental disorders. Dis. Nerv. System *9:* 231-241, 1948.
19. ——, —— AND LEWIS, H. R.: Periodic relapsing catatonia: simplified diagnosis and treatment. Dis. Nerv. System *9:* 330-335, 1948.
20. —— AND ——: Thyroid therapy in some mental disorders. Dis. Nerv. System *14:* 3-13, 1953.
21. GORNALL, A. G., EGLITIS, B., MILLER, A., STOKES, A. B. AND DEWAN, J. G.: Long-term clinical and metabolic observations in periodic catatonia. An application of the kinetic method of research in three schizophrenic patients. Am. J. Psychiat. *109:* 584-594, 1953.
22. MALL, G.: Beitrag zur gjessingschen thyroxinbehandlung der periodischen katatonien. Arch. Psychiat. *187:* 381-403, 1952.
23. LINDSAY, J. S. B.: Periodic catatonia. J. Ment. Sc. *94:* 590-602, 1948.
24. ROWNTREE, D. W. AND KAY, W. W.: Clinical biochemical and physiological studies in cases of recurrent schizophrenia. J. Ment. Sc. *98:* 100-121, 1952.
25. ABBOTT, C. G.: The sun as a regular variable star. Science *105:* 632, 1947.
26. RICHTER, C. P.: The role played by the thyroid gland in the production of gross body activity. Endocrinology *17:* 73-87, 1933.
27. —— AND BISWANGER, L. T.: In preparation.
28. ——: Cyclical phenomena produced in rats by section of the pituitary stalk and their possible relation to pseudo-pregnancy. Am. J. Physiol. *106:* 80-90, 1933.
29. —— AND ECKERT, J. F.: Increased calcium appetite of parathyroidectomized rats. Endocrinology *21:* 50-54, 1937.
30. MCGAVACK, T. H.: The Thyroid. St. Louis, C. V. Mosby Company, 1951.
31. RICHTER, C. P.: Animal behavior and internal drives. Quart. Rev. Biol. *2:* 307-343, 1927.
32. ——: Biological foundation of personality differences. Am. J. Orthopsychiat. *2:* 345-362, 1932.
33. THOMPSON, W. P.: Observations on the possible relation between agranulocytosis and menstruation with further studies on a case of cyclic neutropenia. New England J. Med. *210:* 176-178, 1934.

Discussion of Chapters 1-4

By W. N. SCHOENFELD, Ph.D.*

THIS SYMPOSIUM is another heartening sign of the growing interaction between psychopathologists and experimental psychologists.
It is a simple fact that both categories of workers are involved in the
general science of behavior and both contribute their entries to the
same balance sheet of profit and loss.The American Psychopathological
Association, to its credit, has been a leader in recognizing interaction
among behavioral researchers as a natural and irrepressible outcome
of their mutual interests, and has been a leader in implementing
that recognition by means of meetings like this morning's.

The data and considerations offered in the previous papers (Chapters
1-4) represent a total of many years' work and thought by their contributors, and I am certain that we who listened have found it difficult
to absorb all of this provocative material in so short a time. Being a
discussant, however, is less fun than being a listener, especially when,
as an experimentalist, one is probably expected to be chary with
applause and generous with criticism. If this be the expectation I must
do my best to comply, no matter how often I betray my admiration for
our contributors nor how strongly that admiration urges me to reverse
my function.

II

Doctor Brady summarizes work done on various effects of electro-
convulsive shock (ECS) on "anxiety" in rats, and on the reinforcement-
like effects of electric stimulation in the limbic system of cats. Taken
as a whole the paper is impressive evidence of what can be achieved
today by a behavioral scientist in a proper laboratory. Given good
procedures, conditions, and controls, behavioral measures display such
sensitivity that data from even a single organism are often definitive
for any selected independent variable, that is, they are replicable
in other individuals. Once this was true only of a few areas, such as
psychophysics, but there seems little doubt that we are entering a thriv-
ing period of new advances in our science.

The author's treatment of "anxiety" is one that I, for my part, find

* Department of Psychology, Columbia University, New York City.

very congenial. He does not indulge in the old fallacy of reification which has become the modern sport in handling "anxiety"; nor does he confuse it with stimuli, responses, drives, emotions, or intervening variables. He does give it clear and unambiguous statement in terms of the independent and dependent variables involved.

The experimental manipulations he applies to ECS provide a number of interesting points for discussion and of these I might choose one or two for particular mention. Brady reports that "when . . . a series of experimental extinction trials . . . is administered immediately following attenuation of the response by . . . ECS . . . the 'anxiety' response fails to reappear 30 days later, even though the cessation of lever pressing, crouching . . . do not appear at any time during the course of extinction." The problem of whether a conditioned stimulus's power can be extinguished without the response occurring is one of some importance in current learning theory and has given rise to a small controversial literature, but Brady does not relate his finding to previous work on the question. This omission, probably intentional, is less to the point, however, than his willingness to mention, in connection with that finding, an ambiguous, untestable and pseudo-neurological notion " . . . relative to the independence of the anticipatory functions of the brain and overt behavioral expression." This latter view is, of course, inconsistent with the unassailable position on "anxiety" Brady otherwise adopts, and represents a lapse to an inferior level of discourse. An alternate explanation is available which keeps to the level of behavior and for which some evidence has already been gathered. This explanation, to which I am still inclined, appeals to an interaction between the striate and smooth muscle response systems, an interaction arising from the inclusion, in the conditioned stimulus complex controlling the observed response in one system, of the internal stimulus accompaniments of a response in the other system. Simply put, this means that the proprioceptive stimuli accompanying the autonomically-mediated responses in "anxiety" may acquire partial control, as part of the conditioned stimulus pattern, over the skeletal muscle response of bar-pressing. This would imply that Brady's extinction procedure may have eliminated autonomically-mediated responses to his clicker and thus have led, because of the change in the total conditioned stimulus pattern and the known properties of generalization gradients, to a reduction in the "anxiety response" evoked by the clicker. Be that as it may, Brady's next point is certainly valid, namely, that such an extinction phenomenon can have far-reaching practical implications for psychotherapy if it can be verified on the human level. He is also undoubtedly aware, too, that this possibility goes hand in hand with another idea that has cropped up in many places seemingly independently, that is, that the post-ECS period of "depression" may be taken advantage of as a training period for behavior which is clinically desired but inaccessible for training during a patient's pre-ECS state, or for behavior which is antagonistic and incompatible with the undesirable syndrome expected to reappear after ECS effects dissipate; in short, the possibility that the post-ECS phase may be exactly the time for the most intensive therapy. If this turns out to be the case, experiments like Brady's will have provided some landmarks for a causative analysis.

One final comment on Brady's ECS work. He reports that acquisition of the "anxiety response" (i.e., depression of the bar-pressing rate when the signal→shock sequence is superimposed) is slower for animals whose bar-pressing is under continuous or ratio reinforcement than when it is under variable interval or aperiodic reinforcement; moreover, extinction of the "anxiety response" is faster for the continuous and ratio reinforcement animals than for the interval schedule animals. Such findings are not easily, if at all, predictable from any current theory of conditioning, nor do they conform to the intuitive expectations I believe most workers would derive from already-known effects of these schedules. Thus, the findings not only teach a lesson about rash theorizing and premature judgment, but are all the more interesting for being so unexpected. In addition, this negative correlation between acquisition and extinction rates as among different reinforcement schedules should find a place in the general literature concerning acquisition-extinction correlations.

Turning to the studies of limbic system stimulation, I find it difficult to know what to say. This work is intriguing, but it is still in an early stage and its implications for behavior theory lie in the future. The data seem clear that response-produced limbic stimulation can maintain a response, and in this operational sense it acts as a "reinforcement." The world to which organisms are adapted, that which we call "nature," does not offer direct limbic stimulation as a reinforcement contingency, and it may perhaps turn out that such stimulation will create anomalies and conundrums for behavior theory requiring separate treatment. A similar case is that of direct faradization of muscle tissue by electric shock, which also does not appear in "nature" as a contingency and sometimes seems to create difficulties for behavior theory. In any event, a leap of unknown length appears necessary to pass from limbic "reinforcement" to reinforcements like food or water. Happily, Brady is not the sort of scientist to abandon his phenomenon and his variables for an excursion into fantasy and pseudo-neurology on the basis of the "similar" behavioral effects of reinforcement and limbic stimulation. Such an excursion at this stage could only become mired in *ad hoc* and fictional relations between this stimulation and behavioral principles of secondary reinforcement, motivation, and the like. Much more important is it to concentrate effort on studying the parameters of limbic "reinforcement," making some comparisons with reinforcement parameters of which we already have some knowledge. For example, would limbic "reinforcement" yield a delay of reinforcement gradient, and if so, what kind? What is the effect of amount of stimulation, and of increases or decreases in amount? Can a secondary reinforcer be established by pairing with limbic stimulation, and what are the parameters of such establishment? What behavioral effects are generated by various schedules of limbic "reinforcement"? Someday, perhaps, Doctor Brady will have answers to these questions and more, and we may hope that future symposia will have the pleasure of hearing from him again.

III

Doctor Gantt's historical remarks made an interesting introduction to his talk. Both conditioned cardiac rate changes and the rate changes occurring in the course of other conditioning caught the eyes of Sherrington, Pavlov, Watson, Lashley, and others. None of these men made any systematic study of the effect, but their notice of it showed the sharpness of their observation and, in view of later developments, the shrewdness of their foresight. Among these later developments, Doctor Gantt's own work occupies a prominent place. Although his studies have branched out in several directions, his talk centered on experimentally-induced tachycardia in dogs. Using a "stress" situation, he finds that the heart may be readily conditioned, that the CR is in the direction of tachycardia, and that this tachycardia may be extremely persistent, that is, resistant to extinction.

As Gantt spoke and presented his slides, the "persistence" of his cardiac CR reminded me of the durable effects in Richter's fighting and swimming rats. Although one occasionally encounters the feeling that conditioning with aversive stimulation has more lasting or deepgoing effects than when appetitive stimuli are used, any such general conclusion really is not indicated since, among other things, it ignores the many parameters involved in an appropriate demonstration, and implies a dubious, if not impossible, comparability between amounts or intensities of aversive and appetitive reinforcement. Though psychopathologists often regard themselves as concerned mainly with behavior problems arising from negative reinforcement, is it not true that as many, as long-lasting, and as serious behavioral problems arise from misuse of positive reinforcement? As you know, too, there are some developments of behavior theory which do not include any distinction between "positive" and "negative" reinforcement, but instead treat conditioning phenomena as integrations of reinforcement and extinction effects over response classes defined in certain ways, all the while regarding reinforcement as a monotype. From this viewpoint the aforementioned conclusion is even more clearly subject to parametric qualifications.

Regarding the tachycardia Gantt observes, I cannot help thinking that affairs in this field are currently in a curious state of seeming inconsistency. For many years, our conception of a stressed organism has been that of Cannon, namely, the "adrenalized" organism. As part of this conception we routinely expect that an organism under stress will show increased cardiac rate, and that it is this increased rate which will be the CR to a stimulus initiating stress, that is, a stimulus signalizing aversive stimulation. During the past few years, there have been reported a number of studies on human subjects involving measures of cardiac CR in a "stress" situation. Subjects were exposed to a sequence of signal→electric shock, and systematic acquisition, extinction, and other data, were secured on cardiac CR to the signal. The consistent finding was that the cardiac CR comprised a drop in rate rather than a rise, on occurrence of the signal, and this finding has since been corroborated at least twice by independent investigators. Faced with such discrepant findings we must conclude either that one or the other of the two findings is incorrect, which I cannot believe in view of the weight of data on both sides, or that both findings are correct. The second alternative may seem impossible at first blush, but it becomes more palatable on reflection and after a closer inspection of the literature. The apparent discrepancy arises from the variety of experimental procedures and features, and the variety of conditions of measurement of cardiac CR, that have been indiscriminately assigned to the single rubric of "stress". Because we make the initial error of adopting too broad a rubric, we commit the second error of regarding bidirectional findings as discrepant. Faced by seemingly contradictory data, we are reminded of Mach's observation that, in such cases, the truth lies in finer distinctions.

IV

Richter's attention is engaged by behavioral cycles. With these as his dependent variable, and guided by a theory combining endocrines-metabolism-nervous system, Doctor Richter considers first some observations on human cycles and then passes to rat cycles which he feels to be analogues of the human observations. We can perhaps obtain a different perspective if we change this sequence and consider the animal picture first.

Richter's early studies of rhythm in the rat are classic, and give him a voice of considerable authority. In this morning's presentation of later work, activity measures are again used as the behavioral index, but this time in connection with experimental operations chosen presumably as tests of his physiological theory of cycles. The numerous slides offered for our inspection give testimony to the care with which these activity measures were gathered and help to exhibit what Richter has in mind when he says "cycle." He does not mean simply changes in activity over time, though all such changes could be called "cyclical"; rather, he means certain types of change. If we liken his activity curve to a wave plot, we can exhaustively list the possible questions by reference to the form and parameters of the function, and to changes in these as a function of time. Richter does essentially this, but he seems preoccupied more with certain aspects of his waves than with others. Such preoccupation may be only a matter of taste, however, and not binding upon other researchers who decide to join Richter in exploring this area.

The general treatment Richter gives his rat data seems to me to call for two comments. First, he dismisses external events as possible causes of his observed cycles, but this runs headlong into his own discovery of stress (i.e., fighting and prolonged swimming) as an experimental method of producing his cycles. What we need from him here are some definitions of words like "external" and "event" to make clear how he conceives them. Only an intense concentration on his theory could lead Richter, first, to neglect the external referents of "fighting" and "swimming" in favor of supposed internal consequences of these activities, and, second to think we could understand him without further explanation. In the same connection, Richter argues for an internal and presumably permanent upset in the animal resulting from its experimental stress, citing as analogues of the abnormal cycles obtained after stress those obtained after endocrine and neurological invasions. But the analogy is not clear, being drawn on the bases of "abnormality" and "permanence" rather than those of etiology and functional properties. It would seem more desirable to make use of conditioning and extinction parameters in behavior theory to account for these results, before recourse is taken to the remoter levels of gland and nervous system. We may recall, as perhaps akin to Richter's case, the "inextinguishable" avoidance obtained by Solomon and Wynne with severe electric shock, to which the same thought would apply. Incidentally, the reported inaccessibility of Richter's stress-induced cycles to hormone therapy leads one to wonder how they would fare under some of Brady's ECS procedures.

Second, Richter's theorizing about the physiological bases of his cycles is couched in too broad terms, is too lacking in detail, to impart his own conviction to another who, like myself, might have some initial hesitancy about the utility and feasibility of physiologizing the science of behavior. Thus, he speaks of a "target organ" when his actual data are activity measures and define the skeletal muscles as the final "target" no matter how many intermediate "targets" are hypothesized. Again, he speaks of the interaction of a target organ with its glandular opposite number as if there really were such exclusive and one-to-one relations. Moreover he adds the supposition that his experiments cause the "successive states [of this interaction to be] stretched out as in a slow-motion picture," when what he means is that his cycles take longer than he expects of endocrine reactions; hence, since the data will not yield, the play must be on the other more accommodating side of "theory." Or, again, the hypothalamus is regarded as a "site" of hormonal action, as an "energy center" in which important loci are "close together." To my mind, Richter's work is too valuable to be treated this way, and he can be sure that it will survive the ebb and flow of physiological fads.

Before leaving Richter's rat studies, I might risk a suggestion that occurred to me on viewing his slides. In several instances, it seemed to me there appeared a long-term cycle superimposed on the shorter rhythms. It might be worthwhile to submit these data to some of the newer techniques of sequence analysis; with the aid of machine computation, such analysis could check the existence of superposed periodicities with relative ease. Richter's data may contain more than his paper has hinted at, and I shouldn't be surprised if this eminent researcher has suspected it, but has let caution silence him in advance of the quantitative demonstration.

In passing to the studies of human cycles cited by Richter, difficulties are encountered at once. First, some of the earlier work appears questionable as to methodology, and the reliability of the data is dubious, so that we are no longer quite sure of just what is intended by "cycle," and just what the human cycles are, if any, that we are trying to explain. Second, the status of the datum has changed from simple activity measures to complex behavioral patterns including emotional components. Perhaps it is for this reason that Richter includes the hypothalamus in his physiological theory of rat cycles. Despite these and other immediately apparent difficulties, Richter holds firmly to the conviction, not only that cycles in humans are a tractable datum, but that they are the same datum his rats give, both in overt aspect and in etiology. Though one may disagree with our contributor, claiming that the case is not proved, we are instructed by the ideas and observations that accompany the development of his theme; for example, that psychiatric patients and patients with so-called periodic diseases have overlapping syndromes; that physical and emotional symptoms are correlated; that in an early study where some patients were reported improved out of a group subjected to thyroid treatment, no one bothered to determine whether the improved patients had had thyroid deficiency to begin with.

A basic issue in Richter's discussion of human cycles, even more than with the rat cycles, I think, is his strikingly swift dismissal of external events as causes. He is not diverted by the fact that only the grossest attention could be paid to external events in a hospital situation; he cares nothing for the fact that the very complexity of his cited human cycles not only opens the way for subtle external controls over large segments, if not all, of the behavior described, but also greatly increases the likelihood that such controls were indeed present; he is unmoved by his own citation of a finding that German and American workers show a difference in cycle of 31 days as against 34 days, respectively. He is convinced: his cycles are not externally caused. If one day his view becomes accepted doctrine, Richter will be looked back upon with awe.

V

Doctor Scheflen reports an experiment aimed at the extinction of conflict and the extendibility of such extinction from one stimulus situation to another. Though the problem of "extinction generalization" is not new, it is still an important one in behavior theory and probably also, as Scheflen believes, in psychotherapy. She does not relate her experiment to the extensive literature on extinction and generalization, probably for reasons of brevity. But some indication of these relations might have been helpful to those of us this morning who are unfamiliar with that literature.

The experimental data are summarized in one graphic figure. Scheflen's attention to the broad problem of the study leads her to omit consideration of some details of her data which, though perhaps of small interest to a non-specialist, may have bearing on the interpretation of the data and the validity of the conclusions. For example: we note that the control group was lower than the two experimental groups even at the start of original acquisition (no P value is given for this difference); the curve of Group I rises at the start of the "new situation,"—is this spontaneous recovery (see her conclusion No. 6), and if so how much of this rise in Group II's curve is spontaneous recovery?; the curves of Groups I and II do not converge in the trials testing for "spread of effect;" the basis for conclusion No. 5 is not clear.

Aside from such details, however, this interesting paper urges me to five comments, the first two on the experimental conception, the other three on our contributor's broad behavioral views.

First, our contributor conceives of her experiment as a test of original versus new "situations." In the experimental portion of her paper, her own usage of the term "situation" agrees with the proposition that a "situation" is made up of stimuli; in her study, the differences between the two situations came in the height, width and wall reflectance of the alleys. There is nothing transcendental or mysterious about a "situation," and any statement about a "situation" is a statement about stimuli. This is really an experiment on stimulus generalization and extinction.

Second, when once we have grasped the status of the term "situation," we can immediately note that Scheflen's experiment is of the nonparametric sort. Each of the stimulus differences between the two alleys can be investigated as a continuum open to functional analysis, while in this experiment only two values of each variable are studied, and each of those in fixed combination with only one value of each of the other two variables. Functional studies always carry more force and add more to our knowledge of a phenomenon than do two-point studies, but perhaps such a study was not practicable for Scheflen in the given place at the given time.

Third, in the introductory and discussion sections of her paper, Scheflen elects to use a framework and a vocabulary both of which, though widespread in the field, are somewhat muddied. One of the central difficulties is "fear"; our thought stumbles and gropes while this term assumes many faces and shapes by popular demand. "Fear" is a response, a drive, an emotion, and possibly even a stimulus, at the same time. We hear phrases like "generalization of fear," "fear his own drives," "what was originally fear is now anxiety," "fear response," "fear-evoking stimuli are present but the punishment is not"—and each time we must pause to translate, to re-orient, to comprehend. Most of us in this field have inherited confusion of this sort. Scheflen's interest in an experimental approach to these problems should help develop, as it did with others of us, a corrective critical attitude.

Fourth, Scheflen's extrapolations from her experiment to human psychopathology are bold. Naturally, all of us are interested in the possible generality of our findings, and often, too, in gaining some insight into human behavior by extrapolating from infra-human studies. But extrapolation is a tricky business. It requires prudence, and some deliberate judgment as to what type of extrapolation to make and how far to go with it. In the last analysis, I suppose, these are matters for the individual's decision, and Scheflen is certainly entitled to her own; by the same token, the freedom she allows herself seems to me excessive.

Fifth, there appear a few times in her discussion traces of a fundamental non-behavioral philosophy. I do not believe these traces represent Scheflen's actual attitude as a scientist, but rather that they crop up almost as a manner of speaking, as a linguistic hangover from the primitive stages of the science of behavior. If, therefore, I mention the matter here, it is only to point out how easily we can compromise ourselves if we let down linguistic guards. My reference is to phrases like ". . . she was able to work through her anxiety . . ." and ". . . ways by which people try to handle fear and anxiety . . ." Taken literally, such phrases imply a dichotomy between a person and his behavior; they imply an agent inside the person, but outside his behavior, who can manipulate the behavior; they imply a duality in the person, two elements acting in a subject-object, slave-free, director-actor relation; they imply a "little man in the head" taking charge of the body's behavior. I need not labor the point. I feel confident that none of us, whether experimental psychologist or psychopathologist, would subscribe to these implications when they are made explicit. All of us, including our contributor of this morning, will agree that a science of behavior cannot carry the burden of mysticism.

5

EXPERIMENTALLY INDUCED
DEPERSONALIZATION

By OTTO von MERING, Ph.D., KIYO MORIMOTO, M.A., ROBERT W. HYDE, M.D. *and* MAX RINKEL, M.D.*

THE PHENOMENA OF DEPERSONALIZATION, observed in a great variety of psychopathological conditions, have been described and interpreted by many authors, but their nature, etiology, and meaning still remain obscure. In our work[1] with the partially synthesized diethylamide of d-lysergic acid (LSD), which causes a temporary psychotic-like condition, we noted phenomena of depersonalization. An opportunity was thereby presented to re-examine, experimentally, the problem of depersonalization. We gave this psychotogenic compound, LSD, which was developed at the Sandoz Chemical Works at Basel, Switzerland, to more than 100 non-patients, all of whom showed symptoms of depersonalization. In the course of the experiments, we became aware of the importance of this aspect of our observations, and studied it intensively in 48 subjects, who form the basis of this report.

DEFINITION AND PROBLEM

We understand by depersonalization the "depersonalization complex." Its characteristics are: The subject's distortions of his own body-image, of the body-images of other persons in his life space, of objects in the physical environment, in spatial distortions, and in progressive disturbances of thought processes.

The problem of this study is to establish specific criteria for the assessment of depersonalization phenomena and to investigate the psychopathological nature of its many divergent symptoms.

LITERATURE

The first experimental studies on depersonalization were published by Guttmann and Maclay[7] in 1937, in a paper on "mescaline and

* Boston Psychopathic Hospital. Aided by a grant from the McCurdy Company, Rochester, N.Y., and the Geshickter Fund for Medical Research.

depersonalization." They used a synthetic preparation of mescaline which was prepared according to the method of Slotta and Szyszka; .1 to .2 Gm. of this drug was dissolved in a small amount of water and given orally to 11 patients with depression, which was either an endogenous psychosis or the symptom of other psychopathological states. On the basis of their observations, the authors concluded that: (a) "Mescaline depersonalization is identical with this symptom in morbid states . . . "; and (b) "Mescaline is able to improve depersonalization symptoms insofar as they consist of changes of the surroundings (derealization), not of the self." These conclusions, though interesting, were not generally accepted.

Psycho-dynamically oriented psychiatrists and psychoanalysts, during the past thirty years, provided most of the pertinent references. Rosenfeld[13] explains depersonalization as a process which the ego uses to ward off objectionable feelings and sensations. Sadger[14] described it as a form of psychic castration with a strong exhibitionistic component. The castrative element was also emphasized by Nunberg[10] who, at the same time, pointed out that the loss of ego-feeling, detachment of libido, ego-withdrawal from one's self, and therefore from the total environment, often occurs as the result of the real loss of an important libidinal object. Reik[12] called attention to the sado-masochistic aspects of depersonalization. Schilder[16] expressed the opinion that the psychic loss of emotionally over-invested organs or parts of the body is the result of the patient's feeling of having been deprived of a loved person. Federn[4] stated that the "libidinously cathected organ is gradually felt to be outside of the body ego, i.e., a loss." Savage[15] gave 10 to 100 micrograms of LSD to 32 hospitalized patients and six normal patients, and in his recent report he related his observations on Federn's[4] theories of impoverishment of ego libido or ego cathexis.

The problem of how the mentally disturbed handle unacceptable anxiety-provoking cathexes or libidinal wishes has been interpreted in different ways: Bergler[3] suggested that the mechanism involves the development of "increased self-observation." Nunberg[10] stated that "hypercathexis of the ego" arises if part of the ego becomes subservient to the superego. Schilder[16] described it as a condition of "morbid introspection" or "self-scrutiny." Oberndorf[11] referred to it as "eroticized thought."

Malamud[9] reported that depersonalization "is found frequently in all types of mental diseases." Ackner[2] stated, in a recent paper which included a review and discussion of the literature, that "depersonalization types of complaint arise as a result of the relative failure of integration of experience into the total organization of psychic functioning . . . , " and that these complaints "merge with those of many other conditions which involve a change in the relation of the individual to his self, his body, or the outside world." He emphasized that the writings on this subject reveal conflict over interpretation and confusion about whether depersonalization is "a clear-cut clinical syndrome" or "merely a symptom." In his view, it is a cluster of phenomena that "know no boundaries." Lewis[8] stated that disagreements arise from attempts at "schematization without sufficient evidence" and an "uncritical trust in the adequacy of language."

METHOD AND PROCEDURE

Our 48 non-patient subjects were males and females between 19 and 48 years of age. They were college students, hospital personnel, anthropologists, physicists, teachers, psychologists, nurses, doctors, salesmen, and housewives.

Each subject received one microgram of LSD per kilogram of body weight. The LSD was dissolved in distilled water and administered orally at eight o'clock in the morning. The subjects were then observed continuously by at least one and usually two observers for a period from 8 to 10 hours. Symptoms were considered in reference to the particular interpersonal situation during which they occurred. The interpersonal situation comprised the total environment which included the self, i.e., the subject's own body and thought, all people that were present, and the impersonal environment, i.e., all non-human objects. Only perceptual distortions and alterations of feeling and thought, recognized and reported by the subject as a distinct change from his non-LSD control state, are included in this study.

RESULTS

The classification and distribution of the different types of psychotic symptomatology is summarized in Table I.

Table I indicates that the majority of the subjects, 32 (76%), who were examined by a psychiatrist, underwent a schizophrenic-like reaction, and only 10 (24%) showed other types of psychotic reactions.

TABLE I.—*Distribution of Subjects in Psychiatric Syndrome Classification.*

Type of Reaction	Subjects	
Schizophrenic—Turmoil	15	
Schizophrenic—Undifferentiated	5	
Schizophrenic—Affective	4	
Schizophrenic—Catatonic	4	
Schizophrenic—Simple	2	
Schizophrenic Features	2	
Total Schizophrenic Reaction		32
Manic	4	
Depressed	1	
Manic—Depressive—Mixed	1	
Undifferentiated	4	
		10
Subjects not seen for diagnosis		6
Total		48

NOTE: The designations are synonymous with those in the *Diagnostic Statistical Manual.*

The subjects in each of the diagnostic categories experienced some type of depersonalizing distortion.

A total of 569 distortions was observed in the 48 subjects. These distortions were classified into four general categories: changes of the self, of others, of objects and physical environment, and of general thought processes. Table II shows the distribution of changes of the "self."

Table II indicates that the most frequently observed changes of the "self" occur in body sensations of part or all of the body. They are manifested in feelings of non-existence, denial, detachment, loss of

TABLE II.—*Distortions of the Self.*

Type of Disturbance	Number of Occurrences
1. Sensations of whole or parts of body	130
2. Organ distortion	19
3. Association of body or parts of body, with animate or inanimate objects	9
4. Voice	3
5. Age	162
Total	1

sensation, changes in size, "sidedness" and feelings of specific kinds of independent motion of parts or all of the body. Organ distortions, i.e., an intense awareness of circulation, respiration, twitching of muscles and nerves, also occurred. Association of the body, or parts of the body, with animate or inanimate objects which the subject expressed in such exclamations as, "I am a hand . . . a shell . . . a foot," occurred rarely. Sensations which indicated the subject's feelings of change in age or voice seldom happened. Distortions of other people are listed in Table III.

TABLE III.—*Distortions of Other People.*

Type of Distortion	Distortions of Specific Individuals	Distortions of People in General
1. Face	22	14
2. Whole body and parts	18	13
3. Age and voice	5	3
4. Figure—ground	6	12
5. Association of others with animals or inanimate objects	3	3
6. Feelings of spatial removal of other people	2	19
	56	64
Total		120

The most common distortions were related to the physical appearance of a specific person, especially his face. This person's face looked kinder and beautiful, or ugly and frightening. Distortions of the whole body and its parts included changes in size and color. Changes in age and voice occurred rarely. Figure-ground refers to seeing people as one-dimensional pictures with changes in space and illumination. Association occurred in which other people were likened to animal forms, like a cat or a fish, or were perceived as inanimate objects like puppets. Feelings of spatial removal of other people were expressed in the following ways: people having a ghost-like quality so that it was possible to walk right through them, people on a stage, or a glass partition existing between the self and others. The subjects distorted particular individuals about as often as they distorted groups of people. Table IV reveals that most subjects experienced a heightened awareness of the external environment. They were predominantly fascinated and preoccupied with sounds, smell, form, color, light, texture, or composition of objects. Changes or movements of objects, which were

TABLE IV.—*Distortions of Objects and Physical Environment.*

Type of Distortion	Number of Occurrences
1. Heightened awareness of external environment	41
2. Changes or movement of objects	16
3. General perceptual disturbance	15
4. Changes in specific spatial "size"	11
5. Changes in distance and size of objects	12
6. Denial of environment	3
7. Changes in shape of objects in general	2
8. Ego-merging with object	1
Total	101

much less frequently experienced, included phantom motion, rippling drapes, walls undulating, or books moving across the floor. Under general perceptual disturbances were individual expressions such as "peripheral blurring," "difficulty in focusing," "things look fuzzy." Experiences which indicated changes of spatial "size" were expressed as "room closing in," "things jumping around in space," or "room more spacious." Changes in distance or size of objects were also quite frequent. They were expressed in phrases like, "the pool balls look like peas"; objects looked higher or lower, nearer or farther, longer or shorter, but occasionally fluctuated. Infrequently noted was denial of environment, i.e., being "unconscious of the environment," having the sense of "spacelessness" or the feeling of "things disappearing." Changes in the shape of objects may be illustrated by one subject's seeing the recording machine twisted out of shape. The classification of ego merging with object could be made in only one instance in which the subject described himself as feeling that he was a tool and not an independent human entity.

In Table V are listed the types of disturbances which occurred in general thought and speech processes.

TABLE V.—*Distortion of General Thought Processes*

Type of Distortion	Number of Occurrences
1. Thought	66
2. Speech	33
3. Thinking about self and the world	30
4. Concept of time	30
5. Feelings of unreality or estrangement	27
Total	186

Changes in thought included retardation, acceleration, repetition, or blankness. Difficulty in concentration, in recall and in dissociation of thought from feelings; the inability to follow others' questions, are also included. The subjects frequently said that "thoughts come so rapidly, I can't keep up with them," or, "my mind is a blank," or, "I'm crying but I don't feel sad." Changes in speech were shown by retardation, acceleration, repetition, difficulty of expression, disconnectedness, and inability to verbalize thoughts. Distortions in thinking about self and the world may be demonstrated by the following phrases: "I have an awareness of an awareness of an awareness," "the world takes on a haggard look" and grandiose conceptualizations expressed in terms of, "I have the world in a jug," "my head is the universe." Changes in concept of time were in terms of "time seems to be telescoped," or, "time means nothing,—everything is timeless," "time is slow," or, "every minute is a year." Feelings of unreality or estrangement were described as, "I seem to be floating along in a dream," "realistic situations seem unrealistic," "I feel unreal . . . all is magnified . . . I feel strange."

DISCUSSION

We have found that in the psychotic-like conditions resulting from LSD, depersonalization occurred in all diagnostic categories. The classification system used in this study differentiates among distortions of the subject's own body image, of body-images of other persons in his life space, of objects in the physical environment, in spatial distortions, and in progressive disturbances of thought processes. These categories were derived from systematic experimentation to clarify some of the confusion about the depersonalization complex.

In this study it became apparent that the social situation had a marked effect on the type of depersonalization. The changes that the subjects experienced were found to be intimately related to particular demands and expectations of others in the immediate situation. Symptoms of depersonalization became more significant when interpreted in terms of the social situation. Non-supportive or hostile people were seen as 'tiny and boyish," "satanical," or looking like a "jaundiced witch"; supportive people were seen as kinder, younger, and more beautiful.

In other situations when subjects were confronted with specific demands, they tended to cope with them in a variety of ways which involved distortion or dysfunction of body parts. Their hands would become heavy when they were asked to write; their legs would feel detached when they were asked to walk; a choking sensation would be experienced when they were asked to speak.

Other subjects focused upon ideas and resorted to pseudo-logical system-building to explain the immediate human and objective situation which they expressed in statements such as, "everything is zero . . . zero equals minus . . . zero is inert matter." "I have a synthesis of many things about me . . . have more insight . . . lots of things are quite clear"; "all has old meaning, almost as if meaning was substance." "It's a peculiar solution to time and space when the anxiety of mortal man has no significance."

Another method used by our subjects to cope with interpersonal situations was shown by the experience of such feelings as, "I can walk through people"; "people are phony actors"; "people are hollow

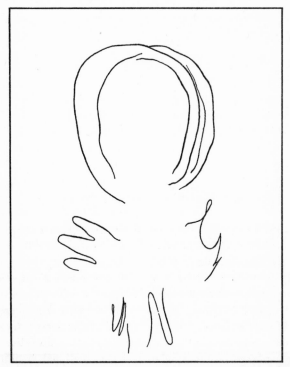

Fig. 1. "I feel all head with my hands like fins." Subject #10.

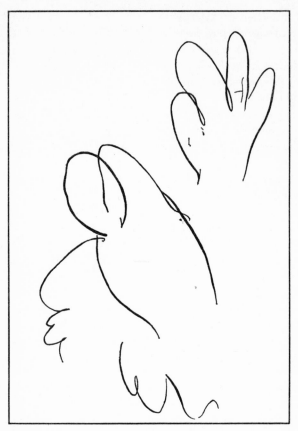

FIG. 2. "I feel all hands now . . . legs are insignificant . . .; they are so pedestrian." Subject #10.

shells . . . their meaning is pushed out"; "people can't move"; "glass partition between me and people." By this method, they were able to consider other people as harmless.

We may assume that some of our subjects gained satisfaction from the experience of being able to feel their thoughts. These thoughts appeared to have a conscious erotic significance. The mere act of thinking became more gratifying and may have served the goal of reducing inner tension, at least temporarily. Selective distortion of one's own body occurred and was related to the emotional significance of these parts. The distortion in Figure 1 occurred when a subject

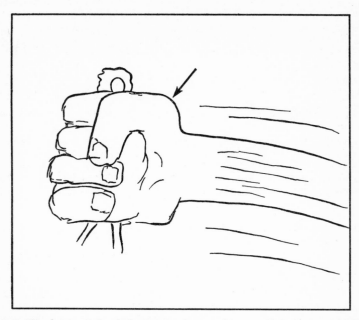

FIG. 3. "I'm huge, my hands have never been so big . . . She's in my right fist."
Subject #28.

was talking to another person who aroused his emotional interest. The subject was asked about his concept of himself at that particular moment. He answered that he felt "all head with my hands like fins". One minute later, when he grasped a doorknob, he suddenly felt "all hands." The observer asked him to draw his experience (see Fig. 2). He was then asked about his legs and feet to which he commented, "My legs are insignificant appendages; they are so pedestrian." We may theorize that these distortions of the body-image occurred not only because the subject was deeply involved in his private feelings and thoughts, but also because they were closely related to immediate outside stimuli.

Another subject (Fig. 3) pictured himself as a clenched fist. While he was being questioned by a nurse, he said, "I'm huge. My hands have never been so big. My hand is on a swivel and turns round and round." He saw the nurse clutched in his hand and felt that he could eliminate her simply by squeezing his fist. The emotional significance of this distortion may be interpreted as indicating his desire to destroy the "attacking" or "threatening" person. Although the subject was initially gratified in seeing himself as master of the situation, he later reported that he was also quite disturbed about depicting such situations.

The figure-ground reversal and the perception of color as a tactile substance seemed to represent a frantic but unsuccessful attempt at feeling withdrawal. Evidence has already been presented that concomitant with such perceptions the momentary "disappearance" of people as separate living entities took place. Many seemed to live in a pathologically concrete and changing world; they had lost the feeling of personal identity. This "loss" made many feel that their thoughts could not be reversed by reality-testing or reasoning, and even less by the reasoning of others.

SUMMARY

LSD, in the amount of one microgram per kilogram of body weight, produces the symptom complex of depersonalization.

A total of 569 distortions was recorded; these were classified in the following four categories: (1) changes of "self;" (2) changes of others; (3) changes of objects and physical environment; (4) changes of general thought processes.

Persons with very strong positive or negative feelings are especially exposed to depersonalization experiences.

The specific distortions are intimately related to the social environment of the individual.

We wish to acknowledge the valuable assistance of Mr. Charles Atwell, Chief Psychologist at the Boston Psychopathologic Hospital, in the preparation of this manuscript and to thank the Sandoz Chemical Works, Inc. who so generously supplied the lysergic acid diethylamide (LSD).

REFERENCES

1. VON MERING, O., et al.: Depersonalization and LSD. J. Clin. Psychopath., 12: 42, 1951; Psychiatric Quart. 26: 33, Jan. 1952; Am. J. Psychiat. 108: 572, Feb. 1952; Dis. Nerv. System, 15: 3, Sept. 1954; Arch. Neurol. & Psychiat. 73: 100, Jan. 1955; Am. J. Psychiat. 111: 881, June 1955; Dis. Nerv. System, 16: 1, Aug. 1955; J. Nerv. & Ment. Dis. 118: 266, Sept. 1953; J. Nerv. & Ment. Dis. 120: 413, Nov.-Dec. 1954.
2. ACKNER, BRIAN: J. Ment. Sc. 100: 837, Oct. 1954.
3. BERGLER, EDMUND: Am. J. Orthopsychiat. 16, 1935.
4. FEDERN, PAUL: Psychiatric Quart. 17, 1943; Ego Psychology and the Psychoses. New York, Basic Books, 1952.

5. FENICHEL, OTTO: The Psychoanalytic Theory of Neurosis. New York, W. W. Norton & Co., 1945.
6. GOLDSTEIN, KURT: Methodological approach to the study of schizophrenic thought disorder.Kasanin, J. S., ed., 1944. pp. 17-40. Language and Thought in Schizophrenia. Berkeley Univ. of California Press.
7. GUTTMAN, E. AND MACLAY, W. S.: J. of Neurol. Neurosurg. & Psychopath. *16:* 193, 1936.
8. LEWIS, NOLAN, D. C.: Am. J. Psychotherapy, 3,4, 1949.
9. MALAMUD, WILLIAM: Outline of General Psychopathology. New York, W. W. Norton & Co., 1935, p. 203.
10. NUNBERG, H.: Internat. Ztschr. f. Individualpsychol. *8,* 1924.
11. OBERNDORF, C. P.: Tr. Am. Neurol. A., 1933.
12. REIK, THEODOR: Psychoanalysis and depersonalization. Vienna, Wie man Psychologe wird, 1927.
13. ROSENFELD, H.: Internat. J. Psycho-analysis, *28,* 1947, p. 130.
14. SADGER, I.: Internat. Ztschr. f. Psychoanalyse, *14:* 315-351, 1928.
15. SAVAGE, C.: Psychonalyt. Rev., *42:* 1-16, 1955.
16. SCHILDER, PAUL: Neurol. centralbl., *38:* 300, 1919; The Image and Appearance of the Human Body; Studies in the Constructive Energies of the Psyche. New York International Univ. Press, 1950.
17. STOLL, W. A.: Schweiz. Arch. Neurol. & Psychiat., *60:* 1-45, 1947.

6

AN INVESTIGATION OF THE
PSYCHOPATHOLOGIC EFFECT
OF SPECIFIC EMOTIONS

By OSKAR DIETHELM, M.D. *and* FREDERIC F. FLACH, M.D.*

VARIOUS EMOTIONS may have far-reaching effects on the psychopathologic picture in any kind of psychiatric disorder. The psychopathologic symptoms, which may be related to specific emotions or groups of emotions, may influence or overshadow the symptoms which are the expression of the psychiatric illness under study. Little consideration is given, in clinical and research literature, to an evaluation of the psychopathologic effect of specific emotions which may be marked and may color the total psychopathology, but are only secondary to the essential core of the illness. Insufficient recognition of this fact is one of the causes for contradictory results in psychologic and physiologic studies of psychiatric illnesses.

There is to be found in the literature a valuable body of pertinent data which is limited because experimental procedures did not permit satisfactory verification in the intricate clinical field. Recent pharmacologic developments have opened new vistas which many investigators are now exploring. The drugs which have been found to be especially valuable in the study which we are discussing are chlorpromazine and reserpine.

Among early clinical psychopathologic studies in this field, E. Bleuler's[1] investigations of the role of emotions in the formation of delusions should be cited. He singled out depressive and elated emotions. The studies of panic reactions by Diethelm,[3] made possible through preceding psychoanalytic investigations of anxiety, demonstrated the far-reaching psychopathologic effects of fear and anxiety. This study singled out transient paranoid and disorganizing reactions which might occur in any psychiatric disorder. After the introduction of insulin treatment, it became possible for Rennie[15] to demonstrate

* Department of Psychiatry, Cornell University Medical College and The New York Hospital (Payne Whitney Psychiatric Clinic), New York.

that anxiety and fear and related paranoid delusions subsided under the influence of insulin. The influence of hostility and resentment, primarily turned against oneself, expresses itself frequently in a paranoid attitude and may dominate a depressive picture, e.g., in what the older authors called involutional melancholia.

Psychologic investigations have not been very productive because of the complex nature of the problem. Studies by means of Rorschach's method have been helpful in demonstrating the presence of strong emotions and their influence on thinking. Further progress was made by Welch[17,18] in experimental studies of the effect of anxiety on reasoning, and of elation on speed of association. (See also Diethelm and Jones.[7])

Physiologic investigations of the role of specific emotions is found in the early literature on hypnosis. Studies on sugar fasting and sugar tolerance (Diethelm[4]) and on leukocytes (Milhorat and Small[13]) are related to the effects of anxiety, fear, and tension. Among the vast psychosomatic literature, few contributions single out the effect of specific emotions. The work of Graham,[10] for instance, illustrates the effect of resentment on itching and on skin diseases. Biochemical assay methods have been used over a period of years by Funkenstein and by Milhorat, Fleetwood, and Diethelm. Funkenstein[11] was able to demonstrate biochemical changes in the presence of the emotions of tension and anger and applied these findings in the selection of psychopathologic disorders for electric convulsive treatment. Milhorat and his group[5] studied biochemical changes appearing in the presence of anxiety, tension, resentment; and later studied by this same procedure the significance of these emotions in chronic alcoholism and in depressive and schizophrenic disorders.

Clinical endocrinologic studies related to specific emotions have not been productive. In the field of psychopathology, Bleuler's[2] approach seems to be the most promising.

Emotional reactions in interpersonal relations, especially in the patient-physician relationship, have been investigated intensively and much valuable knowledge has been acquired. Among contributions in the field under discussion should be mentioned those of Sullivan[16] and Fromm-Reichmann[9] in the psychopathologic studies of schizophrenia.

Pharmacologic studies have been pursued by Milhorat, Fleetwood, and Diethelm,[6] who were able to demonstrate that in chronic alcoholism, alcohol may abolish specific emotions, their psychopathologic manifestations, and related biochemical changes in the blood. The most striking results were obtained in resentment and less frequently in anxiety and tension. Barbiturates seem to be effective on tension. This observation did not come as a surprise since it had been known for over thirty years that continuous use of barbiturates decreases pathologic tension and prevents the development of panic reactions in the setting of mounting tensions.

RESULTS OF CURRENT INVESTIGATIONS

From clinical studies and from our investigations of the psychopathologic influence of specific emotions, the following summary can be presented: (1) Anxiety, characterized by apprehension without an adequately known cause, decreases the span of attention and retention, disturbs sleep, and may cause anxiety dreams. With marked intensity of anxiety, difficulties in thinking and disturbed reasoning may occur leading to pathologic vagueness or confusion. (2) Tension experienced as inner tautness, irritability, and muscle tension, produces disorders of concentration and thinking. Usually intense tension, which produces considerable insecurity, is accompanied by anxiety. Either of these emotions, but especially their combination, may adversely affect grasp, immediate memory, and recall. (3) In fear, with awareness of a more or less definite threat, the effects of anxiety and tension are noticeable. In marked and persistent fear, an extreme state (panic) with delusional and hallucinatory projections, often of a paranoid nature, may be reached. (4) Resentment is a reaction of bitterness with a desire for revenge, with an attitude of hostility, sarcasm, and often suspiciousness. Rejecting others may lead to a feeling of being rejected by others and result in feeling lonely and sad. Projection of varying degree is present and often expressed in paranoid rejection. Inability to tolerate one's resentment may be seen in depressions and expressed in aversion reactions. In relation to resentment, a patient may react with anxiety and sadness, humiliated by his failure to deal with this unacceptable emotion. The fearful reactions of others to the resentful and hostile person may lead to complicated emotional reactions in the patient and to severe abnormal behavior, e.g., anger, attack, withdrawal. Sudden relief from resentment or prolonged tension may be followed by mild elation. (5) Depressive emotions are less understood because anxiety, tension, or resentment may be additional emotions. The subjective descriptions are difficult to evaluate, and psychodynamic factors lead to different depressive reactions. Decreased self-confidence and a pessimistic attitude toward the future are well recognized. Slowness in associative responses and possible decreased distractibility seem to be characteristic but have not been demonstrated satisfactorily through experimental methods. (6) The psychopathologic significance of elated emotions is unclear. An increase of associative activity results in elation. Whether increased distractibility is essentially related to elation or to additional anxiety or to other factors is unclear. Cobb[12] demonstrated that repetitiveness and monotony of thinking are characteristic of pathologic elation and not indicative of wealth of ideas.

The determining of emotions and their evaluation is very difficult in any person but especially so if one deals with a psychopathologic condition. In addition to the type and intensity of the emotions, one must consider their mode of development and their duration. The meaning of the emotion depends on the individual, and the dynamic factors involved may be difficult to recognize. The effect of various emotions on each other is not understood psychologically, physiologically, or psychopathologically. Even so, gradual progress has been made in the understanding of the role of specific emotions.

1. *Observation with the Use of Drugs*

Pharmacologic investigations of emotions, especially in the field of psychopathology and therapy, have attracted attention for many years. The recent introduction of two drugs, chlorpromazine and reserpine, has permitted considerable progress.

Chlorpromazine—The influence of chlorpromazine was most noticeable on resentment and fear and the psychopathologic effects of these emotions. Excitements, sexual and otherwise, were also influenced. This drug, which we gave in high amounts, abolished resentment and the related symptoms of hostility, sarcasm, suspiciousness. It was not always possible to determine whether the delusions of persecution which disappeared were related to accompanying fear and its decrease. In some patients with resentment and without fear, mild delusions of reference were observed to subside.

Anger, which accompanied marked resentment, also subsided rapidly. In one patient whose anger subsided, the underlying tension which had been assumed by us but denied by the patient now became obvious. The effect of the drug on fear and panic reactions was prompt. The psychopathologic symptoms of suspiciousness, fear, fearful paranoid delusions and hallucinations, and disorders of concentration subsided rapidly. Another prompt effect was achieved in sexual unrest, erotic behavior, and in full-fledged sexual excitement with its features of homosexual and heterosexual aggression, irritability, anger, and underlying anxiety.

The psychopathologic picture of these extreme sexual excitements is little understood. The behavior may resemble a panic reaction but fear is absent. Disorganization of thinking, as expressed in incoherence, suspiciousness, delusions of persecution, and auditory and other hallucinations, is characteristic. To what extent this complex psychopathologic reaction is caused by specific emotions, by physiologic factors, or by the setting of the psychiatric illness is at present impossible to state. In some patients a sexual excitement occurs in the setting of a schizophrenic illness, in others with an anxiety or hysterical reaction, and even frequently in a poorly organized psychopathic personality. Whether in other excitements the subsiding of elation is directly affected by the drug or whether it is affected through its influence on underlying anxiety or on other emotions has remained unclear. It was assumed that the effect on overactivity was related to emotional factors but this point has also remained unclear. Overtalkativeness in several patients was related to resentment and possibly to additional anxiety. A persistent aversion reaction, related to intense but poorly tolerated resentment to the patient's husband and to herself, was controlled in one case by chlorpromazine, which barely affected the depressed mood. In a schizophrenic patient with anxiety and resentment, marked blocking of speech was decreased greatly by the drug, which also decreased the emotions. In another schizophrenic patient in a state of excitement with elation, anxiety, overtalkativeness, and incoherence of speech, all symptoms decreased considerably and the incoherence disappeared. In agitated depressions, the agitation, anxiety, difficulties in concentration, and slowness of thinking disappeared, but the depressive mood persisted.

Reserpine—The effect of reserpine was somewhat different from that of chlorpromazine. Reserpine appeared to be more effective on anxiety and on unreality reactions which seemed related to anxiety. Erotic display and sexual excitement, resentment, and fear responded less markedly than they did to chlorpromazine. In one case, anxiety with related physiologic symptoms and paranoid delusions subsided, but underlying hidden resentment became obvious. In several other patients, hidden resentment was expressed after mild anxiety had subsided.

2. Clinical Observations in Chronic Schizophrenic Patients

A study of schizophrenic patients whose illness had lasted from 12 to 30 years gave interesting findings. These chronic patients are being studied at the Montrose Veterans Administration Hospital. They have been in psychiatric hospitals continuously during these years except for a few who had been able to stay in the community for one to three years following a brief first admission. The vast majority presented the picture of simple deterioration. In a few, some catatonic symptoms such as posturing, stereotyped posturing or movement of fingers, or paranoid delusions were observed. About 18 patients soiled themselves by urinating in their clothes or beds; none defecated in their clothes. In these patients, other toilet habits were poor i.e., there was frequent soiling of toilet seats and floor.

There were some observations pertinent to the present discussion. An analysis of the records revealed that in the majority of the patients the illness started with an acute episode which led to the diagnosis of paranoid schizophrenia. From a few months to about two years, the paranoid delusions and hallucinations were not mentioned any longer, but a picture of simple deterioration or hebephrenia was presented. The latter changed after a few more years to simple deterioration. A few patients persisted in their delusional projection and after a period of years were still diagnosed paranoid schizophrenia. Their main emotions were resentment (hostility), sadness, and loneliness. From the records one gets the impression that the acute paranoid phase was primarily related to fear and anxiety in the acute development of the schizophrenic illness. The acute catatonic onset, characterized by excitement, combativeness, anger, hostility, posturing, and occasionally elation, subsided frequently within the first year. In others, periodic excitement, rarely stupor, persisted for several years. The outstanding remaining emotion in these patients was resentment (hostility). Sexual unrest and aggression also usually subsided, except when it was related to homosexuality.

The patients who soiled had done this for many years. They came from hospitals where they had been rejected and neglected. In several patients, soiling did not occur until after transfer to a building in which soiling was common. It is impossible to state what factors contributed to this special type of habit deterioration, but it seems obvious that environmental and interpersonal factors were important, as well as anal-erotic, homosexual, and other factors.

A study of combativeness and destructiveness in this hospital population revealed the emotional background of tension and irritability in some patients whose outbursts were usually provoked by occurrences in the environment. In others, anxiety related to homosexual strivings became stirred up. In a third group, hostility in the setting of chronic resentment was the basis for combativeness. Combativeness rarely seemed related to specific conscious or unconscious motivation. Destructiveness occurred most frequently in an outburst of anger, less frequently as the expression of hostility, and rarely on an unexplained basis. It must be kept in mind that these chronic patients could not be observed sufficiently to give us clues for dynamics.

This study of the long-term development and natural course of chronic schizophrenia is, after two years, still in its preliminary phase. This report therefore does not include observations of, and investigations into, the role of emotional factors in the remaining vast psychopathology of schizophrenic illnesses.

DISCUSSION

The most frequent emotions which we can recognize in psychopathologic symptoms and reactions are anxiety, tension, fear, resentment, depression, and elation. The last two, which until recent years were considered well understood by most authors, present more difficulties in interpretation than the others. Psychopathologic and physiologic studies have demonstrated the role of tension, anxiety, fear, and resentment in psychopathology and have thrown some light on the nature of these emotions. Pharmacologic experimentation has afforded further clarification.

Resentment can lead to various degrees of psychopathologic symptoms, especially seen in attitudes of hostility and aggression, aversion, paranoid projection, and additional emotional reactions of sadness, loneliness, and anxiety.

Chlorpromazine seems to be able to abolish or greatly decrease the above reactions, in whatever setting they occur. The only other drug which has a similar effect on resentment is ethyl alcohol. It is of interest to note that 20 years ago Russian authors recommended large doses of alcohol for the control of schizophrenic excitements. Their therapeutic proposals do not seem to have been followed elsewhere. The effect of chlorpromazine on resentment and excitement supports the earlier Russian observations.

Reserpine seems to have a stronger effect than chlorpromazine on anxiety, and demonstrates in an interesting way the psychopathologic influence of anxiety. Alcohol has demonstrated its ability to abolish subjective anxiety and related biochemical findings in the blood of patients suffering from anxiety neurosis. Disturbed span of attention and retention and feelings of apprehension seem to disappear. It is not known what the influence of alcohol would be on the more severe psychopathologic symptoms related to anxiety.

One should not evaluate merely the direct expression of anxiety in psychopathologic symptoms but also its effect on other symptoms. Anxiety will considerably aggravate the attention and memory difficulties of a patient who suffers from mild or moderate senile changes and thus produce the picture of senile deterioration. In schizophrenic patients, vagueness of thinking will become intensified through anxiety. On the other hand, schizophrenic thinking disorders are little understood and may well be the expression of a special type of anxiety or of a special psychodynamic or physiologic setting.

Some observations on schizophrenic patients bring up the question of the nature of anxiety which is not affected by these drugs. A characteristic description by such a patient related entirely to physiologic symptoms; she was unable to offer a description of experiencing the emotion of anxiety. She stated that she felt, "real tense . . . my heart is racing." On further detailed questioning she repeated that anxiety means, "It's my stomach . . . like it turns over. I am choking, I can't breathe, I can't sit still, I have to walk around." She and another patient were not relieved by chlorpromazine or reserpine. The best explanation seems to be that one deals with a dissociation of the experience of the emotion with awareness of the physiologic effects. From previous experience one is inclined to expect that under the effect of insulin a reintegration might occur.

Similiar dissociative aspects of emotions are seen in hysterical and related psychosomatic disorders. Such patients illustrate difficulties which will arise if one depends too much on the patient's descriptions and interprets too strictly the word symbols. It is also hazardous if one disregards well defined groupings of emotions, assuming that there are innumerable emotional experiences.

Suspiciousness which was not related to anxiety, fear, or resentment was affected but slightly by the drugs. It is possible that suspiciousness may then be a projection of a more deep-seated nature, found in those schizophrenic patients who have a paranoid illness which will change little in future years.

An interesting change occurs in depression when, through the use of suitable drugs, anxiety and other emotions are reduced or eliminated. Under the influence of chlorpromazine a previously very agitated, distraught, depressed woman became quiet and described her mood as "not very good . . . discouraged that I don't feel better." Her later description stressed the "lack of pleasure, the lack of initiative." Her previous marked self-depreciation changed to mild anxiety as to whether she would be able to do things she ought to do. Concentration became good, alertness increased considerably, and there was no indication of retardation. Under the influence of reserpine a severely depressed man with marked anxiety, tension, restlessness, inability to concentrate, and hopelessness became quiet. He described his mood as "sad, depressed" but not unbearable. He was apprehensive of the future because of his poor physical condition. Concentration became good and he was alert in his thinking, but complained about the slowness of passing time. These observations emphasize the need to reconsider the nature of depressive illnesses. Symptoms which in the past have been considered characteristic of depression seem to be related to more incidental emotions.

An interesting observation with the use of reserpine is the ability of some persons to display emotions with little inhibition. This behavior, which is well known in alcoholic intoxication, may also occur with sodium amytal or methamphetamine as well as with habit-forming drugs. It may be a true "acting-out" in the psychoanalytic sense, but more frequently it is a "living-out" of suppressed emotions. In disorganized (usually schizophrenic) or poorly organized, immature psychopathic personalities, specific emotions can present an involved psychopathologic picture. Although these facts have been well known (e.g., in poison reactions) they are frequently misinterpreted. With chlorpromazine and reserpine, erotic manifestations have been observed in two of our patients. This is an interesting reaction of two individuals to a drug which usually decreases sexual desires. It is reminiscent of the sexual unrest which one observes occasionally in toxic reactions of the anaphrodisiac bromide. Other patients may react with an aggravation of hysterical symptoms, bringing up the often discussed factor of willful exaggerations in hysterical reactions.

In passing, it might be mentioned that one should be careful not to diagnose parkinsonism too readily. In a few of our patients under the influence of chlorpromazine or reserpine, a true Parkinson syndrome was observed, but in the majority there was considerable doubt about the interpretation of the neurologic symptoms. It was interesting that the most marked symptoms occurred in catatonic and hysterical-like reactions.

In evaluating the role of emotions, one must keep in mind that a patient may react emotionally to the experiencing of existing emotions. This occurrence has been described in connection with aversion reactions to resentment which is unacceptable to the patient. Depending on psychodynamic factors, a person may react with anxiety (e.g., humiliation, guilt), anger, sadness, or tension to the feeling of resentment.

The complexity of the emotional picture may make it most difficult to single out pertinent specific emotions and their psychopathologic significance. Yet the task, difficult as it may seem, is most important if we want to understand the essentials of psychiatric illnesses. With progress along this line it will become possible to investigate the nature of these many disorders.

REFERENCES

1. BLEULER, E.: Affectivity, suggestibility, paranoia. State Hospital Bulletin, 4, 481-601, 1912.
2. ——: Endokrinologiche Psychiatrie. Stuttgart, Thieme, 1954.
3. DIETHELM, O.: Panic. Arch. Neurol. & Psychiat., 28: 1153-1168, 1932.
4. ——: Influence of emotions on dextrose tolerance. Arch. Neurol. & Psychiat, 36: 342-361, 1936.
5. DOTY, E. J., AND MILHORAT, A. T.: Emotions and adrenergic and cholinergic changes in the blood. Arch. Neurol. & Psychiat., 54: 110-115, 1945.
6. ——, FLEETWOOD, M. F. AND MILHORAT, A. T.: The predictable association

of certain emotions and biochemical changes in the blood. Life Stress and Bodily Disease. Baltimore, Williams and Wilkins, 1950, pp. 262-278.

7. ——, AND JONES, M. R.: Influence of anxiety on attention, learning, retention and thinking. Arch. Neurol. & Psychiat., *58:* 325-336, 1947.

8. FLEETWOOD, M. F. AND DIETHELM, O.: Emotions and biochemical findings in alcoholism. Am. J. Psychiat., *108:* 433-438, 1951.

9. FROMM-REICHMANN, F.: Psychotherapy of schizophrenia. Am. J. Psychiat, *111:* 410-419, 1954; Principles of Intensive Psychotherapy. Chicago, Univ. of Chicago Press, 1950.

10. GRAHAM, D. T.: The pathogenesis of hives: experimental studies of life situations, emotions and cutaneous reactions. Life Stress and Bodily Disease, Baltimore, Williams and Wilkins, 1950, pp. 987-1009.

11. GREENBLATT, M., FUNKENSTEIN, D. H., AND SOLOMON, H. C.: The effect of mecholyl: in frontal lobes and schizophrenia. New York, Springfield Publishing Co., 1953, pp. 296-306.

12. LORENZ, M. AND COBB, S.: Language behavior in manic patients. Arch. Neurol. & Psychiat., *67:* 763-770, 1952.

13. MILHORAT, A. T., SMALL, S. M., AND DIETHELM, O.: Leukocytosis during various emotional states. Arch. Neurol. & Psychiat., *47:* 779-792, 1942.

14. RANCKOW, L. L. AND HARRIS, R. L.: The study of aggressive and destructive patients in a psychiatric hospital. (In press.)

15. RENNIE, T. A. C.: Use of insulin as sedation therapy. Arch. Neurol. & Psychiat, *50:* 697-705, 1943.

16. SULLIVAN, H. S.: The Interpersonal Theory of Psychiatry. New York, W. W. Norton, 1953.

17. WELCH, L., DIETHELM, O., AND LONG, L.: Measurement of hyper-associative activity during elation. J. Psychol, *21:* 113-126, 1946.

18. —— AND LONG, L.: Psychopathological defects in inductive reasoning. J. Psychol., *21:* 201-226, 1946.

7

DISORGANIZATION:
A PSYCHOSOMATIC PRINCIPLE

By D. EWEN CAMERON, M.D., F.R.C.P.*

I AM PROPOSING to put before you a concept of disorganization as a principle in psychosomatic illness. A working concept which is useful in understanding, manipulating, and correcting certain aspects of deviant functioning commonly found in psychosomatic illness.

The concept of disorganization has been used by a number of previous workers, chiefly psychologists like Luria[1] and Jacobsen[2]. For a variety of reasons it has not been taken up by psychiatrists, but a provisional working definition can be extracted from these earlier uses of the concept. We may take first one of the simpler motor skills such as writing. Here it is well known that, under growing stress, considerable disorganization takes place. Tremor makes its appearance and renders letters irregular, misspellings increase in number, and in more advanced stages of disorganization words may be omitted; finally, under great stress, the capacity to write may become disorganized to a point that a person is quite unable to write at all. A sensory pattern is provided by the flicker-fusion test. Here it has been shown[3] that as stress increases the fusion of rotating items takes place at a lower and lower speed. We may take a more complicated pattern in which perception plays the greater part, i.e., the katograph test. Here the individual attempts to trace out a simple pattern connecting a number of predetermined points by a pencilled line. The task is rendered complex by reason of the fact that the individual has to guide his pencil by watching it in a mirror, which reverses all directions. Those individuals who are under stress—particularly those who are anxious—show a great disorganization in their capacity to perform this simple task: errors are made, the pencil mark continually retraces itself to the starting point, and not infrequently, the whole project is given up. A more complex pattern involving the total behaviour of the individual has been demon-

---

* Chairman, Department of Psychiatry, McGill University, Montreal. Director, Allan Memorial Institute of Psychiatry.

strated by Jacobsen, in which he subjected a group of typists to stress in the form of a steadily increasing speed of dictation. By means of electrodes fixed over various parts of their musculature he was able to show a breakdown of the differentiation of tension which had been achieved at an earlier time when they learned to type, and was now breaking down under the pressure of the effort to keep up. As tension spread to involve the total individual, other evidences (among them failure of concentration) became apparent, emotional disturbances set in; some of the girls became very angry, others burst into tears, still others terminated their efforts in a hysterical outburst. Finally, one may refer to reports[4] in regard to children who have suffered head injuries with resulting deficits which became latent, but under such stress as bereavement showed a disorganization of behaviour with a return of the deficit to overt form. From these observations, it is clear that our working concept of disorganization must meet the following requirements:

1. Disorganization is a total phenomenon involving the whole organism but may, however, express itself primarily through one particular aspect of functioning of the individual, as through his motor skills.

2. The working concept must be applicable to the functioning of (a) the normal individual; (b) the individual with an overt deficit, such as an anxiety neurosis; and (c) the individual with a latent deficit, i.e., a child who had compensated the damage produced by his head injury.

3. It must meet the fact that the phenomenon is usually if not always reversible.

4. It must accommodate itself to disorganization as being a common sequel of stress.

Here then is a tentative working definition. By disorganization is meant an impairment of behaviour, usually temporary, which most commonly arises as a consequence of stress. This impairment may accentuate existing defects, bring to light latent defects, and in the individual without defect provide a range of impairment up to and including complete disappearance of one or more patterns of behaviour. Disorganization is commonly reversible as soon as the relevant stress is removed.

I should like most carefully at this time, however, to offset any possibility that the concept of disorganization may be equated with the somewhat unrealistic concept of regression. The breakdown in the organization of behaviour does not necessarily mean a return to a simpler, less highly differentiated and less adequate level of performance. It may sometimes mean the abolition of a pattern altogether or the manifestation of other forms of behaviour which certainly did not appear in the course of the evolution of a more highly skilled behaviour.

Let us then say that while it is true that under stress the behavioural patterns of the individual may break down and at times simpler, more childlike stages of behaviour may appear, at the same time, gross disturbances in performance may show themselves which had no counterpart in childhood years. Of course in using the concept of disorganization one does not fall into the absurdity with which the concept of regression involves us; namely, that if we talk of the totally regressed individual then logically we must expect somebody whose hair has turned black again, whose milk teeth have returned, and whose thymus is once more in functioning form. Even if yielding to the fatal and fallacious charms of this dichotomy we limit ourselves to the level of symbolic behaviour we may point to someone whose behaviour is childlike or even infantile, but at the same time we know very well—and he too can be brought to know—that he is not a child, but rather is acting the part of a child.

CLINICAL PATTERNS OF DISORGANIZATION

Now, having set up a working definition of disorganization, I should like to move from the experimental psychological field and study manifestations in the clinical situation. During the last several years, we have had occasion to study a number of different clinical patterns of disorganization:

1. *Overt Defects and Disorganization*

One of our earliest cases is that of a 56-year-old woman who had shown repeated depressive attacks for which she had been treated successfully by electro-shock therapy. About six months after her last attack this patient, who had suffered in addition from long-term arterial hypertension, had a moderately severe apoplexy which left her with a considerable degree of weakness of the left arm and leg and of the left side of the face. She recovered from this to a point but found that she was unable to get up and down stairs from her apartment. Her husband, who was a somewhat antagonistic person, rapidly lost interest in her. She again became quite deeply depressed and re-entered the

Institute for treatment because she was becoming actively suicidal. When she was examined it was found that her gait was so impaired that she could walk along the examining room, where movies were being taken of her, only by keeping her left shoulder against a wall. She had to support her left arm by her right hand, and she showed a good deal of distortion of her facial contours. After consultation with the department of neurology it was decided to carry out electrotherapy. This was done successfully, and as the patient became free of her depression and her agitation, it was apparent that she was now able to walk much better. She also developed much greater control over her left arm, and in comparing the movies taken before and after her treatment, it was also clear that her facial expression had normalized again considerably. She no longer had to walk supporting herself on the wall, and while she had a limp, could get around reasonably well by herself.

We have seen and dealt with a number of other cases in which overt defect was present and made worse. For instance, one patient was a long-term stutterer and suffered from an intercurrent anxiety state, or an intensification of an underlying anxiety. Here the speech was always made worse, reverting to its former level or to a somewhat better level after the anxiety was removed. The same is true of sensory deficits. We have repeatedly seen individuals who have suffered from hearing deficits of varying degrees, some of which were being managed by means of a hearing aid. When the patient became agitated and depressed the hearing became considerably worse, but returned to its former deficit level as soon as the depression and the agitation had subsided. Anxious and otherwise disturbed patients suffering from defects in functions such as hearing and vision furnish particularly good illustrations of disorganization, since such patients usually already have had their deficits carefully recorded through an ophthalmological or acoustical examination prior to the onset of anxiety or other disturbances. Measured during the period of disorganization there will be found further deficit; measured again after treatment has been successfully carried out there will be a return to the former pre-disorganizational level of deficit.

2. *Latent Defects and Disorganization*

The best illustrations are furnished by those cases in which a strabismus shows itself only during the periods of disturbed behaviour.

Other illustrations are to be found in the use of stress to bring out latent defects in the electro-encephalogram (EEG) pattern. Here, as is well known, stresses at the biochemical and physiological levels like photic driving, hyperventilation, and intravenous metrazol are commonly used to break down the organization of the brain wave pattern and permit a latent defect (e.g., an epileptogenic focus) to appear.

3. *Disorganization without Prior Defect*

The examples of disorganization appearing in individuals who had no known deficit prior to the onset of stress are very numerous, and range all the way from those who develop conceptual difficulties under stress, amounting at times to actual delusional formation, to those who show disturbances in psychomotor function.

Learning, both motor and verbal, is impaired in anxious patients. Tension and concentration are also interfered with.[5] We all are aware from clinical experience of other effects of stress such as increasing feelings of sensitivity leading on to actual ideas of reference, these in turn subsiding as soon as stress is reduced, and hence disorganization disappears.

SPECIAL FIELDS OF APPLICATION

From these basic observations we can proceed to apply this working concept of disorganization to the exploration of several other fields. First, with respect to schizophrenia, we have found a number of patients who have gone through an acute schizophrenic upset, who have recovered either spontaneously or under treatment, and who then have gone on living reasonably adequate lives with little or no discernible deficit. However, during a period of stress there sets in a return of the schizophrenic symptoms.

Illustrative of these cases is a 36-year old man who had first shown a schizophrenic breakdown as far back as 1950. He had been admitted to the Institute at that time, but insisted upon leaving against advice before treatment had been carried out. Two years prior to his readmission to us he had received a lobotomy in another city and had got along tolerably well until a month or two prior to admission. Apparently insecure over his job, he had grown increasingly tense and anxious and displayed anew precisely the same delusions as he had in 1950: namely, ideas of reference—personal body odours to which others were objecting. On readmission we decided first to reduce his tension and anxiety in order to determine whether or not his symptoms were largely due to disorganization. This was done by means of largactil and Phenobarbitol and was accomplished within five weeks. He was then discharged and arrangements were made for him to have a more satisfactory home situation, and in particular, to provide him with the necessary support which he had not found when moving around from one job to another. He did well until he came under increasing pressure on the job through a superior who had learned about his hospitalization and who attempted to drive him out of his job on these grounds. The patient once more became tense and anxious, there was a return of his suspiciousness, and he made an appointment to come back to be seen at the Institute. Within the week or two which intervened, however, his father—who had not yet been able to come to Quebec to set up a home for the boy—arrived, and within a week after his arrival the reassurance of his presence had been enough to allay the patient's anxiety; his suspicion subsided, and when he was actually seen there was no evidence of active schizophrenic symptomatology, though he of course showed the defects due to the earlier schizophrenic break-down plus the lobotomy.

A somewhat similar case is that of a 33-year-old married woman who had two schizophrenic breakdowns, both accompanied by symptoms of depersonalization, feelings of being influenced, vagueness of contact, and considerable concreteness of thinking. She was treated on the first occasion by coma and electric convulsive therapy (ECT) and on the second by ECT only. It was then decided that because she relapsed fairly readily on going home, she would be put on a monthly preventive ECT. She has done well under this treatment save that on one occasion about six months ago, she began to feel increasingly tense and anxious again, things became vague and unreal to her, and she feared that her symptoms might return. This was dealt with by giving her a short course of five electroconvulsive treatments spaced over a 10-day period. This broke up her anxiety and tension entirely and since then she has remained well. She runs her household, mixes with friends, gives parties, and carries on a full social life.

It has been our experience that this lighting up of schizophrenic symptomology usually subsides again fairly easily as soon as the stress is removed. Here, too, such relapses have been taken as evidence of reactivation of the schizophrenic process. It is our view, however, that a considerable number of these cases have a quite different origin—

that in actuality what they represent is a breakdown in the individual's compensation of his schizophrenic deficit. Thus we see here a disorganization of a hitherto well-compensated schizophrenic patient; a disorganization during which a latent schizophrenic deficit comes to light.

It is desirable to attempt to differentiate here between disorganization of a hitherto well-compensated schizophrenic patient and further progression in the schizophrenic process itself. From our experience we are inclined to feel that we should consider the disorganization of a compensated schizophrenia to be present where the symptoms shown by the patient are similar to those shown during the first attack, and that one should consider that a genuine lighting up of the schizophrenic process should be considered to be present only when new categories of symptoms appear. Illustrative of the latter would be a case in which distortion of the body image appeared in the second attack and not in the first or where schizophrenic concreteness of thinking began to show itself in the second attack. We consider that the differentiation between the two states; namely, between a disorganization of a hitherto well-compensated schizophrenic and an actual lighting up of the schizophrenic process, is most important from the point of view of treatment. This in turn leads to two important conceptions. The first is with respect to the treatment of this disorganization of the hitherto compensated schizophrenic patient; the second is with respect to its prevention. We have found that our best therapeutic approach is based upon the conception of the rapid reduction of the patient's reaction to the stress situation. That reduction may be achieved by any or all of the usual means; by psychotherapy, the use of Thorazine or barbiturates, or if necessary (as in the case of a depressive response) by electroconvulsive shock therapy.

Turning now to the matter of prevention, we have found that we have been able to maintain schizophrenic patients at exceedingly good levels by regular monthly checks during which a type of relationship psychotherapy is carried on, electric-shock is given on a once-a-month basis if necessary, attention is paid to weight, and in general everything is done to prevent the development of stress and hence disorganization.

A second area to which we have applied this conception of disorganization is in the exploration of isolated symptoms. We have made use here of current premises concerning the method of action of Thorazine: namely, that it blocks the effective components of behavior by acting particularly upon the ascending reticular system. Hence, we have been most interested in exploring what happens to such symptoms as delusion formation and incoherence when the effective component is interrupted briefly by intravenous Thorazine. We have now several instances where the patient has reported either that his delusions no longer mattered or that he could see that they were false, and we have also one or two instances in which, much to our surprise, incoherence disappeared for the half-hour or so while the intravenous largactil was working.

Finally, one may raise some suggestions concerning the possibility of disorganization taking place at other levels. For instance, we have a good deal of evidence in the literature that under stress, anxiety and other aspects of the intensification syndrome, the cardiac action may become irregular as recorded by the electrocardiogram. Moving from there it would seem possible that some of the disturbances which we find under similar circumstances in persons with diabetes and in those suffering from hyperthyroidism may also be seen in the same sense. In other words, we do not yet have a clear idea as to the limits of the operation of the principle of disorganization.

SUMMARY

Disorganization has been used as a working principle for some time by experimental psychologists.

It can be usefully applied in the psychiatric field both clinically and experimentally.

Disorganization under stress may occur (a) in individuals without defect, (b) in individuals with latent defects, (c) in individuals with overt defects.

This concept of the impairment of behaviour, usually temporary, which most commonly arises in response to stress has been applied to schizophrenia.

It has been shown that a certain proportion of relapses in chronic schizophrenic patients are best understood not as a lighting up of a schizophrenic process, but as temporary disorganization produced by a period of intercurrent stress.

Stress-reducing agents suffice to terminate these phases of disorganization in such schizophrenic patients, and their appearance may be in large measure avoided by preventive treatment.

We have also explored the uses of acute interruption of stress by Thorazine and the effects of this interruption upon symptom formation.

REFERENCES

1. LURIA, A. R.: The Nature of Human Conflicts. New York, Liveright, 1932.
2. JACOBSON, E.: Progressive Relaxation. Chicago, Univ. of Chicago Press, 1944.
3. KRUGMAN, H. E.: Flicker-fusion frequency as a function of anxiety reaction. Psychosom. Med., 9: 269, 1947.
4. FABIAN, A. A. AND BENDER, L.: Head injury in children: predisposing factors. Am. J. Orthopsychiat., 17: 68-79, 1947.
5. LEWINSKI, R. J.: Psychometric pattern—anxiety neurosis. J. Clin. Psychol, 3: 214-221, 1945.

8

PERCEPTION OF PARENTS
AND SOCIAL ATTITUDES

By DANIEL H. FUNKENSTEIN, M.D., STANLEY H. KING, Ph.D.
and MARGARET E. DROLETTE, M.P.H.*

THIS IS A REPORT of the close relationship between the social attitudes of healthy college students and their perceptions of their parents. The substantiating data were gathered during a study of 125 randomly selected male students in a large eastern college, and the focus was on the emotional, physical, and social correlates of experimental stress reactions. In this investigation each subject was studied extensively outside the experimental situations by means of psychological tests, psychiatric interviews, and sociological questionnaires. We have reported on various aspects of this study elsewhere[9] and propose in this paper to confine our attention to the association between the perception of parents in authority, affection, and role areas and the scores on a series of social attitude scales.

In brief review it should be stated that the perception of parents in these areas was highly associated with the emotional reactions of the subjects in acute emergency stress situations. When the mother was seen as the chief source of authority and affection the subject usually responded with anxiety; and when father represented both authority and affection the subject usually denied the experience of any emotion. When the subject perceived one parent as being the primary source of authority and the other parent of affection he usually responded during acute stress with anger, directed outward or inward. There was, how-

* Department of Psychiatry, Harvard Medical School and the Boston Psychopathic Hospital; Department of Biostatistics, Harvard School of Public Health. This research was supported in part by a grant from the Supreme Council 33rd Degree, Scottish Rite, Northern Masonic Jurisdiction, through the National Association for Mental Health and in part by Grant M-945, U. S. P. H. S. We wish to express our appreciation for the help given us by D. J. Levinson, Ph.D. and D. C. Gilbert, Ph.D.

ever, a qualitative difference between these two anger reactions in that subjects who directed anger outward had a poor relationship with the father and saw his role as quite different from that of mother. Subjects who directed anger inward had a good relationship with the father and saw less discrepancy between the parents in terms of authority and affection.

The perception of parents was also associated with scores on the Brownfain Concept of Self Test.[2] Here subjects who perceived one parent as being the source of both authority and affection differed little in "best" and "worst" ratings of themselves on a series of traits. Subjects who perceived one parent as the primary source of authority and the other as the primary source of affection had large differences between these two self-ratings.

The perception of parents in authority, affection, and role model areas was also related to scores on social attitude scales—the subject of this report. This association is of great interest in the light of the increasing importance of social attitude studies during recent years. A review of these studies is hardly necessary at this point in view of the excellent report by Adorno, Frenkel-Brunswik, Levinson, and Sanford in *The Authoritarian Personality*[1] and the recent monograph by Christie and Jahoda[3] which reviews this work in detail.

SUBJECTS

The studies reported here were part of a large project carried out in a large eastern private college. One hundred and thirty-five male students in the junior and senior classes were chosen by random numbers from the lists of students living at the college. Ten were eliminated from the study for a variety of reasons such as illness or because they were too busy to give the time. The students ranged in age from 20 to 24 years. Each student was studied for a period of 20 to 30 hours from the standpoint of many disciplines. The data reported here were a small part of the total data accumulated on these students.

PROCEDURE

A biographical questionnaire containing questions about perception of parental roles was administered to 99 of the subjects in the project, and a battery of five social attitude scales developed by Levinson[11] was administered to 79 subjects. It was necessary to introduce these two instruments after the project had begun, hence the discrepancy in numbers.

Questions about the parents were grouped in three areas: how the subject saw mother and father in terms of authority, how he saw them in terms of affection, and how he saw them in terms of a role model for him to follow.*

The questions relating to authority dealt with the following factors: were father and mother stern or mild, fair or unfair; which parent had the final word in most family decisions; which was the chief disciplinary agent; and which parent most frequently punished the subject when he was a child.

The questions relating to role model asked about which parent the subject felt he resembled in personality, which parent had the greatest influence on his becoming the person he was, which parent was admired the most, and which parent he took the part of when his parents had a disagreement.

The questions relating to affection were in the area of the closeness of the relationship felt by the subject toward each parent, the degree to which each parent showed affection, and the perception of each parent on a loving-rejecting continuum.

Altogether there were 12 questions that pertained to the subject under discussion, five on authority, four on role model, and three on affection. The rating of each subject's perceptions of his parents in the three areas followed two procedural steps: first, an inspection of his answers for evidence of clear-cut predisposition toward one parent or the other and, secondly, comparison of his answers with those of the group as a whole.

Many subjects were easy to rate on inspection of their answers owing to the consistent choice of one parent on all the questions in one area. For example, a subject might answer that father was stern in discipline while mother was mild, that father always had the final word in family decisions, that he was the chief disciplinary agent and the person who most frequently punished the child. In this case it

* The exact questions used can be obtained from the ADI Auxiliary Publications Project, Photoduplication Service, Library of Congress, Washington 25, D. C.

would be clear that father was perceived as the chief source of authority. On the questions concerning affection the subject might answer that mother frequently showed strong affection, father sometimes. Rating each parent on a nine-point loving-rejecting scale, with one equalling strong rejection and nine equalling strong loving, he might rate mother as seven and father as four. He might also answer that he felt closer to his mother than to his father. Here, then, it would be clear that he perceived mother as the chief source of affection.

Problems in rating occurred only in connection with subjects whose answers in any one area were sometimes in the direction of father and sometimes in the direction of mother. In order to have a quantitative, relatively objective method for scoring such records, it was necessary to take the second procedural step, the comparison of his answers with those of the group.

To accomplish this, the distribution of responses of the entire group on each question was first tabulated. On the basis of this distribution, weights were assigned to each question so that if a subject answered all questions in one area as indicating one parent dominant he would get a score of 100 for that parent. The ratio of "father" responses to mother responses of the entire group determined the specific value for each question. For example, on the questions relative to affection, let us suppose that the majority of the subjects answered "mother" and that the ratio of "mother" to "father" responses was three to one for the first question, two to one for the second, and five to one for the third. The weights would then be 30 for question one, 20 for question two, and 50 for question three. In each case the score would be assigned to the parent specified in the answer. Since a response of "father" on the third question would be more unusual (in comparison with the whole group) than a similar response on either of the other two questions, the score on this question would be justifiably higher.

For a given area the score for each subject was derived by totaling the score for each parent and then taking the difference between these scores. To continue the example outlined above, a subject who answered "mother" on questions one and three and "father" on question two would receive a total score of 60 in the direction of the mother. He would be given 30 for question one plus 50 for question three in the direction of mother minus the 20 on question two in the direction of father. This would leave a total of 60 toward mother and would indicate that he saw mother as the chief source of affection. Schematically, this case would be scored as follows:

Affection	Mother	Father	
Question 1	30	0	
Question 2	0	20	Total Score Mother: 60
Question 3	50	0	
Total	80	20	

This enabled a quantitative score to be assigned to the importance of one parent in relation to the other in each of the three main percept areas.

As a matter of practical importance, the great majority of men answered a majority of the questions under one heading toward one parent. The quantitative score merely enabled an objective decision to be made in the minority of cases in which the answers were more evenly divided. In several instances, the total score equalled zero, so that it was necessary to assign the particular percept as equal in relation to each parent.

A social attitude battery of 64 items (FERPT Scales) developed by Levinson was used. Three of these scales, the F, the E and the PEC, were derived from forms used in *The Authoritarian Personality*. The other two, the RC and the TFI scales, were later developed by Levinson. These scales were described by Levinson[11] as follows:*

The *Authoritarianism* (F) Scale contains a variety of ideas concerning authority, work, sex, aggression, human nature, and the like. High scores presumably indicate personality trends such as punitiveness, authoritarian submission, stereotypy, and projectivity.

The *Ethnocentrism* (E) Scale deals with intergroup relations within this country and at the international level. High scores presumably indicate a generalized tendency to reject various outgroups such as Negroes, Jews, foreigners and other nations, and to idealize the corresponding ingroups. Low scores are associated with rejection of both outgroup prejudice and ingroup idealization.

The *Religious Conventionalism* (RC) Scale contains a variety of ideas about the church, the Bible, God, prayer, and the like. High scores reflect a conception of God as punishing power figure and of the church as absolute moral authority, as well as a marked emphasis on faith, tradition, and conformity to institutional forms. Low scores, on the other hand, represent a religious humanistic or a nontheistic approach which emphasizes reason, personally

* Copies of these scales may be obtained from D. J. Levinson, Ph. D., Department of Social Relations, Harvard University, Cambridge 38, Massachusetts.

derived values, and a naturalistic rather than supernaturalistic view of the world.

The *Politico-Economic Conservatism* (PEC) Scale provides a measure of general liberalism (low score) *vs.* conservatism (high score) concerning such issues as economic security, taxation, and the government-business-labour balance of power.

The *Traditional Family Ideology* (TFI) Scale deals with husband-wife relations, parent-child relations, conceptions of authority, masculinity and femininity, and so on. High scores indicate strong emphasis on discipline in child-training, on the dominant-assertive male and the rigidly conventional female. Low scores indicate less dichotomous definition of sex roles and greater emphasis on self-expression.

RESULTS

First we will report the family perceptions and the social attitude scores of the group as a whole; then we will present the interrelationship between these two sets of data.

1. *The Family Perception Data*

An analysis of the separate variables of authority, role model, and affection showed that 60.6 per cent of the students perceived father as the chief authority, 69.7 per cent perceived father as their chief role model, and 77.4 per cent perceived mother as their chief source of affection (Table 1).

TABLE 1. *This shows the perceptions of the students of the importance of their fathers relative to that of their mothers as their chief sources of authority and affection and as their role models.*

	Father	Mother	Both
Authority	60 (60.6%)	34 (34.4%)	5 (5%)
Role Model	69 (69.7%)	30 (30.3%)	0
Affection	13 (13.1%)	77 (77.4%)	9 (9.5%)

These results indicated that the great majority of students perceived father as the chief source of authority and as their role model and mother as the chief source of affection. Finding father as the chief source of authority was at variance with the popularly conceived idea of the American matriarchy. However, no generalizations from this sample to the population as a whole can be made because of the highly selective nature of the sample. Then too, these results represent the perception of the students in a highly emotional area. The results might be quite different if the measures were related to the realities within their families.

2. The Social Attitude Battery

The means of the college students were relatively low and well below the mid-point on four of the five social attitude scales (Table 2). In the upper half of the scales there were only *11* (14.1%) on the F scale, *18* (23%) on the RC scale, *14* (17.7%) on the E scale, *56* (71.4%) on the PEC scale, and *10* (12.8%) on the TFI scale.

TABLE 2. *This shows the mean and range of the scores of the students on the five scales of the Social Attitude Battery.*

	F	RC	E	PEC	TFI
Maximum	65	77	81	82	69
Mean	*38.11*	*36.66*	*42.77*	*52.19*	*36.09*
Minimum	12	12	19	19	14

Number of Students 79

These results showed that the college students as a group make scores in the "equalitarian" range. On only one scale was a majority of the students on the conservative side, and this was in relation to political and economic beliefs where the mean score was in the upper half of the continuum. Seventy-two per cent of the students were conservative in their political and economic beliefs. This meant that the vast majority could be described as having flexible "equalitarian" attitudes, liberal religious beliefs, little prejudice against groups with which they were not identified, and little belief in a traditional family ideology. At the same time they were politically conservative.

3. The Relationship of the Family Perceptions to the Social Attitude Scales

The subjects were first divided into two groups in each of the three family perception areas: (1) those who perceived father as the chief source of authority; those who perceived mother as the chief source of authority. (2) Those who perceived father as the chief role model; those who perceived mother as the chief role model. (3) Those who perceived father as the chief source of affection; those who perceived mother as the chief source of affection. The two groups in each family perception area were then compared on each of the five social attitude scales and "t" tests for significance of differences between means were run for these groups.

The men who perceived their fathers as their chief sources of authority were significantly higher on the PEC scale and TFI scale than the men who perceived their mothers as their chief sources of authority, .01 level. The men who perceived father as their chief role model had a significantly higher mean on the PEC scale than men who perceived mother as their chief role model. On the other four scales there were no significant differences, although the difference on the TFI scale was close, at the .08 level. No significant differences were found on any of the scales between the group that perceived father as the chief source of affection and the group that perceived mother as the chief source of affection. These results are summarized in Table 3.

Secondly, the subjects were grouped according to the way they perceived the division between their parents on authority and affection. Assuming that either mother or father could fulfill either or both of these roles, there were four possible combinations:

(a) Father chief source of authority, father chief source of affection
(b) Father chief source of authority, mother chief source of affection
(c) Mother chief source of authority, father chief source of affection
(d) Mother chief source of authority, mother chief source of affection

The men who perceived mother as the chief source of authority and father as the chief source of affection were too small in number for statistical analysis.

The three remaining groups were then compared on the basis of their scores on the five social attitude scales. The men who perceived father as the chief source of both authority and affection had the highest mean score of all the groups on all five of the social attitude scales. The men who perceived mother as the chief source of both authority and affection had the lowest score of all the groups on all five of the social attitude scales. The men who perceived father as the chief source of authority and mother as the chief source of affection had a mean score between the means of the other two groups.

The differences between the men who perceived father as the chief source of authority and affection and the group of men who perceived mother as the chief source of authority and affection were significant on four of the five social attitude scales. The differences between these groups on the RC scale were not significant (Table 3).

On the E scale the difference between the men who perceived father as the chief source of authority and affection and those who perceived father as the chief source of authority and mother as the chief source of affection was significant, .03 level, and the difference between these

TABLE 3. This shows the statistical comparison on the five scales of the students in their perception of the importance of one parent in relation to the other as the chief source of authority and affection and as their role models.

		AUTHORITY					ROLE MODEL					AFFECTION		
		No.	Mean	t	df	p	No.	Mean	t	df	p	No.	Mean	p
1. F Scale	Father	52	38.76	1.14	76	.25	52	37.54	.18	74	.85	12	40.25	Insignificant
	Mother	27	36.00				24	38.00				67	37.4	
2. RC Scale	Father	52	39.79	1.49	77	.15	52	37.50	.12	74	.90	12	37.25	Insignificant
	Mother	27	33.18				24	36.92				67	37.6	
3. E Scale	Father	52	44.73	1.58	77	.10	52	43.42	.55	74	.60	12	49.5	Insignificant
	Mother	27	39.44				24	41.50				67	41.7	
4. PEC Scale	Father	52	54.71	2.70	77	<.01	52	54.62	2.45	74	<.01	12	55.3	Insignificant
	Mother	27	48.04				24	48.17				67	51.9	
5. TFI Scale	Father	52	38.62	2.82	77	<.01	52	37.35	1.75	74	.08	12	39.08	Insignificant
	Mother	27	30.96				24	32.50				67	37.4	

same two groups on the PEC scale was also significant, .05 level (Table 4).

TABLE 4. *This shows the relationship between the variables of authority and affection, as perceived by the students, and the social attitude scales. The number of cases in which mother was the authority and father the chief source of affection was too small for statistical analysis.*

SCALE	Group 1	Group 2	Mean Group 1	Mean Group 2	t	df	p
	FF	MM	43.86	36.18	2.12	27	.05
F Scale	FF	FM	43.86	36.13	——	—	—
	FM	MM	38.13	36.18	——	—	—
	FF	MM	45.43	34.86	——	—	—
RC Scale	FF	FM	45.43	38.91	——	—	—
	FM	MM	38.91	34.86	——	—	—
	FF	MM	55.00	36.68	4.89	27	.01
E Scale	FF	FM	55.00	42.24	2.30	50	.03
	FM	MM	43.13	36.68	——	—	—
	FF	MM	62.00	48.50	3.40	27	.01
PEC Scale	FF	FM	62.00	53.58	1.98	50	.05
	FM	MM	53.58	48.50	——	—	—
	FF	MM	45.43	29.77	3.70	27	.01
TFI Scale	FF	FM	45.43	37.78	——	—	—
	FM	MM	37.78	29.77	——	—	—

F = father
M = mother
First symbol authority; second symbol affection

DISCUSSION

These data indicated a strong relationship between domination by one parent of the roles of authority and affection (as perceived by the subject) and the "authoritarian-equalitarian" personality dimension. Students whose fathers dominated the roles of authority and affection made relatively high scores for their college culture on authoritarianism, ethnocentricity, conservative political and economic values, and traditional family ideology.* In contrast to this, students whose mothers

* Relative differences are referred to because with the exception of the PEC scale, the average scores of the students as a whole were below the mid-point. The "father-related" subjects were near the mid-point on all scales except the PEC, where they were absolutely high.

dominated the roles of authority and affection made relatively low scores on authoritarianism, ethnocentricity, conservative political and economic values, and traditional family ideology.

Originally Levinson[1] interpreted the scales in *The Authoritarian Personality* as follows:

> Some of the variables in the authoritarian syndrome include: idealization of accepted authority; exaggerated concern with power and fear of weakness; extreme self-deception concerning one's own emotional life and insensitivity to the emotions of others; a strong tendency to displace aggression from its original intrafamilial objects to others conceived of as immoral or weak. In general, equalitarian individuals are more flexible in their thoughts, more able to criticize themselves and those with whom they are identified, more concerned with self-understanding and self-expression, more able to accept and to gratify their deeper-lying impulses.

Continuing, Levinson stated that the "authoritarian" individual tends to put more emphasis on discipline in child-parent relationships, keeps closer control on things, maintains respect, and makes clear who is boss. For him standards of morality, of how people act and the goals they set for themselves, always have a locus in some external agent, and all who are subordinate take their cues from this agent of authority. The attitude of the "authoritarian" individual is that if one stays within this pattern he is all right, but if he gets out of the pattern he is in for trouble and will deserve whatever happens to him. He sees the world in terms of black and white.

The "equalitarian" individual leans in the opposite direction from this frame of reference and can be characterized as having more conscious guilt and a stronger internalized conscience. He has more open conflicts and doubts and sees the world in shades of gray.

Since this pioneering work, a number of investigators reported confirmation of this original interpretation of the data. In our project from which the data reported in this paper were drawn, a large body of confirmatory evidence of Levinson's interpretations was obtained. Our data supported the interpretation that high scorers were intolerant or unaccepting of ambiguities; had rigid personalities; were extrapunitive; placed little value on introspection, for which they showed little capacity; were little aware of psychological factors; and had little conscious anxiety or guilt. Further, our data suggested that these attributes were associated with an obsessive-compulsive character structure. Contrariwise, low scorers were tolerant or accepting of ambiguities; had flexible personalities; were intropunitive; placed great value on introspection, for which they had marked capacity; were very much aware of psychological factors; and had conscious anxiety or guilt.

Frenkel-Brunswik[5,6] and others found that high scorers on such social attitude scales differed from low scorers in certain areas of perception. The high scorers were intolerant or were unable to accept ambiguities, whereas low scorers were able to accept such ambiguities. This was interpreted as indicating a rigid personality. In our project evidence of this rigidity together with the inacceptability of ambiguities was found in the data obtained by two techniques: The Brownfain Concept of Self Test and the study of laboratory stress reactions.

In the Brownfain Test[2] the student graded himself in four frames of reference using an eight-point rating scale on 25 different personality items. These frames of reference were as follows:

1. The "optimum" way he sees himself, giving himself the benefit of any doubt and rating himself the highest that he thinks he is, the "Best Self."

2. The "worst" way he sees himself, not giving himself the benefit of any doubt but rating himself the lowest he thinks he is, the "Worst Self."

3. The way he actually sees himself, the "Actual Self."

4. The way he feels that others feel about him, the "Social Self."

It would be expected that men who were unable to tolerate ambiguities would show fewer differences between their gradings of themselves in these four frames of reference than those who could accept ambiguities about themselves. Fewer differences in grading the "self" in these four frames of reference would also indicate an inability to shift from one frame of reference to another, suggesting rigidity of personality. The hypothesis could be stated as follows: high scorers on the Social Attitude Battery show less variance in their four scores on the Brownfain test than do low scorers on the Social Attitude Battery.

In order to test this hypothesis, the men were rank ordered on the basis of their mean Social Attitude Battery scores and compared with the variance they showed on the four parts of the Brownfain test.* The upper fourth of the Social Attitude Battery scorers showed the least variance on the Brownfain test as measured by the "range"; the lower

---

* In order to obtain a valid estimate of the variance of the scores of each subject on the four parts of the Brownfain test, the "range" was obtained. The

fourth of the Social Attitude Battery scorers, the highest variance on the Brownfain test as measured by the "range." When the lower middle fourth and upper middle fourth of the Social Attitude Battery scorers were also considered, it was seen that the variance in the Brownfain scores, as measured by the "range," was related inversely to the Social Attitude scores. A "t" test indicated that the difference in mean "range" between the upper fourth and lower fourth of the Social Attitude Battery scorers was significant at the .04 level (Table 5). Figure 1 shows this diagramatically.

These results indicate that the capacity to tolerate ambiguities and to shift from one frame of reference to another, as measured by the Brownfain test, is significantly related to the Social Attitude Battery scores of the subjects. On the basis of these findings, high Social Attitude Battery scorers would be interpreted as less tolerant of ambiguities and more rigid than low scorers on the same battery of tests. This was further evidence that the social attitudes of a person are but reflections of many aspects of the personality, as others have shown. Brownfain[2] found a high correlation between scores on the F scale and a small difference in the way the men graded themselves on two aspects of his Concept of Self test. This he interpreted as showing rigidity of personality.

All of the students were studied during the three laboratory stress experiments. The very high scorers showed lesser shifts in their reactions from situation to situation in the three stress experiments than did the low scorers, although these differences were not significant. Almost all of the low scorers showed a variety of different reactions during the three stress experiments.

The stress reactions also indicated other characteristics of high and low scorers on the Social Attitude Battery. Although the high scorers most often denied the expression of emotion during acute stress, showing their marked control, they were not hesitant to ascribe their difficulties during the experiments to factors outside themselves, extrapunitive responses. In contrast to this, the low scorers most often responded

---

"range" was the difference between the largest and the smallest of the four Brownfain scores. When only four numbers are used, the "range" gives an excellent estimation of the variance between the scores. The smaller the "range," the less variance between the student's gradings of himself in the four different frames of reference; the larger the "range," the greater the variance between the student's gradings of himself in the four different frames of reference.

TABLE 5. *This shows the average range for the Social Attitude group scores based on the division of the entire sample into fourths. A one-tail "t" test was used because the results were in the direction of the hypothesis.*

Social Attitude Group	Average Range*—Brownfain Group
Upper one-fourth of scorers	41.85
Upper middle one-fourth of scorers	47.58
Lower middle one-fourth of scorers	49.58
Lower one-fourth of scorers	52.60

"t" test (comparing upper ¼ and lower ¼) = 1.78   38df   p = .04 (one tail)

*"Range" gives reliable estimate of *variance.*

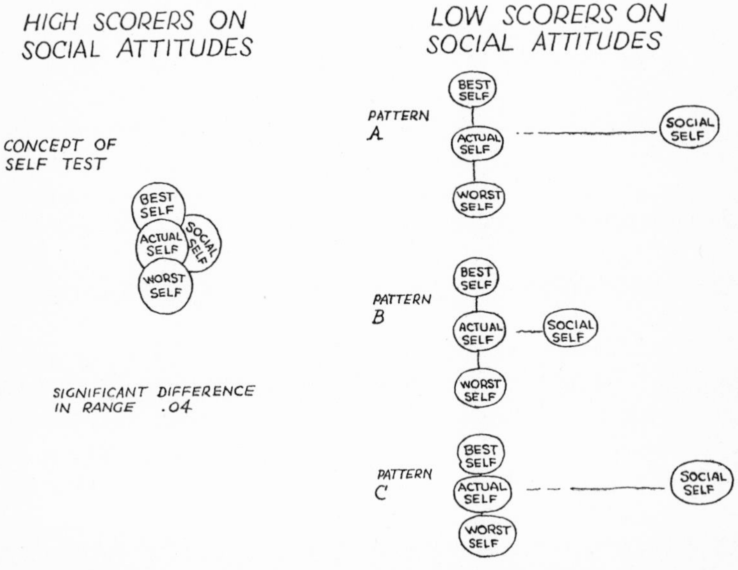

FIG. 1. *This shows diagramatically the variance in the four aspects of the Brownfain Test between high scorers on the Social Attitude Battery and low scorers on the Social Attitude Battery. The high scorers show little variance in the way they score their four aspects of "self." Low scorers fall into three patterns all of which show marked variance in the way they grade the "self" in several frames of reference.*

during acute stress with anxiety or anger directed toward the self and ascribed their difficulties in the test situation to factors within themselves, intropunitive responses.

The little value the high scorers placed on introspection or reflective thinking, as contrasted with the great value placed on this attribute by the low scorers, was seen in another part of the Brownfain test. This measured the relative value placed on certain traits by the students.

The subjects were given a list of 25 defined traits and asked to place a plus (+) in front of the 10 items on which it was important for them to stand high or low and to place a second plus (++) in front of the five of these which were the most important to them. They were then asked to place a zero (0) in front of the 10 items which

TABLE 6. *This shows the value placed on the 25 Brownfain traits between students in the upper one-fourth and lower one-fourth of the scorers on the Social Attitude Battery.*

Brownfain Values

	Upper ¼ of scorers on Social Attitude Battery		Lower ¼ of scorers on Social Attitude Battery			
	++	= 0	++	= 0		
TRAIT	+	00	+	00	x^2	p
1. Intelligence	16	4	18	2	—	—
2. Emotional Maturity	15	5	16	4	—	—
3. General Culture	7	13	11	9	—	—
4. Social Poise	9	11	6	14	—	—
5. Physical Attractiveness	5	15	8	12	—	—
6. NEATNESS	8	12	1	19	5.16	.02
7. Sociability	5	15	2	18	—	—
8. Generosity	6	14	8	12	—	—
9. Manners	7	13	2	18	—	—
10. Cheerfulness	7	13	4	16	—	—
11. Sincerity	12	8	8	12	—	—
12. Consistency	6	14	5	15	—	—
13. Initiative	12	8	7	13	—	—
14. Trustfulness	5	15	5	15	—	—
15. FLEXIBILITY	1	19	9	11	6.67	.01
16. Sportsmanship	6	14	3	17	—	—
17. Individuality	7	13	13	7	2.50	—
18. SELF-UNDERSTANDING	5	15	14	6	6.41	.01
19. Interest in opposite sex	7	13	4	16	—	—
20. DEPENDABILITY	17	3	10	10	4.10	.04
21. Understanding of others	9	11	15	5	2.60	—
22. Self-Acceptance	1	19	5	15	—	—
23. Popularity	7	13	3	17	—	—
24. Prestige	8	12	7	13	—	—
25. Overall Adjustment	14	6	18	2	—	—

they felt most indifferent about in regard to their own standing and to place a second zero (00) in front of the five of these which were the least important to them.

The ratings on the Brownfain Values were consolidated into two groups: one group combined those whose marked a trait with either one (+) or two (++) pluses, thus placing a high value on that trait; and another group which combined those who marked a trait with either one zero (0), two zeros (00) or did not mark it at all, thus placing a low value on that trait.

The men were then rank ordered on the basis of their Social Attitude Battery scores. The high quarter of the scorers on the Social Attitude Battery were then compared with the low quarter of the scorers on each of the 25 values, using chi-square tests. As shown in Table 6, significant differences were found between the high and low scorers on four traits. A significantly larger number of high scorers placed a high value on *neatness* and *dependability* than low scorers; a significantly larger number of low scorers placed a high value on *flexibility* and *self-understanding* than high scorers. It was of great interest that the greatest significant differences occurred on the values of *flexibility* and *self-understanding* since these were two of the traits which Levinson[1] postulated would be quite different in high and low scorers on the Social Attitude Battery.

The ability of a man to engage in introspection or reflective thinking could be gauged by a consideration of his total performance on the Brownfain test. To report these data in detail here is beyond the scope of this paper. However, in summary, the high scorers were interpreted on this basis to show less ability to engage in introspective thinking than the low scorers. This inability to engage in introspection was also shown by the Phrase Association Interviews (14) in these same students to be associated with strong defenses and excessive use of the mechanism of denial.

The personality characteristics associated with a high score on the Social Attitude Battery suggested that these men had personality structures similar to those of obsessive-compulsive neurotic patients. Certainly, only in this type of personality are apt to cluster such personality traits as rigidity of reaction, inability to tolerate ambiguities, denial of emotions, extrapunitive behavior during stress, and underevaluation of introspection with little capacity for such thinking. Still other evidence for this interpretation of these data was found in the

Thematic Apperception Tests and in the Phrase Association Interview results. The fantasies of these men, as determined by the Thematic Apperception Test, were different from those of other men in the project in the amount of aggression appearing in their stories and in the consequences of that aggression, which were almost always guilt feelings. The Phrase Association Interview technique carried out by Ravven and de la Pina, et al[14] showed strong defenses with an almost complete denial of negative emotions; almost all emotional expressions were positive. The directions of the emotions were outward, and their objects apt to be inanimates and abstractions rather than people. All of these data strongly suggested that the high scorers on the Social Attitude Battery were similar to obsessive-compulsive neurotic patients in many of their personality traits.

Finding that the personality characteristics of the students, as determined by these social attitude scales, were closely related to their perceptions of their parents was very intriguing. When the fathers loomed overly prominent in their sons' perceptions, the subjects were apt to be authoritarian. *If* these perceptions represent the internalization of their cultural background, then an over-prominence of father in the family in these areas is associated with too much rigidity of character and too much denial of emotion. An overly prominent mother in the family in these areas is associated with too much flexibility and anxiety. Other data of ours suggest that a more cooperative family in which father, while serving as an adequate masculine model, shares his authority with mother and the mother shares the affection with father, is more optimum for mature development.

In our project the students' reactions during stress were studied from two standpoints: their acute emergency reactions and their ability to handle stress as time passed. The acute emergency reactions and their correlates were interpreted as representing the *basic disposition* of the personality; the ability to handle stress as time passed and its correlates were interpreted as representing the *ego function* of the personality. Both the parental perceptions and the social attitudes correlated very significantly with the acute emergency reactions but were only randomly related to the ability to handle stress as time passed. This suggested that social attitudes are derivatives of the *basic disposition* which is a deeply laid down aspect of personality and which would be very difficult to change by any superficial means.

This has important implications when we consider present efforts to change other cultures to a more democratic viewpoint.

Taylor[17] has written a very stimulating book interpreting history on the basis of the role models of men. According to his thesis, when the majority of men in any period of history pattern their behavior after their fathers (patrists) certain attitudes become prevalent; when the majority of men pattern their behavior after their mothers (matrists) other attitudes become prevalent.

The more prominent characteristics of a patrist period were restrictive attitude to sex; limitation of freedom for women; women seen as inferior, sinful; chastity more valued than welfare; political authoritarianism; conservatism and against innovation; distrust of research and inquiry; inhibition and fear of spontaneity; deep fear of homosexuality, sex differences maximized e.g. dress; asceticism, fear of pleasure; a father-religion.

In contrast to this the more prominent characteristics of a matrist period were permissive attitude toward sex; freedom and high status for women; welfare more valued than chastity; politically democratic; progressive and revolutionary; no distrust of research, spontaneity, exhibition; deep fear of incest; sex differences minimized; hedonism, pleasure welcomed; a mother-religion.

In our studies we could not correlate the social attitude scales to the chief role model except in the area of political and economic beliefs. However, our findings in relation to the group of men who perceived father as the source of both authority and affection were similar to Taylor's findings in regard to *patrists;* and our findings in relation to the group of men who perceived mother as the chief source of authority and affection were similar to Taylor's findings relating to matrists. However, in our students the findings were not as extreme as Taylor's.

In our studies this *ambivalent* relationship with one parent was of great importance and correlated highly with the Social Attitude Battery scores. Reusch[16] found this same ambivalent relationship with one parent in peptic ulcer patients. He called attention to the great difficulties for a child with such a relationship with one parent. When one parent fulfills the roles of both authority and affection it is difficult for a child to rebel without fear of losing his chief source of support. When separate parents fulfill these roles the child may rebel against the parent who represents the authority without the fear of losing his chief source of affection, represented by the other parent.

The association of an ambivalent relationship with father and high scores on the social attitude scales was similar to the dynamics of the sado-masochistic character described by Erich Fromm[8]; Adorno, Frenkel-Brunswik, Levinson, and Sanford[1] used Max Horkheimer's theory to describe this syndrome:

Social repression is concomitant with the internal repression of impulses. In order to achieve, internalization of social control which never gives as much to the individual as it takes, the latter's attitude towards authority and its psychological agency, the super-ego, assumes an irrational aspect. The subject achieves his own social adjustment only by taking pleasure in obedience and subordination. This brings into play the sadomasochistic impulse structure both as a condition and as a result of social adjustment. In our form of society, sadistic as well as masochistic tendencies actually find gratification. The pattern for the translation of such gratifications into character traits is a specific resolution of the Oedipus Complex which defines the formation of the syndrome here in question. Love for the mother, in its primary form, comes under a severe taboo. The resulting hatred against the father is transformed by reaction-formation into love. This transformation leads to a particular kind of superego. The transformation of hatred into love, the most difficult task an individual has to perform in his early development, never succeeds completely. In the psycho-dynamics of the 'authoritarian character', part of the preceding aggressiveness is absorbed and turned into masochism, while another part is left over as sadism, which seeks an outlet in those with whom the subject does not identify himself; ultimately the outgroup . . . ambivalence is all-pervasive, being evidenced mainly by the simultaneity of blind belief in authority and readiness to attack those who are deemed weak and who are socially acceptable as 'victims'. Stereotypy in this syndrome is not only a means of social identification, but has a truly 'economic' function in the subject's inner household. He develops deep 'compulsive' character traits, partly by retrogression to the anal-sadistic phase of development.

It should be emphasized here that these correlations between perceptions of their parents and their social attitudes were obtained in students in a particular college. There is no justification for any generalizations from these results to the population at large or, in fact, to any other college. In other work of ours in progress we have some data suggesting that both the perceptions of families and the social attitudes in some other colleges may be more closely related to ethnic and social class factors. Until such cross-cultural studies are completed it should be understood that these results apply to this one highly selected segment of the population. In fact, the testing techniques used require a certain capacity for introspection. Redlich, Hollingshead, and Bellis[15] found that in families in certain social classes insight is little valued and that psychotherapy designed to produce insight may not work in such patients. These same writers and Parloff, Kelman, and Frank[13] stressed the observation that "insight" or "self-understanding" is highly valued by a limited, intellectually oriented and educated segment of the population. Preliminary data of ours also suggest that the testing techniques used in the studies reported in this article, which require introspection, will not work in ward patients and in students from certain other colleges who belong to a different social and cultural background from that of our students.

The very personality characteristics, particularly self-understanding, intropunitiveness, doubts, few prejudices, a non-belief in authority as a solution for problems, and belief in a family in which women have status, are highly valued by most educators. Reference was made above to the work by others showing that insight is valued by only a limited, intellectually oriented segment of the population. This emphasis in education on introspection was probably first stated by the Socratic dictum "know thyself." A very effective presentation of this viewpoint was made by Kubie,[10] who stated that without self-knowledge "in depth" the master of any field will be a child in human wisdom. Dickey's recent article[4] on the uses of "doubts" in the educational process is another case in point. Our studies suggest that a capacity for introspection, placing a high value on self-understanding, is related to deep dynamic factors within the basic personality. It is in families in which the mother has status that the development of such men takes place.

If we consider such attitudes as more civilized in the best meaning of the word then the mother in most families is the principal civilizing agent. This idea of the woman's role in the family was discussed by Freud in *Civilization and Its Discontents* and was again emphasized by Norris[12] in a recent article in the *Saturday Review*.

This entire field of interrelationship of social attitudes and families has so many implications for psychiatry that it is a fruitful field for further research. The studies reported here are merely a beginning.

SUMMARY

Ninety-nine male students in an eastern college were given a questionnaire designed to measure their perceptions of their parents in terms of authority, affection, and role model. Seventy-nine of these students were also given the FERPT social attitude scales.

1. The majority of the subjects perceived father as the chief source

of authority and as the chief role model, and mother as the chief source of affection.

2. The majority of the subjects had low scores on four of the attitude scales, representing an "equalitarian" attitude toward authority, liberal religious views, low prejudice, and liberal views toward the traditional family ideology. They were, however, more conservative in the political and economic areas.

3. It was found that subjects who perceived father as fulfilling the roles of both authority and affection had the highest scores on the FERPT scales while subjects who saw mother fulfilling both these roles had the lowest scores.

4. Evidence from other data gathered on this subject was cited in confirmation of the hypothesis that high scorers on the FERPT scales have rigid personalities, similar in nature to an obsessive-compulsive character structure.

5. The relationship of domination by either parent in key areas to character structure and social attitudes was discussed, with the reservation that these data are from a highly selected sample and therefore suggest caution in interpretation.

6. The data reported in this article were but a small part of the total material obtained on these same students by a variety of testing techniques. In addition to the interrelationship between social attitudes, perceptions of parents, and Brownfain test results reported here, these same aspects of personality also correlated with fantasies about aggression and its consequences as revealed by Thematic Apperception Test stories and the emotional and physiological reactions of the students during laboratory stress experiments.

REFERENCES

1. ADORNO, T. W., FRENKEL-BRUNSWIK, E., LEVINSON, D. J., AND SANFORD, R. N.: The Authoritarian Personality. New York, Harper & Bros., 1950.

2. BROWNFAIN, J. J.: Stability of the self-concept as a dimension of personality. J. Abnorm. Social Psychol., 47: 597, 1952.

3. CHRISTIE, R. AND JAHODA, M.: Studies in the scope and method of "The Authoritarian Personality." Glencoe, Ill., Free Press, 1954.

4. DICKEY, J. S.: Conscience and the undergraduate. Atlantic Monthly, 195: 4, 1955.

5. FRENKEL-BRUNSWIK, E.: A study of prejudice in children. Human Relations, 1: 295, 1948.

6. ——: Intolerance of ambiguity as an emotional and perceptual personality variable. Journal of Personality, 18: 108, 1949.

7. FREUD, S.: Civilization and Its Discontents. London, Hogarth Press, Ltd., and the Institute of Psycho-Analysis, 1951.

8. FROMM, E.: Escape from Freedom. New York, Farrar & Rinehart, 1941.

9. FUNKENSTEIN, D. H., KING, S. H., AND DROLETTE, M. E.: Mastery of stress. Harvard University Press. [In Press].

10. KUBIE, L. S .:The forgotten man of education. Harvard Alumni Bull., 56: 349, 1954.

11. LEVINSON, D. J.: The intergroup relations workshop: its psychological aims and effects. J. Psychol., 38: 103, 1954.

12. NORRIS, L. W.: How to educate a woman. Sat. Rev., 37: 9, 1954.

13. PARLOFF, M. D., KELMAN, H. C. AND FRANK, J. D.: Comfort, effectiveness and self-awareness as criteria of improvement in psychotherapy. Am. J. of Psychiat., 111: 343, 1954.

14. RAVVEN, R., DE LA PINA, L., KING, S. H., AND FUNKENSTEIN, D. H.: The phrase association interview in "Stress and personality in college students." (In preparation.)

15. REDLICH, J. C., HOLLINGSHEAD, A. B., AND BELLIS, E.: Social class differences in attitudes toward psychiatry. Am. J. Orthopsychiat., 25: 60, 1955.

16. REUSCH, J.: Duodenal Ulcer. Berkeley, Univ. of California Press, 1948.

17. TAYLOR, G. R.: Sex in History. New York, Vanguard Press, 1955.

9

Presidential Address
CONCERNING THE CREATIVE PROCESS IN LITERATURE

By MERRILL MOORE, M.D.*

I N THE FIELD OF PSYCHOPATHOLOGY much attention has in the past been paid to symptoms and behavior of a strictly pathological nature. These studies, usually based on neurotic or psychotic individuals, have led to theories concerning human nature in general. Nearly all the members of this Association at one time or another have made contributions along these lines, and a few have gone even further to study the peculiarities of the artistic personality. Among the early and founding members, Dr. Morton Prince, to mention one, was not unaware of this problem, and Dr. Ernest Jones, who is still active, on several occasions has expressed his interest in the subject. Dr. Adolf Meyer made intensive studies of several artistic and creative personalities, and Dr. George A. Waterman of Boston followed the productive careers of numerous writers and painters over long periods during his active practice. The problems of the artistic temperament and the creative personality were given considerable attention by our late President, Dr. Clarence P. Oberndorf, whose investigations as well as his speculations on this subject are extremely interesting. But even today the knowledge we have that deals with this subject is limited. I shall try to outline it in three parts.

SPECULATIONS AND IMPRESSIONS FROM THE REMOTE PAST

One might as well jump *in medias res*. It is said that Western literature began with Homer, who is an almost mythical figure, and about whom almost nothing is known except the fact that throughout the Near East and the Mediterranean countries it is believed that he was blind. A controversy has raged and will continue to rage concerning the

* Research Associate, Department of Social Relations, Harvard University, Cambridge, Mass.

authorship of the two main works attributed to him. Certain German scholars, for example, have thought these poems to be the work of a number of individuals. I can only say that I have read them both laboriously in school, in Greek, and I have read dozens of translations. To me both poems seem to have a striking uniformity and I prefer to believe that there was an actual poet named Homer, and that he did write the "Iliad" and the "Odyssey." I am also impressed by the fact that they are "true epics"—that is to say, they were written to be spoken or declaimed and it is not impossible, in my experience, to believe that one man might have learned them by heart and spoken them from memory. Also, he might have taught them to others. I have known several actors who have memorized more lines than these two poems contain. And if the poet were blind, perhaps his memory might have been sharper than if he had his sight.

When we study these two masterpieces, we can only wonder. Ancient literature gives us very few clues about the method of composition, why they wrote at all, or why a mythical Homer selected as his subject two such moving topics as the wrath of Achilles and the wanderings of a veteran from the Trojan Wars, who finally reached his home in safety. Least of all do we know any relationship between the documented works and the life of the creative artist.

We are in an identical pickle when we come to consider the works of so recent a poet as Titus Lucretius Carus, commonly known as Lucretius, who is believed to have lived between 98 and 55 B.C. We know almost nothing of his life, and in all there are only four or five reliable references to him in early literature and these are rather vague. On the other hand, we have his remarkable, long poem titled "De Rerum Natura" (concerning the nature of things), which is a completely different poem in every respect from anything ever produced by his eminent predecessor Homer. In this poem there is a great deal that throws light on the personality of the author. It is clear that he was an Epicurean in his philosophy, that he knew a great deal about physics, that he was a student of human nature—in fact, a "naturalist" in his day. Considering the fact that there were no medical schools then, nor doctors as such, nor universities, nor degrees, I would consider Lucretius to be the equivalent of what we call a physician or a psychiatrist in our age. His long chapters on love and sex indicate profound understanding of those subjects and his last chapter on the terrible plague that devastated Athens indicates the comprehension of the medically trained mind even though it is believed that part of it was borrowed from Thucydides. And most amazing is the section in this poem dealing with the atom and electromagnetism.

I cannot possibly imagine how any man living just before the birth of Jesus Christ could have such wide and extraordinary knowledge as Lucretius demonstrated in his masterpiece, "De Rerum Natura." A savant at the Massachusetts Institute of Technology, who is more expert than I, tells me Lucretius showed incredible insight and amazing knowledge of atomic science, that his views implied foreknowledge of electronics even as we know it to-day.

So far as we know, there was in his time no school or known source of this information, and in his own way this creation of his brain is still as remarkable today as the ideas of the farm boy Newton who created the science of calculus or Thomas Alva Edison, who went to school but three months of his life, then sold newspapers on a train when he was thirteen. It is true that in the case of Newton he had the advantage of university associations. He was a professor of mathematics in his mid-twenties. Edison was taught at home by his mother for about five years. But these facts do not explain Edison's invention of the electric light or a machine to record the human voice, to name only two out of more than one thousand patents issued to him by the United States. These inventions are not far from those of literature. The creative literary artist is an inventor in his own way, although his inventions are less obvious.

We know a great deal more about Vergil, the Mantuan. The nature of his main work, "The Aeneid," is completely different from the works of Homer. It is a synthetic epic written down in manuscript to be read and copied by others. Certainly Vergil was partly motivated by imitation when he came to write his long poem in 12 books. He wanted to do for his emperor (Augustus) what Homer had done in his time, but he went about it in a completely different manner. I would say that Homer's poems flowed out of his unconscious, whereas those of Vergil flowed more from the conscious levels of his mind. I think Vergil knew exactly what he was doing and planned it all in advance, which in part accounts for some of the long and tedious passages in "The Aeneid" which might be called padding. There is no padding in the work of Homer; it is all hot stuff! Many scholars have noticed and mentioned this.

It is interesting to note that Vergil held a low opinion of his own works and ordered his manuscripts to be burned after his death. On learning of this, the Emperor looked them over and decided that they should be published because they were highly complimentary to his rule and to the Rome of his day. I would cite this as an early example of conflict in the mind of an author—which might be of interest to any psychopathologist. I think Vergil consciously tried to imitate Homer, and knew he failed even though he wrote a good poem. Also he admitted into his poem a good deal of special "pleading" and some window-dressing. I think Vergil felt guilty about this and for that reason ordered his manuscripts burned after his death. Interestingly enough, it is quite possible that the parts which appealed to the Emperor and led him to order the manuscript published were the inferior parts and not the best meat of the story. We will never know but we can speculate.

Contemporary psychologists have written a good deal about the attitude of the artist toward what he creates. Some artists "love" the things they create and cherish them. Others "hate" the things they create and do not want to see them again. Some even want to see them destroyed. I have seen a sculptor chop to pieces a clay head he was modelling because he could not catch exactly the right expression he thought he saw in the subject he was modelling, whereas I, who was standing by his side, thought he had captured a remarkable likeness. I have known more than one playwright who would never attend one of his own plays once it was produced; and many poets dislike their own poems and refuse to learn them by heart or read them for others. A very wide range of attitudes obtains in the matter of the artist and the things he creates, but I am struck, as others have been, by the fact that the created object might theoretically be classified or compared with anal objects. To put it more simply, the attitude of the artist toward the things he creates may be compared with the attitudes of the child toward his own excrement. It is equally fair to say that some artists appear to have a maternal attitude and look on their books, plays, poems, novels, paintings, etc., as if they were their children. These two possibilities which I have mentioned in simple analogy permit a very wide interpretation when it comes to evaluating the attitude of the artist toward the thing he creates, whatever it may be.

We should not end this section about the implications and impressions gathered from the past without noting the unique place the ballad seems to occupy in the history of literature. True ballads are usually anonymous. They are often folk songs adapted for group singing and sometimes written with stanzas followed by a chorus so that one or more individuals could lead in singing the stanza, while the whole group might join in on the more familiar chorus. From all I have studied of ballads, and there is a vast literature on this subject, I have come to the conclusion that ballads and ballad singing were *the* original group psychotherapy. I believe that in ancient times when groups of people felt nervous, anxious, tense, afraid, or depressed, they gathered together and sang the familiar songs we know today as ballads and felt better after singing them because something of the "togetherness" and the familiarity with the words and the music were reassuring if not supportive.

What Poets Say about Their Own Works and What Critics Have to Say about Them.

Next we may consider what poets and authors have to say about their own works and, along with this, we might consider what others say about them and their works during their own time and afterwards— especially afterwards. For some reason it seems that very few poets receive much personal and critical attention during their lifetimes. Usually a poet has to have been dead quite a number of years before the critics begin their post-mortem examinations.

What poets say about their own work may often reach extraordinary extremes and sometimes much of it is irrelevant. An example is William Butler Yeats' famous sonnet, "Leda and the Swan." In this remarkable poem one hears the rush of mighty wings, practically witnesses strange coitus, and a magical effect is achieved that is unique in power and vitality. However in his own account of the writing of this poem, Yeats merely states that an editor asked him to contribute a poem to a magazine and he, Yeats, finally got around to doing it. There is no hint or explanation of his creative artistry nor does the poet himself give any inkling as to how or why his creative imagination set about its task.

At the other extreme we have the figure of Allen Tate, whose best known poem, "Ode to the Confederate Dead," has occupied his creative attention over a number of years. In one published essay titled, "Narcissus as Narcissus," Tate explains in detail how he came to write the poem, what he meant by it, and outlines as fully as possible his own attitudes concerning his work.

Then there is, in my opinion, that most remarkable of all books written about poetry, "The Road to Xanadu," by the late John Livingston Lowes. This monumental labor represented the essence of his lifetime interests and was published about 1927. It is a study of Coleridge, particularly "The Ancient Mariner" and "Kubla Khan," and more than any published work extant it demonstrates the poetic imagination at work. It delves carefully into the source material from which Coleridge drew for his writing and leans heavily upon notebooks and library references of the period. But all of this might be loosely classified as hearsay. It is not basic evidence and, as the eminent psychoanalyst and editor, Dr. George Wilbur, recently said: "Most of this material is what I would call 'secondary elaboration' . . . it does not get at the heart of the matter, the primary creative process."

There is much truth in what Doctor Wilbur has to say. Today we are far from understanding the heart of the creative process. If you were to ask me about my own writing I would say something like this: I think I know some of the reasons why I write, but it is a long story.

In the light of what I have learned in my personal psychoanalysis with the late Dr. Hans Sachs, I would say the impulse manifested itself at the age of three, when I was an only child. Then twin sisters were born and I felt displaced. I attempted to regain my status in the family circle by learning to read at a very early age. Of course, I was competing with my sisters—"sibling rivalry" you might call it— but then I became preoccupied with words, sounds, meanings, and later with rhyme. Mother Goose and Robert Louis Stevenson were my first poetic experiences. Then came school and more effort to recoup my original status. The goal was to regain parental attention. In preparatory school poems were assigned as homework in composition by teachers I admired and respected. Obviously, they were parent substitutes and the goal was still the same: competition with my schoolmates and an effort to gain the approval of the beloved teachers. This went on in college, and the process was repeated, assuming more validity. What had formerly been imitation or identification (and perhaps some exhibitionism) became a more serious effort characterized by more originality and self-assertion. For example, I can remember distinctly when my teacher, Professor John Crowe Ransom, assigned me a sonnet to write as homework in a class in English composition. He expected me to produce a regular (Italian) or irregular (English) sonnet, both of which were considered legitimate. My results were mediocre.

I found it was not possible in 1921 for me to write in English as

Petrarch had done in Italy, nor yet as Shakespeare had written during the reign of Queen Elizabeth the First. I found the language had changed and the rhythms had altered. No longer did the ancient octet-sestet form seem to suit our times, and even the more relaxed form, three quatrains ending with a rhymed couplet, that Shakespeare used in his monumental series of sonnets seemed stiff and cumbersome. But Professor Ransom was encouraging. He said: "You don't *have* to use the old forms. Why don't you strike out for yourself and try to find your own style?" I did this and the act became a habit. I've been doing it ever since, for 35 years, to be exact, and I feel that I have discovered my own style—a representative sample that might be considered are the "Clinical Sonnets." This took years of laborious effort and could not be sporadic; but had to be sustained.

As for the individual act of writing a sonnet, I find it has much in common with the dream, slip of the tongue, or any neurotic symptom for that matter. Essentially a sonnet is only a short poem, conventionally 14 lines long. I find that certain impressions which can be compared to the "day stimulus" start one off. Then my mind compulsively takes over, continuing the work partly on the conscious level, partly on the unconscious level. As for the unconscious, I believe that since birth my mind has been accumulating and storing impressions in the form of memories and associations. In the creative process, whatever it is that does it (perhaps it is part of the ego) draws freely and heavily upon this material, but consciously it is guided also by the general form one has adopted and by the matter of rhyme or any other devices. Finally, the poem completes itself or is completed. The sonnet is supposed to have a unitary quality and this is usually self-evident. For example, I know when I have failed to complete a poem and I am painfully aware of when I have introduced stuffing or padding to fill out a line. The right word must go in the right place and there is no rule that I know for determining this. It is a matter of taste or style, and "The style is the man."

I could spend a good deal of time and go into extensive detail describing what I believe the creative process to be as observed in myself, but I do not believe the poet's word is enough. Neither are the observations of others very valid when taken alone, particularly when the critics live in another century and never know the deceased artists. Even Freud, who wrote extensively about Leonardo, based his entire thesis on a fragment of a memory and was probably at his weakest in writing this composition. If he hit upon the truth it is likely he did so through intuition rather than through any logical reasoning.

CRITICISM AND ANALYSIS OF CREATIVE WRITERS AND THEIR WORK BY MODERN METHODS

The ideal method for studying creative artists has not yet been determined. Certainly it is valuable, when possible, to have a complete biographical study with full disclosure, but this rarely occurs. In past centuries a few artists have published extremely revealing autobiographies, but every individual has his own blind spots and try as he may his own account of himself and his works is usually slanted in some way for posterity or for his own purposes.

Take the brilliant autobiography of Freud, which for years seemed to be an impeccable masterpiece, and compare it now with the two volumes of his biography that Ernest Jones has published. Note the omissions and the differences in emphasis. I would say that Ernest Jones in his biography has given us a far more complete picture than Freud gave us in his autobiography. The same applies to poets, painters, novelists, sculptors, and devotees of other plastic and dynamic arts. Actually the artist can and should be (pardon the expression) a "guinea pig," because his creative work can now be subjected to many technics of many disciplines, particularly those with which the poet's life can be positively or negatively determined. The poet as an individual can be psychoanalyzed by various techniques. The creative artist, whatever medium he works in, can be subjected to a battery of intensive testing. I think it would be more valuable if we had a careful Rorschach test on Leonardo than Freud's charming but non-objective interpretation of the artist.

Modern psychology has developed so many techniques that when they are considered all together they afford an amazing, almost overwhelming volume of direct and indirect observational data of which part can be quite objective. The day is only beginning to dawn when the creative process may be better understood. In the past we have had what the poet or artist himself said about himself and his work and this may or may not be true. Ninety-eight percent of all "criticism" is subjective, impressionistic, non-systematic, and of dubious value. Only a few critics can be called great and their observations, when objective, are likely as not based on the same common sense and day-to-day experience that characterize the knowledge and wisdom of the bulk of mankind.

I do not think that we would ever be able to "explain" Shakespeare even if we knew who he was for certain. Much more is known about Goethe, for example, who lived in comparative terms but yesterday. Still who was Homer and why did he write? Did one man write the "Iliad" and "Odyssey," or did many folk singers and ancient ballad makers pool their efforts in these two great epics which mark the beginning of Western literature? Personally, I prefer to believe that there *was* a man named Homer, that he had prodigious knowledge and a vast memory, that he wrote or "sang" these epics. But even if there *was* such a man and even if he *did* do this, *why* should he have chosen the theme of the wrath of Achilles and the wanderings of Ulysses? What, if anything, did all this have to do with the belief held throughout Western Europe for two thousand years that he was blind? These and many other questions remain unanswered, but I have tremendous confidence in the powers of psychological investigation and the rich rewards that may result from intensive pursuit of psychology and psychopathology. I believe these two disciplines are intertwined and inseparable. Perhaps together they may one day help us answer some of these questions; not necessarily about the great creative artists of the past who have long since been gathered unto the bosom of Abraham. Possibly in days to come when there is more coordination and integration among all the disciplines, practical and academic, we may learn what contemporary poets and creative artists in general are and what makes them tick. We may even learn the answers to such basic questions as these, about poetry:

Who is speaking? What is he saying and what does it mean? Why is he saying this and not something else? Why is he saying this *at this particular time* and how well does he say it? What does his work mean in relation to his life and to the world around him?

10

AN EXPERIMENT IN INCLUSIVE PSYCHOTHERAPY

By HANS SYZ, M.D.*

IN THIS REPORT I should like (1) to present certain observations and postulates regarding the etiology and structure of neurotic disorders, (2) to relate these observations and postulates to specific modifications developed in the psychotherapeutic procedure, and (3) to draw attention to alterations in the patient's behavior which may validate in a measure significant aspects of the concepts proposed.

The attempt to apply experimental procedure to psychotherapy may appear a hazardous undertaking. Adequate controls and comparisons are difficult to establish in this field, and the principles of the experimental method, as stated by Claude Bernard (1865),[16] cannot be easily applied. According to Bernard, the procedure of the scientist is: to observe a fact; to form a concept with regard to it; to devise an experiment which introduces special factors, based on the theory, into the handling of the subject matter; and to observe the resulting phenomena which may serve to confirm or invalidate the original postulate and thus lead to new conceptions and further experiments. Evidently the factors involved in behavior-disorder and its adjustment are so complex that a strict application of these experimental criteria appears almost impossible. Concern with the patient's immediate needs complicates the situation and deflects interest from investigation and experimentation.

In recent years various aspects of research in psychotherapy and of the evaluation of psychotherapy have been discussed,[47,69,91,144] and rather elaborate setups have been suggested for procedures that would meet scientific standards.[99,111,146] Among the complexities involved is the problem of the multiple variables that should be controlled, difficulty in selecting comparative features, incomplete and often conflicting views regarding psychodynamics, the influence of the therapist's

* The Lifwynn Foundation, Westport, Connecticut; New York Hospital and Cornell University Medical College, New York, N. Y.

attitude toward the patient [140] and his emotional bias in the treatment situation, and the unreliable criteria for evaluating improvement. The forces at work in the therapeutic interchange are inadequately understood and may be at variance with those stressed by the therapist. Also, the results from different methods applied by therapists with different basic conceptions may not vary in a significant manner.[11,68,107] So it has been concluded that therapeutic results can hardly be expected to furnish a reliable test of a theory.

Nevertheless there are significant relations between theory, therapeutic procedure, and behavioral results. We know how concepts, like humoral-physiological and anatomical interpretations, inhibit the development of psychotherapy.[40,109] On the other hand conceptualizations in terms of internal and interpersonal dynamics have given impetus to effective psychotherapeutic handling of behavior-disorders, as evidenced, for instance, in the modern approach to schizophrenia in this country. The favorable results confirm in a measure the dynamic interpretation, though a specific concept of psychodynamics is not necessarily supported in this manner.

Therapists constantly experiment with their conceptual postulates, either intuitively and haphazardly or in a more conscious and organized way.[42,84] Conceptions regarding the dynamics involved in the individual case are used as a guide to treatment. For instance, Diethelm[41] has shown how the therapeutic procedure may be changed in accordance with the changing psychopathology of a patient. The dynamic interpretation of the changing pathology naturally involves conceptualizations which, translated into therapeutic procedure, are brought to experimental test.

Also we find that concepts derived from observations on parent-child behavior, such as parental overseverity and overprotection, were validated to a considerable extent when employed in therapeutic and educational experimentation.

In general we may say then that concepts regarding psychodynamics, when carefully introduced into the therapeutic setting, may lead to alterations in procedure and to behavior modifications which in some measure confirm specific aspects of the postulated conceptions. We may not use the word "proof" in this connection, nor may we overlook the justifiability of alternative interpretations. Even in modern physics alternative formulations—the corpuscular and the wave theories, for instance—may serve at least temporarily as valid models.

The ultimate aim of course is to arrive at a conceptual framework which gives a unified over-all picture.

In the effort to meet scientific standards regarding personality and behavior, inappropriate principles and techniques may be borrowed from other fields. While a careful employment of analogic thinking is a necessary part of scientific procedure,[55] faulty analogies and generalizations have been employed merely because they are in common use and are sanctioned by the recognized scientific community—one need think only of the application of atomistic-mechanistic concepts to behavior.

Another fallacy is the overemphasis upon the complexity of the material and the overvaluation of observational details at the expense of adequate conceptualization. As Henri Poincaré[100] expressed it, "a collection of facts is no more a science than a heap of stones is a house." Thus in the field of behavioral adjustment as in other scientific departments, it is necessary to establish conceptual models[80] which meet the requirements of the material under investigation and make it possible to relate the tremendous multiplicity of phenomena to relatively simple principles.

The need to arrive at unifying concepts regarding personality and behavior has been increasingly expressed in the recognition of convergent trends among various psychopathological and therapeutic schools,[110] and in the efforts to correlate or even amalgamate different dynamic trends.[42,88,98,145] Interdisciplinary symposia in which psychologists, psychiatrists, sociologists, and anthropologists participated[57,71,78] have attempted to develop a common language or common conceptual ground on which different aspects of behavior can be understood and interrelated. Burrow's[33] phylobiological point of view is such an attempt to arrive at a consistent formulation which interrelates individual and social structure, objective and subjective phases of experience, constructive as well as destructive tendencies understood as developmental alternatives on the human level.

It may be well to keep in mind that this tendency toward convergent concepts in the behavioral sciences is part of a larger cultural development. Similar basic laws or functional characteristics have been found independently in different branches of scientific research.[48,118] The recognition of these structural similarities has led to the quest for a general system theory (von Bertalanffy),[18] which seeks to establish analogous principles or patterns on different organizational levels, and thus to arrive at a more unified approach to the diversified material of different scientific fields.

In my orientation regarding behavior problems I employ organismic or configurational criteria. At the present stage of investigation in biology and human behavior, it is hardly necessary to justify the organismic point of view.* But it may be emphasized that the configurational approach, with its recognition of systems in which part and whole are interdependent, helps us to understand how apparently distant and externally different phenomena may be integral components of a common dynamic structure, or may be related to a common denominator. We are thus given a conceptual tool which permits us to understand that what appears to be a localized disturbance always involves the total configuration, and that an adjustment at a pivotal point may bring about constructive changes throughout the total pattern.

II

In accordance with the aforementioned possibility of bringing concepts regarding behavior-disorder to experimental test, I introduced a specific theoretical model or set of interrelated concepts into the treatment of neurotic patients. These concepts were arrived at by correlating with principles of dynamic psychiatry, observations derived from Trigant Burrow's group- or phylo-analytic studies, in which I participated. The application of these concepts to the therapeutic situation and their influence upon the attitude of the therapist often facilitated access to and handling of pathogenic material. Certain features of the patient's behavior observed in the therapeutic setting

* I shall not refer specifically to the vast literature and documentary evidence in biology, embryology, neurology, psychology, and the socially oriented sciences that substantiate the configurational nature of living organisms and the need to take this organismic, integrative quality (Gestalt field) into account in our conceptualizations and approach. In the field of behavior-disorders this point of view has been stressed by Angyal,[9] Burrow,[32] Goldstein,[58] and Meyer.[90] For brief discussions see Riese[108] and Syz.[129] Symposia on these problems are to be found in *Levels of Integration in Biological and Social Systems*,[105] and in *Aspects of Form*.[142]

In this connection we may think also of Goethe's influence on biological thought. In his voluminous writings on natural science, and especially in his concept of the metamorphosis of plants, we find the never-ceasing effort to understand the various forms of organized beings as variations of a basic principle of structure and function.

and in his general life-adjustments were considered to validate in a measure the concepts employed. The working hypothesis includes the following postulates:

1. People in general embody in their adaptive equipment a dynamic constellation which in important aspects is essentially identical with that underlying neurotic disturbances.

2. This constellation may be considered "defective" in that it involves an unrecognized overemphasis upon unrealistic self-symbols and their projections. Socially corroborated preoccupation with the self-symbol is expressed in such interrelated phenomena as authoritarian self-assertion, dependent submission, hostility, and guilt, as well as in neurotic defense-formations. This defective configuration embodies in its social systematization a predisposition to neurotic disturbances and to overtly destructive action-trends.

3. A core of powerful biological, integrative, and socially cohesive assets exists within the personality with which the defective trends are in conflict and whose full expression is thereby impeded. That is, the undue attachment of organismic forces to the self-image ties up or distorts these integrative capacities and thus makes them less available for constructive intrapersonal and interrelational purposes.

4. The therapist's own behavior and his observational processes also embody this adaptive deflection since he is an integral element within the defective constellation which characterizes the normal reaction average. The realization of this circumstance by the therapist, both intellectually and experientially, activates within him constructive forces which aid the therapeutic process.

Before entering upon the therapeutic procedure in Part VI, I should like to take up briefly Burrow's phylopathological investigations (III) which in part shaped the conceptions used in my approach to patients. I shall then consider these concepts in the frame of the distinctive features of human nature as they have been outlined in recent research (IV); supportive evidence from diverse behavioral fields will also be offered (V).

III

Even before Burrow undertook his group investigations, he showed in his early psychoanalytic papers (1912-1918) a divergence from orthodox procedure, in that he called attention to unrecognized, socially disorganizing forces.[24] He suggested that discrepant features of normal, socially accepted behavior be considered in their dynamic interrelation with conflicting trends operative in the neurotic patient. He introduced the term "social neurosis"[29] (1926) to indicate a malfunction in which normal persons everywhere are involved and which had not yet been made the subject of scientific study.* Together with his emphasis on socially disruptive processes Burrow early proposed the concept of the preconscious phase of behavior, the "principle of primary identification" (1917).[25] In the early formulation of this concept the infant's identification with the mother was seen to relate to the phenomena of narcissism, latent homosexuality, and potential neurotic developments. In its later interpretation the primary subjective or preconscious phase was considered rather as the biological matrix of societal continuity and coordination as well as of spontaneous and creative personality processes.[30]

In the method of group-analysis which Burrow developed in the years following 1918 and which he reported on frequently after 1924,[26,28] his altered concepts regarding neurotic conditions were brought to practical test. He invited a group of both normal and neurotic students to join him in an experiment in which the interpersonal attitudes and reactions of the participants, including himself, were systematically examined in laboratory meetings as well as in less formal situations occurring in connection with activities they shared.[133]

These group- or phylo-analytic studies were a forerunner of the now current group therapeutic methods, though they differed specifically from them. In Burrow's group analysis the investigative emphasis was always in the foreground. The observer was from the start included as an interwoven part in a common behavior tissue. The dominant interest was the analysis of the normal reaction structure, with a view to reaching a clearer comprehension of its noxious implications. The goal was not adaptation to the social norm, but the development of concepts and measures that would release healthy function by eliminating destructive or immature aspects also of normal behavior.[131,132]

Setting aside, as far as possible, conventional distinctions based on their social or professional status, the participants attempted to deter-

* The term "social neurosis" was later used by Schilder[114] and by Myerson[97] in a way which differs from that employed by Burrow.[130] These authors used this term to designate a disturbance of social contact characterized by marked timidity and self-consciousness, often accompanied by somatic symptoms and at times related to schizophrenic reactions.

mine the latent content of their various reactions as they occurred in the immediacy of group interchange. The mutually corroborative dynamics of authoritarian and dependent attitudes, of competitive self-assertion and its social disguises, of hostility and moralistic safeguards, and of a host of associated trends were brought up for analytic evaluation. These behavior instances were examined not as isolated occurrences, but in their relation to trends enacted by various participants, or pervading the group as a whole. The purpose was to determine, if possible, a common denominator to which the specific manifestations could be related.

A predominant impression gained in these group studies was the evidence of the marked preoccupation of each individual with his self-image. There was indication of ever ready self-defense, of upholding insistently a preferential self identification within the frame of socially standardized behavior. Self-protective factionalism or subgroup formation was observed as a reflex reaction in this socially reflected scheme of self affirmation. Obsessive preoccupation with the "good" self-symbol was brought to awareness, as well as inconsistency between the alleged socially beneficial intent and the underlying self-centered motivation. All these features were consistently viewed as largely unconscious but socially interactive phenomena that have a common source.[128] From this altered perspective important roots of both guilt-anxiety and hostility came to be understood in terms of an internal but socially corroborated deflection.*

It is evident that the defective constellation to which Burrow called attention is not adequately accounted for by referring to constitutional factors, characteristics inherent in human nature. It is doubtful also whether the essentials of the general malfunction are bound up with specific cultural structures[15,44,74,89] or with specific historical periods within cultural developments.[50,119,141] In spite of the endless variety of individual characteristics and of cultural forms, we find a universal structure in man's emotional attitudes and gestural expressions,[38] and perhaps also at the base of his exaggerated tendency toward self-enhancement and associated defensive devices.[96] According to Bidney[19] and Spiro,[121] the creation and transmission of culture demands a

---

* The social aspect of these studies is indicated in the name of the organization founded in 1927 to sponsor them: "The Lifwynn Foundation for Laboratory Research in Analytic and Social Psychiatry."

generic human nature or psychobiological structure that is independent of specific conditioning and learning. Likewise a generic and socially corroborated miscarriage of adaptive processes (Burrow) should be considered as an important cause of behavior-disorder.

In the attempt to understand the essential features of this malfunction, Burrow's analysis led to biological formulations.[31] He suggested that, coincident with the development of symbol and language, organismic drives and total feeling-processes had been wrongly channeled into the cortic and cephalic regions.* An upsurge of basic organismic impulses into the symbolic segment had occurred which led to a divisive self identity, to internal decentration that interfered with the organism's integrative and phylically cohesive function. A broad distinction was made by Burrow between two major types of adaptive attitudes, the self-referent orientation (*ditention*) and organismically integrated function (*cotention*). These two adaptive modes were found to be related to internally perceivable tension patterns. Through sensory discrimination of these intraorganismic patterns a tensional integration could be brought about which was accompanied by constructive shifts of interest, feeling, and motivation. Concomitant modifications in physiological part-systems (respiration, eye-movements, electrical brain potentials) were recorded.

I shall not go into these physiological aspects of the phyloanalytic studies as I have not attempted to apply them to the psychotherapeutic work with patients, except as they may be embodied in my own attitude. But the formulations referred to do offer the possibility of viewing physiological and psychological aspects in a consistently interrelated and complementary manner.

As mentioned, an essential feature in these group investigations was the circumstance that each observer's own experience and action trends were part of the material to be observed. His own functions of observation, perception, and interpretation were open to challenge. The concurrent frustration of his established values and affect-attitudes naturally was often met by powerful resistance expressed in a variety of defensive measures. But these difficulties of procedure had to be

---

* Brief references to disrupting effects of symbol-usage have been made by a number of authors, for instance, von Bertalanffy,[17] Cassirer,[36] Spiro.[121] In a more elaborate fashion pathogenic influences related to symbolization have been discussed, among others, by Buber,[23] Klages,[77] Korzybski,[79] Kubie,[82] Whyte.[141]

worked with as unavoidable concomitants of the general research project.*

Burrow's early insistence that the observer include himself as a participant was expressed in his demand for what he called "consensual observation" (1925).[27] The aim was to reach a consensus or a "phyletic principle of observation" that would aid in correcting the observer's biased vision and permit the examination of the noxious implications of the normal behavior-average.

The requirement that the observer function as a participant has in recent years been emphasized, though in a modified form, in psychiatric,[126] psychological,[34] and sociological[112,117] contexts.† The need for taking into account the observer's bias is evidenced in the attention given to countertransference,[4,45] the demand for analysis of the analyst, the mutual analysis practiced in certain group-therapeutic techniques, and more generally the tendency at some medical centers to train the students to observe the unfortunate influence their own emotional attitudes may have upon their contact with patients. These widespread efforts toward analytic self-correction might well be broadened to include a revaluation on the part of the observers of their participation in socially sanctioned bias and behavioral inadvertence.

IV

In order to amplify the conceptual model here proposed, I shall offer a few additional observations regarding human nature which may assist in understanding in what way a miscarriage relating to man's image-symbol capacity may be a potent factor in the genesis of behavior-disorder. There has been much discussion regarding the differences in cognition, emotion, and behavior between humans and animals; and in how far these differences are of quantitative or qualitative nature.

---

* Though there is a "tremendous resistance of man to new ways of thinking and life" (Carlson[35]), experimental findings, for instance in the field of modern physics, have led to new possibilities of thought[66] and to the increasing necessity of inventing concepts that are theoretically more adequate and pragmatically more effective. Accepted "common sense" is thus replaced by a common sense that is more inclusive. Similar criteria apply also to research and reorientation in the behavioral field.

† A parallel situation has been described in modern physics in which "the observer must somehow be included in the system" and in which "it is in fact meaningless to try to separate observer and observed" (Bridgman[22]).

In a recent symposium on "The Non-Human Primates and Human Evolution" (1954) in which comparative anatomists, anthropologists, and animal psychologists participated, W. L. Straus[125] expressed the opinion in his closing remarks that man's greatest distinction consists in the fact that he is a time-binder and a tool-maker—capacities believed to be the basis for making "long-range plans by which our ultimate goals are more efficiently approached." As far as the significance of tools is concerned, other investigators have pointed out that even in animals we find the beginning of tool making but that man is the only mammal which is continuously dependent on self-made tools for his survival.[13] There is general agreement that in animal life there are few or no manifestations which can be characterized as cultural.

In any case there is no question that humans show a decided advance over prehuman primates in the complex way in which they use the capacity of symbolization. According to L. A. White[138] this capacity represents a fundamental difference, not merely a matter of degree, and leads to a new order of superorganic phenomena: articulate speech and communication of ideas; cultural values and the perpetuation of civilized forms of interchange. As Cassirer puts it, man "lives, so to speak, in a new *dimension* of reality . . . Man cannot escape from his own achievement . . . Instead of dealing with the things themselves man is in a sense constantly conversing with himself. He has so enveloped himself in linguistic forms, in artistic images, in mythical symbols or religious rites that he cannot see or know anything except by the interpretation of this artificial medium."

It is evident that man's symbol capacity is closely linked up with the enormous development of his brain, especially of its cortic regions.[37] Also the rapid cerebral increase during the first few months of life has no parallel in other animal forms. But the evolution of human characteristics cannot be understood in terms of simple correlations. An unusual combination of anatomic, developmental, and socio-adaptive factors, of structure and function took place which has to be considered in its complex interrelations. It has been suggested, for instance, that the use of tools had an influence upon the cerebral development, that the employment of extraorganic implements and devices stimulated the growth of specific cerebral areas (Greenman)[61] through the process described by Ariens Kappers as neurobiotaxis.[73] The human brain, with its remarkable imaginative and retentive capacity, shows a great plasticity in its responses and there is little evidence in the infant of instinctive fixation upon environmental patterns such as we find in most animals (von Uexküll).[134] Portmann[101] emphasized the very immature, really "foetal" condition in which the human infant is born and is exposed to the influence of environmental stimuli. With the rapid physical and cerebral development, however, a creature emerges at the end of the first postnatal year which begins to show essential human characteristics: erect posture, speech, and an objectivating, insightful type of thinking and acting. In subsequent years human development is unique through its unusually slow physical and mental growth, making it possible for complex cultural traditions to be learned and absorbed. In discussing these processes and their relation to studies of animal behavior, Bally[12] has shown how continued parental and social protection creates a field in which the human infant is relieved of urgent need tensions. Free range is given to appetitive behavior, to play activities which make it possible to explore outer objects as well as one's own body from many angles. Where the world is approached and handled in this playful manner, free from immediate need satisfaction and fears, new aspects and relationships can be discovered and things begin to appear as relatively constant and independent objects.

While some indications of this objectivating process (*Vergegenständlichung*) may also be observed in animal life, it has become, in human development, a basic factor in separating the "self" from the objective world. Besides play activity in the tension-relaxed field, other dynamic processes contribute to establish the ego-boundary, such as the denial or delay of need gratification. Another important issue often referred to is the upright posture, which brings about an altered attitude toward the world.[49,123] As E. Straus[124] points out, upright posture with the associated free use of arms and hands lifts us from the ground; puts us opposite things and at a distance from each other. It is a prerequisite for creating a new mode of being-in-the-world which goes along with changes in the central nervous system, with transformation of sensory and motor processes, with a change of form and function.

In considering these interwoven aspects of the specifically human development it is important to realize how profound an alteration has been brought about by the symbolic process which is interlinked with or part of the various structural and functional aspects mentioned. Cassirer[36] has given a comprehensive description of the different kinds of symbolic activity, and Susanne Langer[83] has shown with especial lucidity that the translating of experiences into symbols is a primary human need. There are several types or levels of symbolization and one has to distinguish between sign function and symbol function which are both engaged in our language, thinking, and action. In sign function, which man shares with animals and which is the basis of animal intelligence, the sign, natural as well as artificial or conditioned, stands for a situation or object reacted to; whereas in symbol function, which animals possess only to a limited degree, the symbol stands for a conception which may or may not refer to an object. Animals have no need for elaborate symbolic transformation of experience, while the human organism has an inherent urge to complete the brain's symbolic process in overt action. Complex symbolization is a characteristic and natural human activity, a higher form of neural response which cannot be adequately explained in utilitarian terms, though the sublimation of instinctive drives, tension discharge, and the effort to eliminate anxiety may merge with the symbolic process and use it in various combinations.

As pointed out by Langer[83] symbolism is not restricted to highly developed discursive devices like language and thought, but appears also in non-verbal, presentational form. It is found in the very act of sensory perception, in motor performances from which rituals may arise, in dreams and images that form the bases of myth and religion, and in representations of inner experience expressed in the various arts. All these creations manifest man's ceaseless quest for conception and orientation. They spring from his constructive and ever-developing effort to define his unique position in terms of symbolic and cultural formations which are interlinked with or reflected in the structure of his self.[120] The extrinsic symbolic systems make it possible for groups of human beings to share and transmit a common meaningful world which is closely intermeshed with their physical and biological environment (Hallowell).[63]

Goldstein's [59] experiments on brain-injured patients (especially those with injuries to the frontal lobes) corroborate the importance of abstraction or understanding symbols for the human type of existence. He and Scheerer[60] have shown how the elimination or reduction of this capacity impairs the individual's ability to detach himself from the outer world and from his own inner experience. The lack of abstract attitude destroys an individual's spontaneity and creative power;

makes it impossible for him to grasp the essentials of a given whole and to isolate or synthesize the parts of a total pattern. It obstructs the ability to plan ahead ideationally and to appreciate the meaning of the past, future, and of what is merely possible.

We thus find that symbolic activity and abstraction are essential not only in man's orientation and communication, but also in bringing about his unique position in the world. Image- and symbol-activity, in connection with the aforementioned structural and developmental alterations, make it possible for man to objectivate external things and himself; to sense himself as different from or even opposed to the world, to develop a self and become aware of it (Scheler).[113] This delimitation of the self, in which language and conceptual thinking play important roles, results in a new relatedness to the environment. A self-identity develops which is open to the world and is marked by creative initiative, the capacity for choice, planned handling of the self and of others, and the emergence of responsibility and guilt.

Man's spontaneous symbol activity may be considered as an outgrowth or facet of the organismic configurational process that is basic in the physiology and organic life of all living creatures and that shapes their self-maintaining and creative functions as well as their adaptive and affiliative processes. In a larger view we may see here expressions of a pervasive formative principle whose manifestations have been increasingly observed also in the world of inorganic phenomena (Weyl,[136] Whitehead,[139] Whyte[143]).*

Indications of the intrinsic neural activity, which we may assume to be an energetic basis for the brain's inherent integrative and symbolic functions, may be seen in the ever-active electric brain potentials. As a source of the energetic processes involved we may think also of the self-exciting, reverberating neural impulses.[56] These continuous neural processes may not only relate to certain pathological phenomena, but they may also constitute an important dynamic core for autonomous and constructive personality processes.

In a rather sweeping and summarizing way, then, we may say that

---

* Erwin Schrödinger[116] writes that in modern physics "the *new* idea is that what is permanent in these ultimate particles or small aggregates is their shape and organization. . . . They are, as it were, *pure shape*, nothing but shape; what turns up again and again in successive observations is this shape, not an individual speck of material."

one has as basic human attributes on the one side the urge to become an independent entity, and on the other the inherent quest for symbolic orientation, for establishing relations with the environment in a novel fashion. This development in which symbolization functions in a setting of structural and functional modifications cannot proceed smoothly, however, without proper integration with the organism's biologically integrative and interrelating propensities. It is here within the relationship between symbolic functions and basic organismic processes that the postulated malfunction seems to have occurred.

Man's self- limitation and relative severance from the outer and partly self-made world embodies the danger of isolation. Inadequate relatedness means anxiety, and implies the threat of annihilation. The human being cannot stand alone; his life consisting of dynamic interrelations with his surroundings. The fear of losing contact or love is undoubtedly a powerful incentive for bridging the threatening gap. But this problem of keeping in contact with others and with the world is not a simple matter. It has become complicated not only by the emergence of guilt and hostility due to specific repressions and frustrations, but also by the application of bridging devices or means of intermediation that are inherently inadequate.

At this point I should like to return to our original proposition as suggested by Burrow, that in his present state of development man embodies an inadequate adaptive constellation. In his attempt to maintain identity and contact in his self-made world man has had much difficulty in adequately integrating his newly developed powers of image- and symbol-usage with his organismic resources. This difficulty is embodied in the self structure which we experience and employ in our contact with the environment. It appears that man has attached his organismic processes in an inept manner to socially systematized self-percepts. This attachment is accompanied by an undue transposition of the sense of reality into these self-symbols. Sign, image, and symbol thus given 'magic' power have come to play an exaggerated role in motivation and behavior. With this affect-image impetus modifications occur throughout the entire personality configuration. That is, the undue attachment of organismic forces to socially corroborated self-images not only imposes upon man's spontaneous behavior but ties up, distorts, or mischannels basic integrative capacities, making them less available for constructive, maturational and interrelational needs. There is a drive toward the periphery resulting in a rather unstable internal balance which calls for constant compensatory movements. These compensatory movements and the underlying organismic deflection are expressed psychologically in a variety of behavioral manifestations and defensive measures. They appear in what is called "selfishness" or authoritarian assertion, in sentimental dependence or self-protective partisanship, in overt hostility or in socially structuralized disaffection or detachment, and in neurotically protective compromise-formations.

In the structure and experience of the self, sign reaction and symbolic meaning are both engaged as deeply interlinked stages of the total symbolic process. The self-symbol is reacted to and thus given subjective reality, while at the same time it and its outer extensions (gesture, face, language) may stand for something for which there is no objective reality. This is the case with the good-bad signals which closely tied up with the self-image and powerfully reenforced by the threatened loss of love or other penalties, are used in the process of social conditioning. These moralistic symbols, determined largely by custom and parental convenience and supported by social authority, are reacted to by the child and accepted as realities; but the child in turn uses them for his own advantage and security. An undue dependence upon the moralistic social image develops, so that the peripheral sign or symbol is allowed to dominate unduly over inherent organismic drives. In a peculiar vicious circle the impetus upon the socially approved self-image furnishes dynamics of guilt and repression, while at the same time it generates hostile forces which again have to be repressed. There is thus opened a tremendous opportunity for the development of conflicting reactions, for self-deception and the deception of others, and for repression and substitutive devices. The misuse of image, symbol, and language has been complicated further by the fact that image-symbol processes and related psychological forces operate to a considerable extent on unconscious and preconscious levels and are incompletely accessible to conscious evaluation and control.

We know how the child's early biological dependence becomes transformed into dependence upon the parent-image, and we assume that in healthy development this image tie gives way to the gradual integration of constructive symbolic orientation with basic organismic assets. However, we see generally that the affect-image amalgamation within the self-experience continues to play an important role as expressed in self-preoccupations, in assertive and submissive self-en-actments, and in the predominant part played by image-dependence in establishing security and social contact. The undue attachment of biologically rooted impulses to personally and socially systematized image formations, with the counterpart of hostility and detachment, is elaborated and reenforced in the generally accepted forms of social interaction.

There is a question whether educational processes which corrobor-ate this self-referent trend are the only possible forms of socialization, or whether other forms of child training might not be more in keep-ing with man's basic nature (Read).[104] If we do not artificially set individual and society apart as separate abstractions, but treat them as an indivisibly interwoven complex the parental method and the child's reaction to it may be seen to embody an identical image-de-pendent constellation. We may ask who conditioned the conditioner. While conditioning plays an important role in reenforcing the adaptive defect, while it may occur in innumerable social and cultural varia-tions, we may conceive here of a more general evolutionary mis-carriage. We may think of a developmental alternative brought about accidentally in human evolution by the marked impetus in the direc-tion of images and symbols resulting from the phyletically rapid ex-pansion of the symbolic process and of self-awareness. Such a generic conception of behavior-disorder, however, does not necessarily imply that we are dealing with unalterably set dynamic formations. Recog-nition of the functional processes involved suggests instead the possi-bility that man may reach a stage of development in which he can take an active and constructive hand in guiding his own evolution.

V

Before entering upon the application of these concepts to therapeutic situations, I should like to present a few corroborative data concerning basically cohesive and integrative assets as here postulated. I shall refer also to manifestations and concepts which relate to the destruc-tive or disintegrative aspects of human behavior.

In recent years there has been increasing emphasis upon powerful constructive forces which may be considered the dynamic matrix of personality maturation as well as the source of those bonds which establish contact with the world and other human beings on mere biological grounds. There is evidence from observations on "hospitalism" (Spitz)[122] and on otherwise neglected[21] or isolated[39] children, that without a properly responsive environment in early childhood, especially during the first year of life, the organismic assets essential for personality growth as well as for social contact cannot develop adequately. Serious personality disorders may occur where these constructive forces have not been allowed to develop in an adequate early setting.

Much evidence has been presented from animal life, by Allee,[6] Emerson,[43] Portmann,[102] Schneirla,[115] W. M. Wheeler,[137] and others who have shown that animals are integrated in different forms of aggregations and in the complex group formations in which they enact many inherent, socially significant behavior patterns. Kropotkin[81] presented much material corroborative of innate cooperative trends. In his experiments with chicks, Levy[85] found indications of an elementary cohesive force which is preliminary to dominance order and to sexual activity, and which he considers to be the basis of all processes of identification. He concludes that the primitive need for contact is a basic component of all social behavior and constitutes a powerful force without which animal species could not evolve. Galt[53] has summarized much information on innate cooperation, emphasizing especially studies on children which suggest that cooperative behavior is primary to the competitive response. My own observations of children indicate that in early years instances of spontaneous behavior occur which give evidence of a remarkable sense of inclusion or identification with others that cannot be explained in terms of secondary socialization.

Montagu[92,93] has reviewed much pertinent material to show the existence of deep-seated potentialities toward socialization or of an organic need for cooperation. He points out that biological propensities to positive affiliation and to love have commonly been overlooked or understressed. Moreno[94] has postulated a specific capacity which is responsible for the cohesion of individuals within groups. However, many of the socializing forces referred to by group-therapists appear to be based on dependent, self-protective, and competitive identifications rather than on an inherent affiliative drive. An original instinct of tenderness, affection, social symbiosis was discussed by Suttie,[127] but he seems to have linked the outcome of these affiliative trends in an exaggerated manner to the special way in which the mother handles the child's need to overcome separation anxiety.

While Freud[49] considered man to be fundamentally antisocial other analysts were less pessimistic. Jung's[72] concept of the "collective unconscious" postulates generic personality dynamics which imply an impulse toward basic continuity. Adler's[2] emphasis on community feeling and Ferenczi's[46] stress on the individual's need for adequate relatedness express a recognition of deeply rooted needs for social affiliation.

We may also consider here the views of Martin Buber,[23] who emphasized the primary quality of connectedness with the environment and with other human beings, although this interrelation is specifically structured by man's unique position in the world. He pointed out that while the "I" and the "you" exist as relatively independent and constant entities, at the same time they merge in a specifically human type of dynamic "two-ness." Related to Buber's conceptions and partly influenced by them are the views of a group of existentialists, most prominently represented by Ludwig Binswanger,[20,135] who lay great stress on the fundamental nature of love, "togetherness," or what they call the experience of "we-ness."

In general one can say that there is an increasing tendency among psychiatrists, group psychotherapists, and sociologically or culturally oriented observers[51,95] to reckon more definitely with the urge for cooperation and social affiliation as a primary human drive, not merely as a derivative of the sexual impulse or the result of learning. However, one has to be cautious in the appraisal of supposedly primary affiliative drives in the behavior of social man. As Burrow pointed out, the urge toward organic rapport or phylic solidarity has commonly become deflected or interrupted in the course of normal growth and adaptation. The process of socialization does not consist only of constructive integration within the cultural setting. Very often it embodies a systematization of self-centered and potentially destructive trends which interferes with basic social cohesion.

These socially congruent powers are closely interlinked or identical with the integrative resources which form the biological foundation of creative and self-determined personality development. There has been increasing emphasis upon this phase of constructive personality assets which are related to what Burrow called the "organic persona."[30] Gordon W. Allport[7,8] has stressed the conception that the psychodynamics of the personality are to a large extent "functionally autonomous" though continuous with early motivational formations. He drew attention to war studies[62] which show that the ego is a dynamic process of great positive power which can withstand a remarkable degree of fatigue, fear, anger, apathy, and conflict. Also in psychoanalytic theory we find a movement toward more dynamic ego concepts.[64,103] On the basis of her extensive experience with problem-children, Bender[14] concludes that the child has an inherent drive toward healthy development which is hard to block or divert by his own pathology or adverse outer conditions. Even in serious disorders one finds indications of an inborn capacity for interrelating and identifying with others, for taking an active and creative part in social activities and experiences. The basic human drive to stand up as an individual entity and to confront the world is expressed in various efforts toward self-determination (K. Lewin).[87] The child's insistence on establishing an erect posture is part of this development. Levy[86] points out that oppositional behavior which occurs at several maturational stages (first at 10-11 months) is of an adaptive nature and may be an essential part in the growth of self-reliance and self-determination. There are transitions, however, to defensive patterns and to negativism which may cripple the personality's spontaneity and capacity for affection. We may be confronted with combinations of basically constructive and neurotically adaptive patterns in which it is difficult to discern the composite factors.*

Naturally every physician must depend in large measure upon organismic resources which are a determining force in health as well as in disease. Some psychiatrists and investigators have given them explicit attention in their theories and procedures. Klaesi,[76] for instance, has reported how he specifically utilized the self-healing tendency in serious personality disorders. The postulates of "self-actualization" (Goldstein)[59] and the various ways of bringing the "real self" to awareness and operation, are examples of these efforts (Fromm,[51] Fromm-Reichmann,[52] Horney,[70] Jung[72]). But here again we must ask the question: How far can a basically constructive personality core be reached and maintained where important aspects of the self—in

---

* Some personality theories have overemphasized the role of security operations, self-appraisals,[126] sublimations, efforts of solving conflict,[67] and have neglected the importance of autonomous and constructive assets. The actual predominance of these defensive systems in personality and culture, and our emphasis upon them may be the expression of a general bias or decentration which constitutes an essentially neurotic type of adaptation.

the therapist as well as in the patient—are tied in with a social systematization that embodies unrecognized pathogenic implications?

In considering behavioral evidence for what is regarded here as
a socially pervasive defect of adaptation, i.e., Burrow's "social neurosis," phenomena of hostility are among the most impressive aspects.
It is superfluous to elaborate on the occurrence of hostility and aggression between individuals and groups in present day society. The more
dramatic instances of antagonism, neglect, and destructiveness are
in everybody's mind and a glance through a daily paper gives striking
examples of the existing social pathology. What is less commonly
recognized, however, is the prevalence of egocentricity, oppositeness,
and detachment in the network of customary interchanges that form
one's social milieu. There is an inevitable "blindness" or perceptual
resistance to the behavioral inadequacies of the reaction average of
which one's own self is a functioning part. The "now emerging science
of social pathology"[1] tends to neglect distorted processes embodied
in the observer's own adaptive constellation.

The problem of aggression and hostility is complex and there is
considerable divergence of opinion regarding the processes involved
(Bender,[14] Hartmann et al.,[65] Karpman[75]). Freud's conception of
aggression as an entity traceable to a fundamental drive is now thought
to have been an unjustified abstraction. Among the factors to be
considered are primary muscular activity in the effort to master the
world, the rage pattern, reactions to instinct denial and to other frustrations, and reactions in defense of one's favorable self-evaluation.
These different trends may merge with each other and with other
drives, especially the sexual, to form complex behavior patterns. Terms
such as self-love, narcissism, autism, or unresolved childish omni-
potence indicate different concepts which are tied in with certain
aspects of the tendency to self-enhancement.* As Gardner Murphy[96]
points out in his comprehensive review of these problems the autistic
tendency, to which hostility and neurotic dynamics are significantly

* Regarding the problem of self-esteem and its perversions, it is evident that
a sense of self-worth is essential for adequate human functioning and that serious
personality disorders may result where an appropriate sense of one's value has
been undermined or has never been allowed to develop. But it is difficult to differentiate self-evaluations based on constructive autonomy and self-expansion from
a compulsive trend to self-enhancement, especially where these phenomena occur
in socially sanctioned forms. While various types of self-exaltation and omnipo-

related, does not seem to vary much in its fundamental structure from one society to another though the methods of institutionalizing the worthy self may differ profoundly.

These functional concepts corroborate our observations of behavior reactions in groups, which show that the habitual emphasis on the favored self-image is a powerful factor in generating hostility. In fact, it is not only that the thwarting of these impulses brings hostility to overt expression, but the autistically emphasized self is inherently opposed to other selves. We can understand the processes involved in terms of a dynamic constellation in which motivation, attitude, and interrelational behavior are interlinked as parts of a consistent pattern. The configuration in which organismic impulses are unduly attached to the self-image may generate guilt as well as hostility; it may be expressed in both authoritarian and dependent attitudes; and is an incentive to projective reactions. Instead of overt hostility, phenomena of detachment or repression may be in the foreground expressed either in socially standardized forms or in individual personality-disorders. Where basic organismic powers and symbolic-orientative drives have been interfered with by the interposition of these image-affect systems, internal personality integration as well as one's relation to the world are bound to be impeded or distorted. In the thesis here proposed such an inadequacy or defect within the adaptive constellation is a general characteristic of man's present level of development.

VI

These concepts, based in part on Burrow's work, were applied in the treatment of many patients. The psychotherapeutic setting was used as an experimental situation into which modifications were introduced based on the modified concepts of psychodynamics. Certain manifestations observed in the altered therapeutic situation and resulting changes in the patient's life adjustment appeared to validate aspects

---

tence[11] may have a function in the child's attempt to overcome its early helplessness and to compensate for real or imagined inferiorities, and while they can thus be considered necessary, though transitory, stages of development, their fixation may become a potent factor in personality disorder. Distortions of self-regarding functions, however, may occur not only in this individually reactive and retarded setting, but also on the basis of a generic and socially systematized misuse of the image-symbol capacity with its concomitant deflection of attention.[54]

of the conceptions and procedure employed. But it goes without saying that this work is in an experimental stage and that the theoretical model requires further test regarding its applicability to a variety of cases and situations.

By introducing the concept of a general adaptive defect related to the over-accentuation of the self-image, important aspects of neurotic disorder were seen as variations of a socially pervasive deflection of attention or feeling. Thus symptoms, defenses, and characterologic action trends were regarded as interdependent aspects of a total maladaptive configuration—internal and interrelational, which was dynamically related to a common denominator. Guilt-hostility and dependent-authoritarian reactions were viewed as partial manifestations of a dynamic constellation in which a deflection of organismic impulses played an important role.

In applying the above perspective the therapist not only carried into the therapeutic situation an altered conceptual orientation but also embodied an altered attitude toward the patient. Owing to his actual participation in group-analysis and to the consequent modification in his views regarding psychodynamics, the therapist approached the patient with a specifically inclusive attitude. The term "inclusive" is applied to this therapeutic approach because the therapist includes in his procedure, conceptually and experientially, the recognition of his own participation in the self-referent social reaction tissue. This attitude does not consist merely of empathy or identification but embodies a positive reorientation, a shift of attention on the part of the therapist that permits a revaluation of social malfunctions in which both patient and therapist are involved.*

From this background the patient's reactions are not focussed upon as features characteristic only of his type of personality or due only to his special life experience. Instead they are considered with him as continuous in structure and function with important trends in the environment, with the attitude of significant persons past and present, and with action tendencies observable in the larger social setting as well as in the therapist himself. For instance, attitudes of hostility and resentment are seen as automatic reactions to real or fancied impositions—especially to the authoritarian trends of parental figures.

---

* The principles of this inclusive approach to neurotic disorders were outlined by the author in an earlier report, 1936.[129]

But these parental inadequacies are again placed in the larger social frame of self-assertive bias as enacted in habitual interchanges everywhere although covered up in a variety of disguises. In addition to this broadening and depersonalizing inclusiveness the discrepancy between the socially cooperative appearance and the undercurrent of competition or self-centered drives is brought to awareness. Thus a reinterpretation is offered which recognizes defensive self-deceptions not only in the patient but also in the behavior of normal, well-adapted, and supposedly mature individuals.

In introducing this altered orientation to the patient it is not necessary to make elaborate explanations. It suffices to indicate briefly how his reactions interrelate with the trends of his immediate and more extended environment. Significant aspects of the total neurotogenic configuration will almost inevitably come up during the first interview, either in the patient's immediate behavior or in the story he relates. It does not matter much from what point the total configuration is approached. The therapist will be guided by the material the patient presents in his reactions toward him as well as in his report of past events. The therapist does not follow a specific technique that is merely planned intellectually with regard to his attitude and to the problems that may arise. On the basis of the analysis of his own habitual reactions and in taking account of the patient's personal characteristics and his educational and cultural level, he will sense in what way some of the important interconnections can be brought to awareness.

Regarding the therapist's concomitant revaluation of his own authoritarian trends he need merely refer to it incidentally. But such casual references have value only if they express an attitude of actual inclusiveness. That is, he takes account of his ever-present tendency toward moralistic or parental self-enactment not merely in terms of an intellectual acknowledgment but rather as a feeling recognition of the destructive implications of these action trends. This inclusive attitude lessens the need for counterassertion on the part of the patient. Less "resistance" is generated in him because of the therapist's consistent recognition of his own self-assertion and personal bias. Not only is the therapist's counter-transference thus included in a socially comprehensive manner, but the patient's expressions of positive as well as of negative transference can readily be viewed as partial manifestations of the reaction complex in which the therapist is also a participant.

No insight is ever forced upon the patient and no theories regarding behavior. He is placed rather in the role of a responsible student who may consider from a new frame of reference with the therapist some of his accustomed reactions. He is given the opportunity to observe and sense the inadequacy of his neurotic adaptation in its relation to an underdeveloped or maladaptive social reaction tissue. It is left to him to test and decide in how far the altered evaluation may give a more accurate picture of the dynamic interrelations under consideration.

At times it is of value to place emphasis at first on attitudes of parental figures and refer to the patient's own reactions only by implication. In this way the patient may more easily enter upon phases of experience within the general interreactive structure which has been of special importance in his life and which has contributed significantly to a need for building up neurotic defenses. He may welcome the opportunity to recognize the hostile-authoritarian or autistic-overprotective nature of parental trends to which his resentful or indulgent response appears to have been an almost inevitable reaction. Consideration of these antagonistic tendencies in their socially interreactive setting and in their relation to flattering self-deceptions seems to relieve some of the moralistic impetus involved in the hostility-guilt complex. The more tolerant attitude toward other persons thus developed automatically spreads to or includes one's own impulses and tends to undermine the need for repression and other defenses. It prepares the ground for the acceptance and altered evaluation by the patient of his hitherto unacceptable strivings.

This revaluation within the social field may embody for the patient an element of startle or surprise, but in my experience it arouses no anxiety or resentment. Rather the reaction may be one of relief at being able to interpret unacceptable trends in non-moralistic terms; to sense them as quasi-mechanical responses to external pressures. That is, the socio-individual revaluation here outlined tends to mitigate fixation upon the moralistic self-image, thus dissipating important incentives to guilt and hostility, and reducing the forces which cause anxiety and defense reactions and which separate the individual from others. Infantile and neurotic means of gaining security and satisfaction begin to be replaced by more constructive types of function and adaptation.

In this procedure an over-all view of pathogenic dynamics is developed which does not disregard socially destructive forces to which the patient may be especially sensitive,[5] though their disruptive nature may be well disguised. At the same time the powerful role of the organism's basic integrity is always taken into account. The patient is enabled to understand conflicting trends in himself and in others, not as unalterable behavior-characteristics but as reactions related to a deflection of attention which is due in part to unfortunate conditioning and can be dealt with therapeutically. This integrative understanding of what appeared to be disparate and incompatible tendencies helps to remove confusion, insecurity, and anxiety, and merges with the aforementioned reconstellating forces.

To demonstrate how these concepts and the associated procedure are applied in the treatment of specific patients, I shall mention first the case of a seven-year-old boy who had been troubled for two years by severe tic-like movements of face and shoulders, had shown spells of antagonistic and destructive behavior, and was generally difficult to manage. He was an only child who had always been a poor eater, somewhat overactive, and self-assertive. His mother, a rather timid Finnish woman of 43, was greatly concerned about the boy's behavior and symptoms. She and her carpenter husband had a fairly happy marital life, and both parents cooperated well in the treatment situation. Mother and son were seen separately by the therapist and also in a few joint sessions. In the first interview the mother appeared tense and apprehensive, she said that she had been depressed ("I cry almost every day") and very irritable for a year and had almost continuous headaches and frequent pains in the heart region for four months. An overprotective attitude toward the boy was evident in her report of his difficulties, as well as in her reactions during the interview. The boy himself was a healthy-looking and intelligent youngster, somewhat shy but friendly, who made a rather good contact with the therapist. There was no serious school problem.

While the details of the boy's development and family situation were not obtained in the first interview, significant data were secured to enter therapeutically upon important dynamics. The interrelation between the mother's over-anxious and irritable tendency and the boy's dependent and, at the same time, rebellious attitude was taken up immediately with the mother and a beginning was made in explaining to her the unfavorable influence of her reaction-tendency upon the boy. Their attitudes were considered as interactive variations of a basic theme. In addition the mother's attention was drawn to discrepancies and flattering self-deceptions embodied in her behavior trends. For example, what she considered her thoughtfulness and love for the boy was reformulated in terms of concern for her own convenience and emotional gratification. Her egocentric or self-defensive tendency was brought up for observation together with the essentially identical trends she criticized in the behavior of her son. This could be done without giving offense, as the discrepant behavior trends were not focussed upon as specific to the mother or to the boy. They were immediately related to similar authoritarian tendencies observable in *other* parents and in the social setting generally. The therapist did not emphasize what errors the mother made, but endeavored to observe together with mother and boy familiar events from an altered viewpoint—in their relation to a quite generally distributed but not generally recognized inadequacy of adjustment. In this way, without the therapist giving specific advice, the mother and in a limited way the son were given the opportunity to observe the inadequacy of their own adaptation, and to sense the possibility of more constructive interrelations.

To give a trivial example: During an interview with the mother, a boy (not her son) brought into the room a piece of paper he had taken from the registrar's desk. After he left, the mother remarked with some irritation that she would not allow *her* son to steal. This incident was immediately utilized as material for observation and the mother was asked whether in her irritation she was not acting at the moment in the same way. This remark was elaborated in simple terms indicating how in a reaction of anger one assumes a false authority over other people, and in this way takes something to oneself which belongs to another. The prevalence of such an intrusion on the part of people everywhere was also touched upon. This interpretation startled the mother somewhat but she was able to grasp the gist of it without indications of resentment or marked self-reproach.

The mother reacted quickly to treatment. After two appointments her headaches and the pains in the heart region disappeared, and there was a marked decrease in irritability and depression. She reported that she did not try to control her emotions but that she just did not feel angry or apprehensive any more. "I don't feel like getting mad, it is not that I control it. I have to laugh when I think that

I had to be so mad and now I don't need to be that way. Now I just leave him alone." There was also a change in the son's behavior. "I did not tell him not to do any of these nasty things any more but he just dropped it. When I don't get mad he does not get excited." Likewise the boy mentioned that he did not tease his mother so much now and that for some reason the mother had stopped screaming at him. The boy's tic disappeared, mutual cooperation gradually increased, and no further treatment was necessary after seven appointments. A check-up six months later showed that the boy was getting along well and that the mother continued to have a constructive attitude toward him. It was not possible to follow up the case in later years as the family had moved and their address was not known.

In this case, then, no detailed tracing of the adaptive difficulty to earlier events was attempted. The available information regarding past interactions was used for concrete amplification of the reinterpretation of current action trends in mother and child. In this way a large area of emotional experience was included in the process of reevaluation. Although positive transference was not encouraged and noxious implications of dependent behavior in its symbiotic as well as oppositional expressions were included in the therapeutic consideration, a vital relationship was maintained between mother, son, and therapist. It is of interest that on the basis of this relatively direct approach to psychodynamics rather rapid and far-reaching shifts occurred in the direction of more composed and cooperative behavior. These constructive alterations appear to be connected with a mitigation or partial dissolution of authoritarian-dependent self-enactments and of associated hostility-guilt reactions. A recentering of attention appeared to take place, a withdrawal of emotional emphasis from the moralistic self-image, which reduced internal conflict and resulted in a better coordinated type of interaction.

Another example of emotional reconstellation related to the inclusive or socially reinterpretative procedure also demonstrates the possibility of taking up important emotional issues therapeutically in the first interview. The patient, a woman of 44, displayed symptoms of an obsessive-compulsive disorder of nine years' standing. There were phobias regarding crowds, open spaces, subways, thunderstorms, and travelling in fog. There were no prominent schizoid features. In addition to the phobias there was great anxiety, tension, depression, pressure in the head, and loss of sleep. Though she asserted that her husband behaved thoughtfully, the underlying mutual hostility was readily brought to awareness and was immediately taken up in a socially revaluating manner. She reported her marital situation had been unsatisfactory in earlier years because of her husband's alcoholism and abusiveness. Though he had given up drinking eight years before he continued to be sullen, severe, and forbidding toward her and their three daughters; the patient responded to him with bitter resentment.

At the second interview her depression and tension had practically disappeared, and she reported regular sleep of eight hours which continued thereafter. After a few appointments she volunteered the information that she had reacted very calmly to an incident of offensive behavior on her husband's part which previously would have caused her to have weeping spells and temper tantrums for several days. She expressed surprise at the objectivity with which she was able to handle a previously unmanageable situation. The relationship with her husband had not been submitted to a detailed genetic analysis, but merely to inclusive revaluation. No advice had been given her and the change in her reaction was not a matter of conscious emotional control. Her phobias regarding crowds and thunderstorms had disappeared, whereas other fears (regarding driving in fog) remained but were somewhat lessened. The contact with this patient had to be interrupted after five appointments as she moved to another location and she could not be reached. In further treatment more early conditioning factors would probably have been included. But the question remains in how far the reduction of guilt and hostility through inclusive analysis of a significant current relationship may lessen the need for defensive devices throughout the entire neurotic systematization.

The possibility of overcoming initial resistance by this procedure was demonstrated in the case of an unmarried girl of 20, a mail-desk worker who had been hospitalized for "thrombophlebitis" of the right arm intermittently present for two years. After conflicting appraisals by different specialists, and in view of the varying neurological findings, she was discharged with a diagnosis of conversion hysteria. She was of a fairly sociable personality type, somewhat inclined to day dreams, with a history of a mild early speech disorder which was later corrected. Five years previous to her present illness there had been intermittent pains in the right lower abdominal region whose etiology was not clear, being perhaps partly psychogenic.

At her first interview with me there was pain on active and passive movements of the arm, hyperalgesia to pressure, and marked weakness and slowness of voluntary movements. Her behavior was rather apathetic with a strong undercurrent of resentment, especially against people connected with the hospital. She refused to answer "personal questions," said she did not need psychiatric treatment, and was unwilling to talk of emotionally significant situations. However, I spoke briefly of the interrelation between physical symptoms and emotions, especially of hostility and guilty feelings understood in their larger socially interactive dynamics. There was no evidence of a positive response, but a return appointment in six weeks was suggested. At this second visit the patient reported that her symptoms had disappeared a few days after the first interview, and a great deal of significant material came to light—especially her hate for an alcoholic, domineering father whom she had struck on one occasion, four years before. Her hostility and the guilt related to it, were taken up immediately in a desensitizing and socially revaluating manner. There were two more interviews at two-week intervals. She cooperated well, began to feel less guilty and hostile, and developed a more constructive attitude toward her father. While a great deal of emotional material volunteered by the patient was considered with her, one wonders whether improvement arrived at in the few appointments can be lasting. A check-up a year and a half later showed that the patient was perfectly well. A year after that the internist noted a *transitory* recurrence of mild pain and weakness in the arm. Attempts to check up four years after the patient's first contact with the therapist were unsuccessful as she had moved and left no forwarding address. Here again it is of interest that the direct reinterpretative approach to an outstanding conflict with only limited genetic analysis was followed by a constructive emotional reconstellation.

That this more direct procedure may facilitate rather rapid shifts in longstanding emotional habituations in older persons as well was demonstrated in a sixty-year-old German woman, a widow for twenty years. She had a history of depression and tension, severe headaches for almost two years accompanied by nausea and vomiting, mild pain in feet and shoulders, and more recently *pruritus vulvae*. She was greatly worried about her only son (single, 30) who was living with her, upon whose support she was partly dependent, and of whose standards of living she did not approve. She had always been greatly overprotective of her son and her irritable-possessive attitude had been aggravated by the conflict between her conventional continental standards and his less rigid American outlook. The patient had no relatives or close friends and recently no occupation except her housework. She was an essentially active and intelligent personality with a capacity for good social rapport, and not without some readiness to reconsider the validity of her long-established prejudices and habits of feeling.

While the information necessary to assess the main features of her difficulty was obtained in the first interview, at the same time active therapeutic steps were taken. The patient's possessive attitude was considered in relation to the son's rebellious or defensive behavior (he had no personal contact with the therapist), and both were viewed in the setting of a generally defective type of interrelation from which the psychiatrist did not exclude his own reactions. No specific advice was given to influence the patient's conduct and it was left to her whether and in what way she would make use of the revaluation offered in the interview.

In the second interview three weeks later the patient showed marked improvement. The depression had practically disappeared, and there was less worry and irritation with her son. She became more tolerant and began to accept the fact that her son had to live his own life, that her possessiveness expressed an "egotistical" attitude very similar to that noticeable in her son's indifference or self-defense. The patient showed a more constructive and positive approach toward her difficulties; the headaches, intestinal disturbance, itching, and pains disappeared. She reported that her son's relation to her had also changed, that he began to be more friendly and thoughtful as her critical attitude decreased. The patient had been referred to the social worker and while she did not follow the latter's suggestions regarding social and occupational interests, this contact probably encouraged further an active and positive attitude toward her problems.

A third interview seven months later served mainly as a check-up, and confirmed the more cooperative relationship between the patient and her son. That is, a far-going reconstellation of long standing prejudices and emotional attitudes occurred largely on the basis of one interview in which a crucial interrelationship was handled by inclusive revaluation. It is interesting that the altered attitude of the patient led to an altered, less noxious attitude on the part of her son.

This indirect type of social therapy is of special value where the therapist is not in direct contact with the patient's social setting.

For further demonstration the case of another woman, forty, may be mentioned briefly. She showed a condition of depression and tension in an exceedingly unsatisfactory and difficult marital situation. For many years her husband had been neglectful and violently abusive toward her. Her possessive reactions to his authoritarian and self-centered behavior were considered with her in their larger social setting. There were three therapeutic appointments at two-week intervals and a checkup visit four months later. Her reaction of resentment and despair changed to a more composed and tolerant attitude and the depression disappeared. Instead of being overwhelmed by what had seemed an intolerable situation, she was able to respond to her husband's behavior with more objective and even sympathetic understanding, and to take charge of the difficulties with which she was confronted. In this case the husband's attitude showed no marked change.

As will be evident, while I approach patients with the orientation described and while I often take up important psychodynamic aspects therapeutically in the first interview, I do not fail to gather the routine information regarding clinical and personal history. Early and current frustrations, accidental or especially noxious conditioning, discrepancies between assets and life situation, are of course also taken into account. Where hostility is deeply anchored in the character structure or where one deals with disorganized or dependent conditions, supportive measures may temporarily have to be in the foreground. But even in such cases, I found that the inclusive revaluating procedure leads at times to more ready responses than expected. Dependency needs are not disregarded but they as well as various other dynamic factors and characterological trends are viewed in the over-all frame of the total maladaptive constellation as here conceived.

I fully agree that great caution is needed in approaching issues which the patient has not been able to master and which are important factors in his disorder. Nothing could be more unwise and possibly harmful to the patient than an attempt to apply, as a mere intellectually learned technique, the principles here proposed. For along with the conceptual orientation there is needed an adequately integrated feeling-relatedness in order to apply the procedure in a way that will avoid adverse responses. On this basis the self-inclusive method often permits a relatively direct approach and revaluation which, in my experience, has had no untoward effects.

The approach here described does not directly interpret the patient's symptoms or defensive measures of which he is in need in order to ward off anxiety and maintain his precarious stabilization; nor does it consist of an attempt to bring about the reexperience and detailed analysis of early adaptive miscarriages as they are transferred into the relation with the therapist. The procedure takes up instead a revaluation of emotional reactions which are relatively accessible to conscious consideration and which reflect or are continuous with the individual's early inadequate interrelational experience. In this way important dynamic forces which cause anxiety and defense are revaluated and attenuated. The acceptance of objectionable trends, awareness and reintegration of early experiences, the work with characterological inadequacies thus facilitated, appear as partial phases of the more general reconstellating process.

In accordance with our conceptual postulates and their therapeutic application therefore, the features of the maladaptive constellation especially considered consist of hostility and guilt in the frame of authoritarian and dependent attitudes tied up with the moralistically overaccentuated self-image and the associated emphasis upon social approval. These characteristics are considered as interrelated aspects of a total dynamic configuration, not as separate attributes or isolated behavioral qualities. They are approached as interdependent processes of a general adaptive misconstellation which are variously actualized. They may appear as reactive or characterologically fixated phenomena, as subjective experiences or interrelational manifestations, as individual and socio-cultural formations. In this configurational conception various psychodynamic features which have perhaps been given a too one-sided emphasis in different psychopathological formulations are understood as interdependent parts in a total constellation that relates to a basic deflection of attention.

The revaluation here considered involves a form of insight that embodies an interwoven complex of conceptual and attitudinal processes. All insight,[106] of course, entails the acceptance of certain concepts regarding behavioral processes—even where it is limited to basic ideas regarding the interrelation of emotional experience and neurotic or somatic symptoms. Where the concepts involved in insight are consistently confirmed by clinical evidence and by the processes occurring in the therapeutic setting, one is justified in assuming a significant correspondence between theory (insight) and the processes referred to insofar as they can be conceived from the contemporary cultural and scientific background. But one needs always to take into account that through the application of an altered frame of reference established psychodynamic conceptions may again have to be changed no matter how well they seemed to be supported by the available evidence.

The therapeutically effective insight or revaluation in our procedure embodies a corrective emotional experience[3] in which the relation to the therapist is specifically involved. Very often an emotional reaction is evident where significant neurotogenic features are placed in the altered conceptual frame. But the startle or jolt observed in many patients in this connection does not result in anxiety or resentment, owing partly to factors inherent in the reinterpretation and partly to the patient's relation to the therapist. The fact that the therapist includes his own self-referent trends in the revaluation he proposes increases the possibility of the patient's working along with him and accepting without resentment a fargoing reassessment of his accustomed self-appraisal. On this basis there is developed a positive and not dependently clinging relation to the therapist. The latter is not merely permissive, nor does he attempt to reach an unattainable objectivity. Instead he introduces a revaluation not only of the neurotically distorted expressions of transference and counter-transference, but also of the image-dependence and image-enactment characteristic of the normal reaction average. In this way the patient is placed in the role of a responsible participant in the study of his behavioral inadequacy as it relates to an underdeveloped or maladaptive social constellation; he is taken seriously as a member of the community. His fundamental value and capacity are respected not by verbalization but by the operations inherent in the therapeutic situation. These interrelational experiences together with the socio-analytic revaluation are powerful agents in the emotional reconstellation. They are reenforced by the patient's recognition of his increasing objectivity and independence in his life adjustment, which at times is noted by him as a new and surprising experience. It may be suggested that this type of constructive relationship and adjustment rests largely on the activation of basic integrative capacities and not merely on modifications of image-dependent and self-affirmative relatedness.

There are indications that processes similar to the revaluation here suggested play an important role also in other forms of dynamic psychotherapy. In our procedure, however, the revaluation is employed in a rather direct and specifically organized manner and encompasses in a consistent pattern a large range of normal and neurotic manifestations.

SUMMARY

By correlating observations on interrelational behavior arrived at in group-analytic studies (Burrow) with findings of dynamic psychiatry, a conceptual model is developed which postulates an identity in significant dynamics underlying neurotic and normal behavior. The concept is proposed that basic integrative forces are impeded by a self-referent deflection of attention which constitutes an important cause of behavior-disorders as well as of social disaffection and conflict. The over-accentuation of the moralistic self-image, with its entail of authoritarian and dependent reactions, and the associated dynamics of hostility, guilt, anxiety, and defense-reactions are interpreted as internally and socially interactive expressions of a dynamic constellation in which both patient and therapist are involved. Supportive evidence for some aspects of the theory is offered from diverse behavioral fields. The function of concepts in guiding therapeutic procedure is briefly considered, together with the question in how far the therapeutic setting can be used for evaluating theories regarding behavior-disorder.

The treatment of several neurotic patients is outlined to demonstrate how the conceptual postulates are translated into therapeutic action and are applied to the dynamic processes presented. An important modification consists in the specifically patterned inclusive attitude of the therapist toward the patient. The therapist, being part of the social reaction structure, includes a revaluation of his own self-referent trend in relation to the self-referent or hostile attitude of the patient and his environment. This orientation frequently permits a relatively direct approach to and revaluation of hostility, guilt, and associated factors in accordance with the criteria of the postulated behavioral model. On the basis of this procedure marked and often lasting changes were observed in the patient's symptomatology, interrelational attitude, and personality organization. These constructive and at times rapid reconstellations are brought about in a therapeutic setting that is relatively free from sympathetic or oppositional dependence. In accordance with the conceptual postulates, these behavioral modifications are interpreted as a withdrawal of organismically rooted impulses from moralistic image formations with a coincident release of basic integrative assets. So one might say that a reconstellation takes place within the total personality configuration and its relation to the environment through which biologically constructive forces are increasingly activated as their fixation upon defensive image-formations is weakened or dissipated.

In general it is concluded that the regular sequences observed in the interactions of the therapeutic setting and the type of behavior modifications shown by patients indicate that the proposed concepts are a valid approximation to important processes occurring in behavior-disorder and their adjustment. In any case there is evidence that these concepts have positive operational value.

It should be added that therapeutic improvements, while important for the patient and gratifying to the therapist, appear from the phylobiological frame of reference (Burrow) as incomplete adjustments. Although they alleviate the patient's behavior- or personality-disorder, they fail to modify the socially structured inadequacy of the reaction average in which everyone participates. In view of the destructive and wasteful implications of this general adaptive defect, the study of the larger problem is an important scientific goal and a natural extension of our present concern with individual neurotic disorders.

REFERENCES

1. ACKERMAN, N. W.: Psychoanalysis and group psychotherapy. Group Psychotherapy, *3:* 204-215, 1950.
2. ADLER, A.: Understanding Human Nature. New York, Greenberg, 1927, p. 286.
3. ALEXANDER, F. AND FRENCH, T. M.: Psychoanalytic Therapy. New York, Ronald Press, 1946, p. 353.
4. ———: Current views on psychotherapy. Psychiatry, *16:* 113-122, 1953.
5. ALEXANDER, L.: General principles of psychotherapy Am. J. Psychiat., *106:* 721-731, 1950.
6. ALLEE, W. C.: Cooperation Among Animals. New York, Schuman, 1951, p. 233.
7. ALLPORT, G. W.: Geneticism vs. ego-structure in theories of personality. Brit. J. Educ. Psychol., *16:* 57-68, 1946. Reprinted in "The Nature of Personality: Selected Papers." Cambridge, Addison-Wesley Press, 1950, p. 158-169.
8. ———: The trend in motivational theory. Am. J. Orthopsychiat., *23:* 107-119, 1953.
9. ANGYAL, A.: Foundations for a Science of Personality. New York, Commonwealth Fund, 1941, p. 398.

10. APPEL, K. E.: Psychiatric therapy. In Personality and the Behavior Disorders, J. McV. Hunt, ed. New York, Ronald Press, 1944, pp. 1107-63.

11. AUSUBEL, D. P.: Ego Development and the Personality Disorders. New York, Grune & Stratton, 1952, p. 564.

12. BALLY, G.: Vom Ursprung und von den Grenzen der Freiheit. Basel, Schwabe, 1945, p. 141.

13. BARTHOLOMEW, G. A., JR. AND BIRDSELL, J. B.: Ecology and the protohominids. Am. Anthrop., 55: 481-498, 1953.

14. BENDER, L.: Aggression, Hostility and Anxiety in Children. Springfield, Ill. Thomas, 1953, p. 184.

15. BENEDICT, R.: Patterns of Culture. New York, Houghton Mifflin, 1934, p. 291.

16. BERNARD, C.: An Introduction to the Study of Experimental Medicine. New York, Macmillan, 1927, p. 226.

17. BERTALANFFY, L. VON: Vom Sinn und der Einheit der Naturwissenschaften. Der Student, Feb. 1, 1948, p. 10-11.

18. ———: General system theory. Main Currents in Modern Thought. 11: 75-83, 1955.

19. BIDNEY, D.: Human nature and the cultural process. Am. Anthrop. 49: 375-396, 1947.

20. BINSWANGER, L.: Grundformen und Erkenntnis Menschlichen Daseins. Zürich, Niehans, 1942, p. 726.

21. BOWLBY, J.: Maternal Care and Mental Health. Geneva, W.H.O. Monograph Series No. 2, 1951, p. 179.

22. BRIDGMAN, P. W.:Science and common sense. Scient. Monthly, 79: 32-39, 1954.

23. BUBER, M.: Das Problem des Menschen. Heidelberg, Schneider, 1948, p. 169.

24. BURROW, T.: Psychoanalysis and society. J. Abnorm. & Social Psychol., 7: 340-346, 1912-1913.

25. ———: The genesis and meaning of "homosexuality" and its relation to the problem of introverted mental states. Psychoanalyt. Rev., 4: 272-284, 1917.

26. ———: Social images versus reality. J. Abnorm. & Social Psychol., 19: 230-235, 1924.

27. ———: Psychiatry as an objective science. Brit. J. M. Psychol, 5: 298-309, 1925.

28. ———: The laboratory method in psychoanalysis—its inception and development. Am. J. Psychiat., 5: 345-355, 1926.

29. ———: Psychoanalytic improvisations and the personal equation. Psychoanaly. Rev., 13: 173-186, 1926.

30. ———: The Social Basis of Consciousness—A Study in Organic Psychology. International Library of Psychology, Philosophy and Scientific Method. New York, Harcourt, Brace, 1927, p. 256.

31. ———: The Biology of Human Conflict. New York, Macmillan, 1937, p. 435.

32. ———: The organism as a whole and its phyloanalytic implications—an organismic approach to disorders of human behavior. Australasian J. Psychol. & Philos., 15: 259-278, 1937.

33. ——: The Neurosis of Man—An Introduction to a Science of Human Behavior. New York, Harcourt, Brace; London, Routledge & Kegan Paul, 1949, p. 428.

34. CANTRIL, H., AMES, A., JR., HASTORF, A. H., AND ITTELSON, W. H.: Psychology and scientific research. I. The nature of scientific inquiry; II. Scientific inquiry and scientific method; III. The transactional view in psychological research. Science, 110: 461-464; 491-497; 517-522, 1949.

35. CARLSON, A. J.: Science versus life. J.A.M.A., 157: 1437-1441, 1955.

36. CASSIRER, E.: An Essay on Man. New York, Doubleday, 1953, p. 294.

37. CORNER, G. W.: Ourselves Unborn: A Embryologist's Essay on Man. New Haven, Yale Univ. Press, 1944, p. 189.

38. DARWIN, C.: Expressions of the Emotions in Man and Animals. New York, Appleton, 1916, p. 372.

39. DAVIS, K.: Extreme social isolation of a child. Am. J. Sociol., 45: 554-565, 1940.

40. DIETHELM, O.: A historical review of psychiatric treatment. Psychosom. Med., 3: 286-294, 1941.

41. ——: Dynamische Psychotherapie in Depressionszutänden. Monatschr. f. Psychiat. u. Neurol., 125: 337-346, 1953.

42. ——: Treatment in Psychiatry. 3rd ed. Springfield, Ill. Thomas, 1955, p. 545.

43. EMERSON, A. E.: The biological basis of social cooperation. Ill. Acad. of Science Trs., 39: 9-18, 1946.

44. ERIKSON, E. H.: Childhood and Society. New York, Norton, 1950, p. 397.

45. FLESCHER, J.: On different types of countertransference. Internat. J. Group Psychotherapy, 3: 357-372, 1953. Other articles on countertransference in this issue.

46. DE FOREST, I.: The Leaven of Love. A Development of the Psychoanalytic Theory and Technique of Sándor Ferenczi. New York, Harper, 1954, p. 206.

47. FRANK, J. D.: Group psychotherapy in relation to research. Group psychotherapy, 3: 197-203, 1950.

48. FRAZER, W. R.: Some indications of unity among the sciences. Philosophy of Science, 22: 135-139, 1955.

49. FREUD, S.: Civilization and Its Discontents. International Psycho-Analytical Library. London, Hogarth Press, 1951, p. 144.

50. FROMM, E.: Escape From Freedom. New York, Rinehart, 1941, p. 305.

51. ——: Man For Himself. New York, Rinehart, 1947, p. 254.

52. FROMM-REICHMANN, F.: Principles of Intensive Psychotherapy. Univ. of Chicago Press, 1950, p. 246.

53. GALT, W. E.: The principle of cooperation in behavior. Quart. Rev. Biol., 15: 401-410, 1940.

54. ——: Recent views on attention. Present-Day Psychology, A. A. Roback, ed. New York, Philosophical Library, 1955, ch. 5, pp. 103-115.

55. GERARD, R. W. AND EMERSON, A. E.: Extrapolation from the biological to the social. Science, 101: 582-585, 1945.

56. ——: Neurophysiology in relation to behavior. Mid-Century Psychiatry, R. R. Grinker, ed. Springfield, Ill., Thomas, 1953, pp. 23-32.

57. GILLIN, J., ed.: For a Science of Social Man. Convergences in Anthropology, Psychology, and Sociology. New York, Macmillan, 1954, p. 289.

58. GOLDSTEIN, K.: The Organism: A Holistic Approach to Biology. New York, American Book Co., 1939, p. 533.

59. ——: Human Nature in the Light of Psychopathology. Cambridge, Harvard Univ. Press, 1940, p. 258.

60. —— AND SCHEERER, M.: Abstract and Concrete Behavior: An Experimental Study with Special Tests. Psychol. Monog., *53:* 2, 1941, p. 151.

61. GREENMAN, E. F.: The extraorganic. Am. Anthrop., *50:* 181-199, 1948.

62. GRINKER, R. R. AND SPIEGEL, J. P.: Men Under Stress. Philadelphia, Blakiston, 1945, p. 484.

63. HALLOWELL, A. I.: Personality structure and the evolution of man. Am. Anthrop., *52:* 159-173, 1950.

64. HARTMANN, H.: Ich-Psychologie und Anpassungsproblem. Internat. Ztschr. Psychoanaly. u. Imago, *24:* 62-135, 1939. Tr. and reprinted in Organization and Pathology of Thought, D. Rapaport, ed. Columbia Univ. Press, 1951, xix, pp. 362-96.

65. ——, KRIS, E., AND LOEWENSTEIN, R. M.: Notes on the theory of aggression. The Psychoanalytic Study of the Child, 1949, *3* & *4,* p. 9-36.

66. HEISENBERG, W.: Wandlungen in den Grundlagen der Naturwissenschaft. Zürich, Hirzel, 1949, p. 112.

67. HENRY, J.: Review of personality in nature, society, and culture. C. Kluckhohn and H. A. Murray, eds. Am. J. Orthopsychiat., *19:* 714-715, 1949.

68. HINSIE, L. E.: Concepts and Problems of Psychotherapy. New York, Columbia Univ. Press, 1937, p. 199. Cha. v by C. Landis, A statistical evaluation of psychotherapeutic methods.

69. HOCH, P. H., ed.: Failures in Psychiatric Treatment. New York, Grune & Stratton, 1948, pp. 241.

70. HORNEY, K.: Neurosis and Human Growth. The Struggle Toward Self-Realization. New York, Norton, 1950, p. 391.

71. HSU, F. L. K., ed.: Aspects of Culture and Personality. A Symposium. New York, Abelard-Schuman, 1954, p. 305.

72. JUNG, C. G.: The Practice of Psychotherapy. Essays on the Psychology of the Transference and Other Subjects. New York Pantheon, 1954, p. 377.

73. KAPPERS, C. U. A.: Further contributions on neurobiotaxis. J. Comp. Neurol, *27:* 261-298, 1917.

74. KARDINER, A.: The Psychological Frontiers of Society. Columbia Univ. Press, 1945, p. 475.

75. KARPMAN, B.: Aggression. Am. J. Orthopsychiat., *20:* 694-718, 1950.

76. KLAESI, J.: Psychotherapie in der Klinik. Monatschr. Psychiat. u. Neurol., *124:* 334-353, 1952.

77. KLAGES, L.: Der Geist als Widersacher der Seele. Leipzig, Barth, 1933, p. 1478.

78. KLUCKHOHN, C. AND MURRAY, H. A., edrs.: Personality in Nature, Society, and Culture. New York, Knopf, 1950, p. 561.

79. KORZYBSKI, A.: Science and Sanity. An Introduction to Non-Aristotelian Systems and General Semantics. International Non-Aristotelian Library Pub. Co., 1933, p. 798.

80. KRECH, D. AND KLEIN, G. S., eds.: Theoretical Models and Personality Theory. Durham N. C., Duke Univ. Press, 1952, p. 142.

81. KROPOTKIN, P.: Mutual Aid: A Factor of Evolution. New York, Knopf, 1922, p. 240.

82. KUBIE, L. S.: The distortion of the symbolic process in neurosis and psychosis. J. Amer. Psychoanal. Assn., 1: 59-86, 1953.

83. LANGER, S. K.: Philosophy in a New Key. New York, Mentor, 1942, p. 248.

84. LEVINE, M.: Principles of psychiatric treatment. In Dynamic Psychiatry, F. Alexander and H. Ross, edrs., Univ. of Chicago Press, 1952, p. 307-366.

85. LEVY, D. M.: The strange hen. Am. J. Orthopsychiat., 20: 355-362, 1950.

86. ——: The early development of independent and oppositional behavior. In Midcentury Psychiatry, R. R. Grinker, ed., Springfield, Ill., Thomas, 1953, pp. 113-21.

87. LEWIN, K.: A Dynamic Theory of Personality. New York, McGraw-Hill, 1935, p. 286.

88. MASSERMAN, J.: Practice of Dynamic Psychiatry. Philadelphia, Saunders, 1955, p. 790.

89. MEAD, M.: Cooperation and Competition among Primitive Peoples. New York, McGraw-Hill, 1937, p. 511.

90. MEYER, A.: Inter-relations of the domain of neuropsychiatry. Arch. Neurol. & Psychiat., 8: 111-121, 1922.

91. MILES, H. H. W., BARRABEE, E. L., AND FINESINGER, J. E.: Evaluation of psychotherapy: with a follow-up study of 62 cases of anxiety neurosis. Psychosom. Med., 13: 83-105, 1951.

92. MONTAGU, A. M. F.: On Being Human. New York, Schuman, 1950, p. 125.

93. ——: The Direction of Human Development: Biological and Social Bases. New York, Harper, 1955, p. 404.

94. MORENO, J. L.: Inter-personal therapy and the psychopathology of inter-personal relations. Sociometry, 1, 9-76, 1937.

95. MULLAHY, P., ed.: A Study of Interpersonal Relations. New York, Hermitage Press, 1949, p. 507.

96. MURPHY, G.: Personality: A Biosocial Approach to Origins and Structure, New York, Harper, 1947, p. 999.

97. MYERSON, A.: The social anxiety neurosis—its possible relationship to schizophrenia. Am. J. Psychiat., 101: 149-156, 1944.

98. NOYES, A. P.: Modern Clinical Psychiatry. Philadelphia, Saunders, 1953, p. 609.

99. OBERNDORF, C. P., GREENACRE, P., AND KUBIE, L.: Symposium on the evaluation of therapeutic results. Internat. J. Psychoanal., 29: 7-33, 1948.

100. POINCARÉ, H.: The Foundations of Science. New York, Science Press, 1929, p. 546.

101. PORTMANN, A.: Biologische Fragmente zu einer Lehre vom Menschen. Basel, Schwabe, 1944, p. 140.

102. ——: Das Tier als Soziales Wesen. Zürich, Rhein-Verlag, 1953, p. 378.

103. Rapaport, D.: The autonomy of the ego. Bull. Menninger Clin., *15:* 113-123, 1951.

104. Read, H.: Education Through Art. London, Faber and Faber, 1943, p. 320.

105. Redfield, R., ed.: Levels of Integration in Biological and Social Systems. Biological Symposia. Lancaster, Pa., Jacques Cattell Press, 1942, viii, p. 240.

106. Reid, J. R. and Finesinger, J. E.: The role of insight in psychotherapy. Am. J. Psychiat., *108:* 726-734, 1952.

107. Rennie, T. A. C.: Prognosis in the psychoneuroses: benign and malignant developments. In Current Problems in Psychiatric Diagnosis, P. H. Hoch and J. Zubin, eds., New York, Grune & Stratton, 1953, pp. 66-79.

108. Riese, W.: The principle of integration. Its history and its nature. J. Nerv. & Ment. Dis., *96:* 296-312, 1942.

109. ——: An outline of a history of ideas in psychotherapy. Bull. Hist. Med., *25:* 442-456, 1951.

110. Rosenzweig, S.: A dynamic interpretation of psychotherapy oriented towards research. Psychiatry, *1:* 521-526, 1938.

111. Ruesch, J.: Experiments in psychotherapy. I. Theoretical considerations. J. Psychol., *25:* 137-169, 1948, II. Individual social techniques. J. Soc. Psychol., *29:* 3-28, 1949.

112. —— and Bateson, G.: Structure and process in social relations. Psychiatry, *12:* 105-124, 1949.

113. Scheler, M.: Die Stellung des Menschen im Kosmos. Darmstadt, Reichl, 1928, p. 115.

114. Schilder, P.: The social neurosis. Psychoanalyt. Rev., *25:* 1-19, 1938.

115. Schneirla, T. C.: Problems in the biopsychology of social organization. J. Abnorm. & Social Psychol., *41:* 385-402, 1946.

116. Schrödinger, E.: Science and Humanism: Physics in Our Time. Cambridge Univ. Press, 1952, p. 68.

117. Schwartz, M. S. and Schwartz, C. G.: Problems in participant observation. Am. J. Sociology, *60:* 343-353, 1955.

118. Sinnott, E. W.: Cell and Psyche, The Biology of Purpose. Chapel Hill, N. C., Univ. of North Carolina Press, 1950, p. 121.

119. Sorokin, P. A.: S. O. S.: The Meaning of our Crisis. Boston, Beacon Press, 1951, p. 175.

120. Spiro, M. E.: Culture and personality. The natural history of a false dichotomy. Psychiatry, *14:* 19-46, 1951.

121. ——: Human nature in its psychological dimensions. Am. Anthrop., *56:* 19-30, 1954.

122. Spitz, R. A.: Hospitalism: The Psychoanalytic Study of the Child, 1945, I, 53-74.

123. —— and Wolf, K. M.: The smiling response: a contribution to the ontogenesis of social relations. Genetic Psychology Monographs, *34:* 57-125, 1946.

124. Straus, E. W.: The upright posture. Psychiat. Quart., *26:* 529-561, 1952.

125. Straus, W. L., Jr.: Closing remarks on symposium, The non-human primates and human evolution, Human Biol., *26*: 304-312, 1954.

126. Sullivan, H. S.: The Interpersonal Theory of Psychiatry. New York, Norton, 1953, p. 393.

127. Suttie, I. D.: The Origins of Love and Hate. New York, Julian Press, 1935, p. 275.

128. Syz, H.: Socio-individual principles in psychopathology. Brit. J. Med. Psychol., *10*: 329-343, 1930.

129. ———: The concept of the organism-as-a-whole and its application to clinical situations. Human Biol., *8*: 489-507, 1936.

130. ———: The "social neurosis." Am. J. Sociology, *42*: 895-897, 1937.

131. ———: Phylopathology. Encyclopedia of Psychology, P. L. Harriman, ed. New York, Philosophical Library, 1946, pp. 519-23.

132. ———: New perspectives in behavior study: a phylobiological reorientation. J. Psychol., *31*: 21-27, 1951.

133. Thompson, C. B. and Sill, A. P.: Our Common Neurosis. New York, Exposition Press, 1952, p. 210.

134. Uexküll, J. von: Umwelt und Innenwelt der Tiere. Berlin, Springer, 1921. p. 224.

135. Weigert, E.: Existentialism and its relations to psychotherapy. Psychiatry, *12*: 399-412, 1949.

136. Weyl, H.: Symmetry. Princeton Univ. Press, 1952, p. 175.

137. Wheeler, W. M.: Emergent evolution and the social. Science, *64*: 433-440, 1926.

138. White, L. A.: The symbol: the origin and basis of human behavior. Philosophy of Science, *7*: 451-463, 1940.

139. Whitehead, A. N.: Science and the Modern World. New York, Macmillan, 1925, p. 304.

140. Whitehorn, J. C. and Betz, B. J.: A study of psychotherapeutic relationships between physicians and schizophrenic patients. Am. J. Psychiat., *111*: 321-331, 1954.

141. Whyte, L. L.: The Next Development in Man. New York, Holt, 1948, p. 322.

142. ———, ed.: Aspects of Form: A Symposium on Form in Nature and Art. New York, Pellegrini & Cudahy, 1951, p. 249.

143. ———: Accent on Form: An Anticipation of the Science of Tomorrow. New York, Harper, 1954, p. 198.

144. The objective evaluation of psychotherapy. Round table, 1948. Am. J. Orthopsychiat., *19*: 463-491, 1949.

145. Psychodynamics. Ch. II, pp. 15-48 of The Psychiatrist: His Training and Development, 1952 Conf. on Psychiat. Educ., Am. Psychiat. Assoc., 1953.

146. Research in psychotherapy. Round table,, 1947. Am. J. Orthopsychiat., *18*: 92-118, 1948.

11

STUDIES IN HUMAN ECOLOGY: FACTORS GOVERNING THE ADAPTATION OF CHINESE UNABLE TO RETURN TO CHINA

By LAWRENCE E. HINKLE, JR., M.D., JOHN W. GITTINGER, M.A., LEO GOLDBERGER, M.A., ADRIAN OSTFELD, M.D., RHODA METRAUX, Ph.D., PETER RICHTER, M.D. and HAROLD G. WOLFF, M.D.*

HUMAN ECOLOGY, as the term is used here, refers to the relations between man and his environment in the broadest biological sense. We feel free to concern ourselves with any aspect of the environment to which man must adapt and with any aspect of the adaptive processes which go on within individual men, or within groups of men. Although we are specifically concerned with how man's relation to his environment affects his health, we do not limit ourselves to those studies which are usually included within the medical sciences. We feel free to call upon any discipline which can help us understand man, his environment, and his adaptation to it.

One of the problems with which we have been concerned is the problem of what is called "life stress." It has been postulated that man may encounter situations in his social environment to which he reacts with the development of illness. Such situations are said to be "stressful" because they lead to "stress" within the individual, which is thought to result in illness. Leaving aside the mechanism through which such illness may be produced, we asked ourselves the question: "Can it be demonstrated that there are certain types of social situations to which men react with illness and, if so, can these situations be defined?"

To explore the problem we selected a group of adults ostensibly

* From the study program in Human Health and the Ecology of Man; and the Departments of Medicine and Psychiatry, New York Hospital-Cornell Medical Center.

Saunders, D.R. An outline of Zettinger's personality theory as applied to Kaf Wechsler.

I. The subtests considered separately.

Res Memorandum 59-3 Princeton, N.J.: Educational Testing Service, 1955.

Schucman, Helen (She forc...) Adv. #19(?)... the press.

Wagner, R.F. An explanation of Zettinger's in Eemelizn dimension by factor analysis based upon personality measures. Unpub. doct. dissen. Geo Wash Univ, 1967

Shetford, J.M. Symposium presented at APA, L.A. Sept 974

" " presented at APA Philadelphia Sept 1963

Schucman & Saunders Shetford Paper at APA St Louis Sept 1962

Saunders D.R. Some conclusions drawn from research stimulated by the PAS. Paper presented at Amer. Calling Personnel Assoc. Dallas, Mar. Flg. 7.

Amer. Coll. Personnel Assoc. Dallas, Tex. 1967

similar in education, cultural background, and present situation, all of whom had been, separated from their native cultural environment, dislocated in their social position, and separated from the individuals in their lives with whom they had their most intense and enduring personal relations. The group we selected was made up of Chinese graduate students and professional men who were in this country at the time of the Communist Revolution in China in 1949 and who since that time have not returned to their homes and families because of their class background, political beliefs, or material difficulties. Members of this group have been intensively studied by a team of anthropologists, psychiatrists, psychologists, and physicians. The scientists from each discipline have worked independently, using their own tools and concepts and collecting their own data in their own way; but at all stages the members of the team have compared their information and each has sought to clarify and complement that which the others have obtained.

We shall present to you at this time some findings related to three typical members of the group of Chinese whom we have studied. I shall call upon a representative of each discipline to present the data assembled by his colleagues. Dr. Metraux, representing the cultural anthropologists, will report first; Dr. Richter, representing the psychiatrists, will report second; Mr. Gittinger, representing the psychologists, will report third; and finally I shall present the medical findings and a few tentative conclusions at which we have arrived together.

SUMMARY OF ANTHROPOLOGICAL DATA

Each of the Chinese informants spends from sixteen to twenty hours over a period of two weeks or more working with the several members of the research team; four to six or eight hours are given over to work with the anthropologist.

The task of the cultural anthropologist is a fourfold one: First, to get from each informant a careful *life history* which, together with other social data, will serve to place all of them in a social and cultural matrix; second, to explore with these Chinese informants and with others who may have special knowledge facets of Chinese culture, the analysis of which will provide us with a coherent version of contemporary Chinese culture; third, to provide from analyses of informant and other source materials—observations of inter-personal behavior, autobiographies and biographies, novels and films, and other cultural artifacts—an understanding of the dynamics of Chinese cultural character; and fourth, to place the research material within a broader cultural framework which will enable us to understand the specific emphases of Chinese culture and personality as they are related to health, and to make the research results available for purposes of cultural comparisons.

The Chinese men and women whose lives we are studying all have lived through the uncertainties of change and turmoil in China. Older and younger alike, wherever they were born and grew up in China, all have been exposed to culture change, social strain, and physical hardship. Their lives were disrupted by the Japanese invasion and all of them have been deeply affected by the Communist Revolution and the removal of the Nationalist Government from the mainland to Formosa. In one way or another, all have mastered difficulties—difficulties which left others, one may assume, by the wayside—in order to come to the United States. All have made a working adjustment to living here.

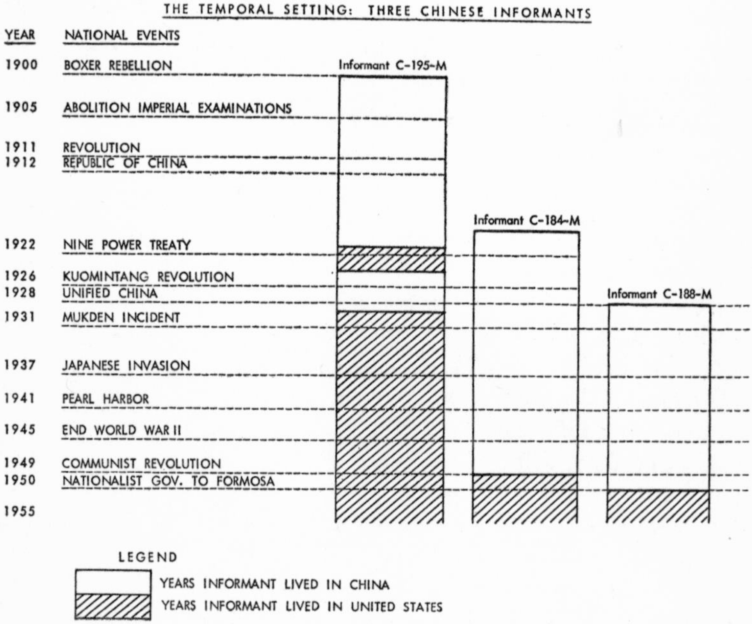
THE TEMPORAL SETTING: THREE CHINESE INFORMANTS
YEAR
NATIONAL EVENTS
1900
BOXER REBELLION
1905
ABOLITION IMPERIAL EXAMINATIONS
1911
REVOLUTION
1912
REPUBLIC OF CHINA
1922
NINE POWER TREATY
1926
KUOMINTANG REVOLUTION
1928
UNIFIED CHINA
1931
MUKDEN INCIDENT
1937
JAPANESE INVASION
1941
PEARL HARBOR
1945
END WORLD WAR II
1949
COMMUNIST REVOLUTION
1950
NATIONALIST GOV. TO FORMOSA
1955
Informant C-195-M
Informant C-184-M
Informant C-188-M
LEGEND
YEARS INFORMANT LIVED IN CHINA
YEARS INFORMANT LIVED IN UNITED STATES

FIG. 1.

The three cases which we shall present are intended to suggest the kinds of individuals, personality structure, and problems which we have encountered in the first months of our work. These three individuals are all men, whom we shall refer to as 195M, 188M, and 184M respectively.

The three men are some years apart in age. The eldest, 195M, was born in 1900 and first came to the United States in 1921; he has made a professional career in this country which has kept him in close contact with China. The next, 184M, was born in 1919; he has a short academic and administrative career behind him in China, and he came to the United States in 1948 for further training. The third, 188M, was born in 1927; he came to the United States in 1950 as a student.

The three men come from different parts of China and from different social milieux. 195M was born in a small village in Northeast China. There, at the turn of the century, at the time of the Boxer Rebellion, he lived in the traditional "big family" of several generations and many relatives. His grandfather and father were scholars. After the

THE SOCIAL SETTING: THREE CHINESE INFORMANTS

	INFORMANT C-195-M	INFORMANT C-184-M	INFORMANT C-188-M
FAMILY BACKGROUND			
REGIONAL ORIGIN:	NORTHEAST CHINA	NORTH CHINA	SOUTH CHINA
COMMUNITY TYPE:	SMALL VILLAGE	SMALL VILLAGE	LARGE CITY
SOCIAL POSITION:	SCHOLAR-GENTRY	SMALL LANDOWNERS	WEALTHY INTELLIGENTSIA
FAMILY LIVING GROUP:	"BIG" FAMILY ("Many Relatives")	"DIVIDED" FAMILY (Grandparents, Parents)	"DIVIDED" FAMILY (Nuclear Family)
PATERNAL ASCENDANTS			
FATHER'S FATHER:	SCHOLAR	SMALL LANDOWNER	HIGH GOVERNMENT OFFICIAL
FATHER:	SCHOLAR-MINOR OFFICIAL TOOK PART 1911 REVOLUTION STUDIED IN JAPAN	SMALL LANDOWNER STUDIED MISSION SCHOOL CONVERTED CHRISTIANITY	ENGINEER STUDIED IN UNITED STATES
INFORMANT			
POSITION IN FAMILY:	YOUNGEST CHILD, 3 SIBS ONLY SON	ELDEST LIVING CHILD, 4 SIBS ELDER SON	ELDEST CHILD, 3 SIBS ELDER SON
EDUCATION:	CLASSICAL EDUCATION MODERN EDUCATION (China and United States)	SOME CLASSICAL EDUCATION MODERN EDUCATION (China and United States)	SOME CLASSICAL EDUCATION MODERN EDUCATION (China and United States)
MARITAL STATUS:	DIVORCED AND REMARRIED (Both Wives of Choice)	DIVORCED (Wife of Choice)	SINGLE
CHILDREN:	FOUR IN UNITED STATES	ONE SON IN CHINA	

FIG. 2.

Revolution, in which he took part, his father studied in Japan. 195M was given a classical as well as a modern education, and he feels himself deeply rooted in traditional Chinese life. However, his grandparents and parents died when he was young, so that he did not carry out his traditional responsibilities but came abroad in 1921. Here he married a wife of his own choice, a woman of Chinese-American background; the marriage failed. Later he married a much younger Chinese woman with a background similar to his and this marriage has been successful. He himself, in his own lifetime, has made the transition from the life of the scholar-gentry to modern Western living.

188M comes from a wealthy and upper-class Chinese family originally from the South. Both grandfathers were high officials in the Chinese government; one was an important figure in the 1911 Revolution. His father was an engineer, trained in the United States. His parents met in the United States and married here, later returning to China. 188M grew up in a small family, but had a great deal of contact with his larger family, especially his grandmother. This family, very traditional in its organization and modern in its outlook, attempted to integrate the new Western and modern attitudes and forms of behavior into the old. The attempt failed and the family broke up; 188M's parents were divorced. Twenty-three years old when he came here in 1950, 188M is left with no very clear view of how his broken past can be woven into a new future.

184M comes from a small village in North China. His grandfather and father were small land owning farmers in the traditional style. The break with the past was essentially made by his father when he was converted to Christianity, got some modern education in a mission school, and founded a small modern village school. 184M had some traditional, but mainly a modern education and became a professional man with a dedicated interest in Chinese social life. He made a marriage of choice in China and has one son. After he came to the United States in 1948 his marriage was used as pressure to force him to return to China and, when he did not go, ended in divorce. It is clear to him that he now could not, if he would, return to mainland China. In his thought and behavior, 184M has been motivated by aims derived from his father's decisions and acts so that although of the three men discussed here he has moved the greatest distance from his home, his life shows the greatest continuity.

SUMMARY OF PSYCHIATRIC DATA

The language barrier, cultural skepticism, and curiosity about psychiatry, have presented problems necessitating a full flexibility in interview techniques. Informants have been seen in from three to five interviews—usually of an hour's length, occasionally clustered within a two to three week period but frequently more widely scattered. On reaching a final clinical evaluation we have not relied solely upon material from our own interviews, but have drawn as well from material obtained by the other research teams, reserving the right to make our own interpretations of their data.

The three men being discussed today share one significant similarity of background: each has enjoyed the advantages and suffered the handicaps of being an eldest son; for one the position was reinforced by the early death of several older siblings. The other two are eldest sons of eldest sons and first male grandchildren.

195M, who has been in this country periodically over the past 35 years, is now in his mid-fifties; a hard working administrator holding a position of considerable prestige and responsibility. He is restless, guarded, fears criticism, speaks of himself as a chronic worrier.

As a child he enjoyed being spoiled by his mother, grandparents, and older sisters, while he remembered his father best for his infrequent presence and heavy hand. In his adolescence he lost first his grandparents and later his parents; and for several years following the mother's death was anxious, insomnic, withdrawn, and worried about his poor health. He emerged from this to make an unsuccessful marriage. With his wife he was clingingly passive, unhappy, but resisted stubbornly her attempts to divorce him. He turned to drinking heavily, suffered a recurrence of the symptoms which followed his mother's death. About 15 years ago when his wife finally obtained a divorce, his symptoms were most disabling. Since his successful remarriage they have not recurred. With his second wife he is more active, feels he is stronger; his behavior towards his children has been patterned after his father's punitive behavior towards him.

Throughout 195M's adult life he has suffered rather severe recurrent depressions whenever his strong passive needs have not been satisfied, first following the death of his mother and grandparents and later with his first wife's failure to respond to these needs. In his second marriage he has found some resolution of this conflict, has assumed a more active role.

188M is a single graduate student in his late twenties; articulate, polished, ambitious, a bit aloof. His ancestors were men of letters, wealth, and influence.

As a child he was irritable and sickly, was moved often, and saw little of either of his parents who quarreled frequently. His strongest attachments were to an elderly governess and to his sickly grandmother. At nine, following the death of the grandmother and the loss of the governess, he remembers little warmth within the household and was not allowed outer contacts, but brought up much as a feudal prince. His parents divorced and during his late adolescence, and at the time of the Japanese Invasion he found himself faced with the responsibility of caring for an infantile, impractical mother who maintained the illusion of her previous wealth and social status. He matured rapidly and painfully, became practical, opportunistic, and somewhat suspicious. Subsequently he has made his own way and is embittered towards his parents. For a short period after his arrival in the United States he attempted to recapture the grandeur of the past, acting out the part of a playboy prince, but has abandoned this.

188M's identifications have been primarily with a class, a way of life, rather than with individuals. Considering his early background and uneven maturation, he has emerged with rather remarkable strengths and resiliencies, and though discontent with his present lot has become intensely practical about his future.

184M is a doctoral student in his middle thirties who came to the United States about five years ago. He is friendly, direct, open, occasionally jolly. His childhood was spent in a small rural village where his father had gained first notoriety and later prestige for having broken with his Buddhist heritage to form the first Christian School in the County. He describes his father as a wise, kind, energetic, inspired and inspiring man and his relationship to him has been that of both disciple and son. The mother is seen in a subservient role, as the father's faithful helper.

During his student days in China he was a leader, a student organizer. He was happily married to a fellow student who initially shared his religious and social ideals but whom he later lost to the Communists when he came to the United States. Following their divorce he became despondent, ruminative, and unable to concentrate upon his studies. He temporarily suspended them and kept himself busy with a menial job until the depression had subsided.

184M's history is remarkable for its freedom from any serious psychopathology. His successful identification with the strong father has left him with little ambivalence in his relationship with other people and though his psychic life is dominated by a rigid conscience, his ego strengths have been sufficient to meet these demands promptly and pleasurably.

SUMMARY OF PSYCHOLOGICAL DATA

The psychological aspect of this study has three goals: (1) to accumulate systematically psychological test data on a variety of individual Chinese; (2) to evaluate these data in order to derive empirically differences in test performances that might be culturally and/or clinically significant; and (3) to evaluate independently each series of protocols and relate these analyses to the total data derived.

The test battery selected was determined by a need to include measures on which there was a body of normative data against which a comparison could be made, as well as unstructured "measuring" devices from which hypotheses could be derived. Consequently, within the framework of the time available to test informants, the following tests were selected and have been systematically administered: (1) the Wechsler-Bellevue Intelligence Scale, Form I; (2) the Thurstone Tem-

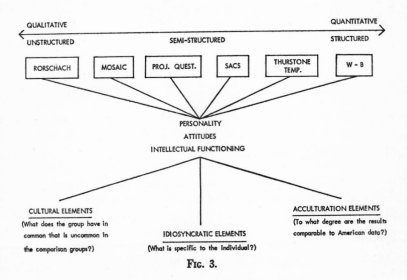

PSYCHOLOGICAL TEST BATTERY

FIG. 3.

perment Scale; (3) the Rorschach; (4) the Lowenfeld Mosaic; (5) the Sachs Sentence Completion; and (6) an adaptation of the Projective Questionnaire as described in *Assessment of Men.*

The testing procedure has been to administer the tests in standard forms, carefully documenting the test behavior item by item and test by test. Even though their "first" or native language is Chinese, all of our informants are essentially competent in English. The test materials have been administered in this language and one of our objectives is to determine the effects of this type of stress on their test performance.

We were interested in discovering whether test differences between normative groups are systematic and therefore predictable from group to group, as well as selective and therefore useful as clues to individual adjustment. If we should isolate significant cultural differences, we should like to try to devise an "Index of Acculturation," i.e. a method of projecting the extent to which a given individual has identified with the new cultural milieu to which he has been forced to adapt.

It may be of interest to report on some impressions gained to date. As a group, these Chinese seem to be considerably more threatened by the completely unstructured personality projection devices than their prototypes in the American culture. The Rorschach is a particularly difficult test and the typical manner of response is a guarded, W—oriented, very low production record. Literalness, tipping that is very close to edging, high P production and rationalization through pleading language difficulty are common manifestations. The instructions to the Mosaic are almost routinely resisted, but once the task is undertaken, unusually creative and dynamic designs are produced. The semi-structured projective devices are usually responded to in a literal but very revealing manner, particularly when the subjects are asked to fill them out in writing alone. The presence of the examiner increases the resistance to these tests, but as yet there is little evidence of a cultural pattern in this resistance as revealed by the words they ask to have defined or the concepts explained.

The Wechsler is the least threatening test, but appears to produce the most tension. There is considerable need for intellectual achievement among our group by virtue of the nature of the sample. Consequently in the Wechsler situation they are more anxious than they are guarded. The motivation towards the test situation is almost opposite to that of the less structured tests, and although in the strict sense the quantitative scores may be less precise than might be desired the patterning of responses is yielding rich data for interpretation and the building of hypotheses.

The quantity of data available makes it impossible to dwell at length on the test-expressed psychodynamics of the three informants who are our focus of attention in this paper. However, the following summaries of impressions may be useful.

195M is an intellectualizing male with a WB IQ of 121 who reflects considerable anxiety in interpersonal relationships. He is quite vulnerable to threats of loss of prestige. He is active in gaining leadership and somewhat pedantic; intellectual rationalization and identification are his primary psychological mechanisms. Depression is very threatening to him and considerable amounts of his psychological energies are devoted to the control of depression.

188M is a passive, dependent male with W-B IQ of 122 who exploits his dependency in a highly socially acceptable manner. He plays the social role demanded of him in any milieu effectively and is accepted as a well-behaved, socially integrated person. He is passive in gaining leadership, reacts against hostile authority but seeks supportive authority. Intellectual rationalization and socially acceptable introjection are his primary psychological mechanisms. Loss of support is very threatening to him, but since he is so effective in gaining support this loss occurs infrequently. When it does occur it tends to be disabling because of his lack of experience dealing with it.

184M is a socially pedantic and "proper" male with a W-B IQ of 126. He evidences considerable drive and energy in effecting social reform and is inclined to deal with persons as prototypes rather than as individuals. He deals with mundane things with considerable originality but shows little creativity. Repression is his primary psychological mechanism. Social isolation is very threatening to him, and his psychological energy is devoted to group activity rationalized on abstract and idealistic terms.

SUMMARY OF MEDICAL DATA

Each of these informants was interviewed extensively by a physician and a thorough medical biography was obtained from each. The family history, the story of birth and development, and all pertinent medical episodes were inquired into at length. The age at which each illness occurred and the circumstances surrounding its occurrence were carefully described. A complete physical examination was performed in every case. Laboratory diagnostic procedures were also carried out when these were pertinent.

The medical data relating to these three informants is summarized in outline form in the charts.

195M: Informant 195M was essentially healthy during childhood. He had three of the childhood exanthemata which could be identified by name and description. He could recall no other illnesses or accidents of any sort until he was 16 years old, nor could any be uncovered by the physician, who questioned him carefully. During the period from age 16 to age 24 he had recurrent and moderately severe symptoms of anxiety, tension, and depression accompanied by intractable insomnia, recurrent constipation, and hemorrhoids. This period of illness coincided with the disruption of his family and with his coming to the United States as a student. Throughout this time he was in severe conflict about his relation to his family and his ability to fulfill the role which he had outlined for himself.

195M had few symptoms of illness from age 24 to 29 and considered himself to be essentially healthy. This period coincided with his return to China and his participation in the hazards and discomforts of the Kuomintang Revolution.

From age 29 to age 43, 195M experienced a recurrence of his previous psychological symptoms with steadily increasing severity. His bowel symptoms returned also. In addition to this, he developed severe hay fever and also had four or five disabling upper respiratory infections per year, each lasting about a week. During the latter part of this period he began to drink increasingly in order to relieve his tension. He also immersed himself in driving, compulsive overwork. The well-documented case of hepatitis, which began within a week atfer his divorce, took place after a period of intense overwork, sleeplessness, fatigue, emotional conflict, and excessive alcoholic intake. This period of illness coincides temporally with the period of his unsatisfactory first marriage.

From age 43 to 47 this informant's psychological symptoms gradually subsided. He gave up drinking and cut down upon his excessive business activity upon the advice of his physician. During this time he had typical and moderately severe episodes of gout, involving several joints.

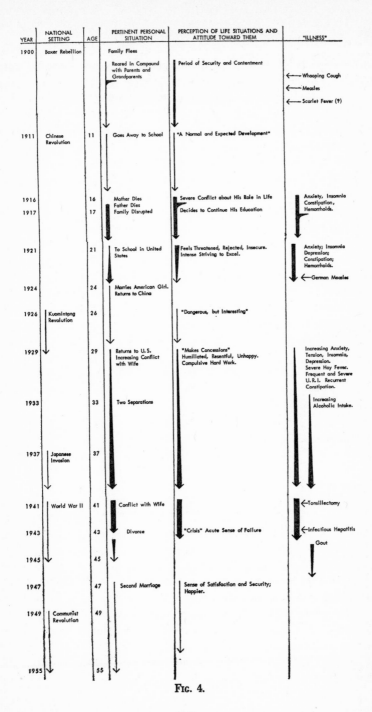

FIG. 4.

From age 47 to the present time (age 55) this informant has been largely symptom-free. This period of relative good health coincides with the period of his second and more satisfactory marriage.

188M: Informant 188M appears to have been essentially healthy up until his seventh year of age. We have no evidence that he did not enjoy a normal development up to that time. This period of

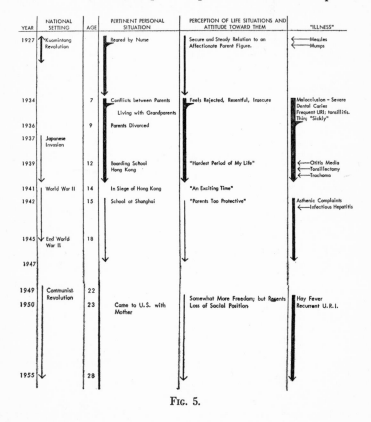

YEAR	NATIONAL SETTING	AGE	PERTINENT PERSONAL SITUATION	PERCEPTION OF LIFE SITUATIONS AND ATTITUDE TOWARD THEM	"ILLNESS"
1927	Kuomintang Revolution		Reared by Nurse	Secure and Steady Relation to an Affectionate Parent Figure.	Measles Mumps
1934		7	Conflicts between Parents	Feels Rejected, Resentful, Insecure	Malocclusion – Severe Dental Caries Frequent URI; tonsillitis. Thin; "Sickly"
			Living with Grandparents		
1936		9	Parents Divorced		
1937	Japanese Invasion				
1939		12	Boarding School Hong Kong	"Hardest Period of My Life"	Otitis Media Tonsillectomy Trachoma
1941	World War II	14	In Siege of Hong Kong	"An Exciting Time"	
1942		15	School at Shanghai	"Parents Too Protective"	Asthenic Complaints Infectious Hepatitis
1945	End World War II	18			
1947					
1949	Communist Revolution	22			Hay Fever
1950		23	Came to U.S. with Mother	Somewhat More Freedom; but Resents Loss of Social Position	Recurrent U.R.I.
1955		28			

FIG. 5.

relative good health temporally correlates with a period of undisturbed and secure relationship to a stable interpersonal environment.

From age seven to age 14 this informant was subject to recurrent illness. He had frequent severe respiratory infections, recurrent tonsillitis and otitis media. His permanent teeth erupted irregularly; he developed a marked malocclusion and had painful dental caries. He also developed trachoma, which was successfully treated. This period of illness coincided temporally with the disruption of his family, a profound disturbance of his relations with his parents, and his separation from the governess who had reared him up to that time.

From age 15 to age 22 his general health improved but he continued to have periods of fatigue and asthenia. This was a period of great physical hardship for him, during which his interpersonal relations became established on a more secure basis although they were still not entirely satisfactory.

Following his arrival in the United States in 1949, most of his asthenic symptoms subsided; but he has developed hay fever of moderate severity and has again begun to have two or three upper respiratory infections each year, each of which disables him for a few days. This period in the United States has been one of less physical hardship and greater freedom from parental restrictions. However, he has had some difficulty in adapting to his loss of social position and in settling upon a satisfactory career in this country.

184M: Informant 184M has had few detectable evidences of illness throughout his entire life. Although undoubtedly he had some minor illnesses during his childhood, he can recall none until he was 14 years of age. At this time he developed mild chronic lower abdominal pain which, by the clinical description, appears to have been the result of a disturbance of the lower bowel function. His appendix was removed by a surgeon who thought that this might relieve his symptoms. This period of minor symptomology coincided with the time when he was first sent away to boarding school. He felt somewhat insecure and threatened by the new environment in which he was striving to excel in both studies and athletic pursuits. His symptoms at this time were in fact minor and not disabling. They subsided by his 16th year and have not recurred since.

During the period from age 16 to age 30 he was entirely free from symptoms. One can find no evidence that he had an illness of any sort. This was a period in which the physical aspects of his life were seriously dislocated by the war and in which he was subjected to recurrent physical exposure, hard work, danger, and occasional lack of food. He had a variety of jobs, all of them involving responsibility and requiring him to cope with a number of new situations in various parts of China; he transferred from China to the United

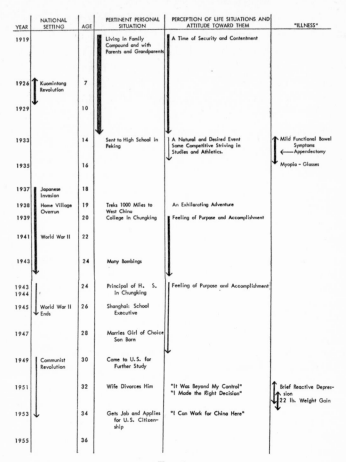

YEAR	NATIONAL SETTING	AGE	PERTINENT PERSONAL SITUATION	PERCEPTION OF LIFE SITUATIONS AND ATTITUDE TOWARD THEM	"ILLNESS"
1919			Living in Family Compound and with Parents and Grandparents	A Time of Security and Contentment	
1926	Kuomintang Revolution	7			
1929		10			
1933		14	Sent to High School in Peking	A Natural and Desired Event Same Competitive Striving in Studies and Athletics.	Mild Functional Bowel Symptoms ←—Appendectomy
1935		16			Myopia – Glasses
1937	Japanese Invasion	18			
1938	Home Village Overrun	19	Treks 1000 Miles to West China	An Exhilarating Adventure	
1939		20	College in Chungking	Feeling of Purpose and Accomplishment	
1941	World War II	22			
1943		24	Many Bombings		
1943 1944		24	Principal of H. S. in Chungking	Feeling of Purpose and Accomplishment	
1945	World War II Ends	26	Shanghai: School Executive		
1947		28	Marries Girl of Choice Son Born		
1949	Communist Revolution	30	Came to U.S. for Further Study		
1951		32	Wife Divorces Him	"It Was Beyond My Control" "I Made the Right Decision"	Brief Reactive Depression 22 lb. Weight Gain
1953		34	Gets Job and Applies for U.S. Citizenship	"I Can Work for China Here"	
1955		36			

Fig. 6.

States and adapted himself to the American environment. Throughout this time he had a strong feeling of satisfaction in accomplishment related to his goals in life.

When this man was forced to choose between returning to China and being divorced by his wife, he had a relatively short period of preoccupation, insomnia, and depression. The reaction was appropriate to the situation in which he found himself and, considering the serious consequences of the choice he had to make, his recovery from these symptoms was rapid.

GENERAL SUMMARY AND CONCLUSIONS

We are not prepared to draw any definitive conclusions from our studies at this time. The primary purpose of this communication is to provide a description of our methods and to give some illustrative examples from the material we are dealing with. However, we do feel free to comment upon some of the phenomena which we are observing.

From the point of view of the anthropologist it seems clear that the informants are individually different in their background, life experience, and personal attitudes; but all of them have maintained their sense of personal identity through a period of change. Their adaptation to life in China and in the United States has been one of continual situational adjustment. What we are seeing, essentially, is the effect of rapid and diffuse culture change on the total personality of the individual. In modern China, change has taken place at different speeds and has had a different impact on different individuals, on the family, and on larger social groups; and change has had a different content and has been differently interpreted. For our informants, coming to the United States and adapting to life here seems to represent not a sudden and dramatic break with a stable cultural and social background, but another episode in the rapid and continuous cultural and social change which has been going on throughout their lifetime. So, studying the lives of individuals, we are inevitably concerned not only with the dynamics of character formation and with the effects of life experiences on individuals, but also with the whole problem of cultural and social process.

From the point of view of the psychiatrist it may be said that these informants do have certain similarities in behavior, attitudes, and value systems, but they are quite different from each other in their fundamental personality patterns. The types of fundamental personality which we have encountered, and the types of symptom formation which we have seen, appear to be no different from those which we commonly see among people from Western cultures.

From the point of view of the psychologist it may be said that the test materials appear to yield valid results with this group of informants, and they can be utilized and interpreted without great difficulty. It is too early to state what are the culturally determined regularities in the responses, what their importance may be.

From the point of view of the physician there are several noteworthy phenomena. First, some of these informants have experienced many illnesses of various types involving a number of organ systems; others have had very few illnesses of any type. Most of those whom we have seen have had some illnesses, but not a great many. Illnesses, when they occur, seem to occur in clusters over a period of years. During such periods the informant will display a number of illnesses of several types; during other periods of his life he will be largely asymptomatic and apparently free from all illness. Among these informants, periods of illness correlate most closely with periods of disruption of significant interpersonal relationships or with conflicts arising out of these. Social change and cultural change appear to be related to the development of illness primarily through their effect upon significant interpersonal relationships. Geographical changes, changes in the physical environment, and exposure to hazards and increased opportunities for infection appear to be much less frequent causes of periods of illness.

Discussion of Chapters 10-11

By LEO ALEXANDER, M.D.*

IT IS A PLEASURE and a privilege to discuss Doctor Syz' excellent
paper, for it is an unusual combination of the philosophically
perceptive and the clinically sound. His extensive and thoughtful
development of theory requires and merits careful study.

Dr. Syz develops his concepts against the background of organismic
field theory in which part and whole are considered interdependent,
forming a system of functioning in which alteration in any part will
lead to alteration in the whole pattern or system. He applies this concept both to functioning within the individual personality and to the
highly complex interactions between the individual and his environment. He also employs to a considerable degree Trigant Burrow's concept of the "social neurosis" as a universal human maladaptation
arising from over-emphasis on maintaining and constantly enhancing
a socially acceptable self-picture. This process may absorb too much
energy from other, more constructive elements in the personality and
lead to asocial and neurotic reactions.

In this approach, Doctor Syz is in remarkable accord with the views
propounded many years ago by Karen Horney[1] and with modern
existentialist thought as expressed by Heidegger,[2] Plessner,[3] Binswanger,[4] Sonneman,[5] and others; views which have made greater
inroads into psychotherapeutic thinking in Europe than in this country.

Doctor Syz believes the common denominator of neurosis to be
an undue and overvalent drive to maintain a socially acceptable self-
picture, which may be carried out at the expense of the basic constructive, integrative, and affectional drives with resulting distortion to
the entire personality configuration that may lead to various neurotic
manifestations and defensive maneuvers. Moreover, the effort to maintain this distorted and unrealistic self-image brings these individuals
into increasingly inadequate relatedness with others that in turn generates anxiety, since no human being can stand alone; the essence of
human life consists of dynamic interchanges between the individual
and those around him.

* Clinical Instructor in Psychiatry, Tufts University Medical School, Boston,
Mass.

I agree with the author—and he with me[6]—that the psychotherapeutic process must be founded on feeling-relatedness of therapist and patient independent of theoretical assumptions, and that this feeling-relatedness may produce good results quite irrespective of the therapist's theoretical leanings. But I also agree wholeheartedly with Doctor Syz in his opinion that pithy goal-directedness in therapy can greatly accelerate its effect. In fact, the most important therapeutic derivative of his organismic concept is his recognition of the clinically important fact that readjustment at a pivotal point in a current problem may bring about constructive changes in the total psychodynamic pattern. This view is also in agreement with Gurjiew's[7] to whom mental illness meant a state of impaired harmony of functioning that could be brought about by disturbance of even one small segment of the personality, while the total vast richness of the remainder of the personality apart from this one segment remained at least latently unimpaired. Hence restoration of harmony by stimulating this small part to normal functioning was to him the decisive step, if not the secret, in restoring health.

Similarly, Irving Rosen and I[8] found that resolution of specific issues in neuroses and psychoses has far-reaching effects; a fact prompting the conclusion that anxiety may act simultaneously both as symptom and as secondary cause for further dysfunctioning. This is in accordance with Jerome Frank's[9] and Fenichel's[10] findings concerning the secondary disruption of the ego by anxiety. I believe that Doctor Syz' emphasis on the crucial importance of pivotal points is based on the same clinical recognition that malfunctioning, whatever its relationship to early genetic issues, is organized in the present around certain pivotal points of disharmony within the personality and between the person and his social environment.

Doctor Syz—in line with Lauretta Bender, David Levy, Ashley Montagu, and others—believes there is a powerful inherent drive toward healthy development, social interrelatedness, love and harmony which is hard to block or divert either by the patient's own psychopathology or by adverse outer conditions. He notes that in contrast to this primary propensity toward integrity and affiliation there are strong forces that make for egocentricity, oppositional behavior, and emotional detachment in the network of customary interchanges that form one's social milieu. He believes that hostility is not a primary drive, but rather an initially constructive reaction that has become secondarily defensive—or, as he says, it is "an adaptive faux pas".

In his practical therapeutic work, Doctor Syz makes a concerted attack on what he calls the "socially favored self-image." This is perhaps another way to describe "perfectionism" which I feel is an important cause of emotional disorder,[11] and which I believe must be dealt with psychotherapeutically in a very direct manner. It is essential to help the patient to give up unattainable and unrealistic perfectionistic goals and standards. In this connection it is important to point out that Stainbrook,[12] in a very perceptive sociological study, has found ideas of status to be the mainspring of depressive reactions.

I find it a particularly attractive feature of the author's method that by exploring with the patient, as he does, the artificial self-image common to all mankind which arouses certain common emotional reactions and defenses, he helps to depersonalize the patient's reactions of hostility and guilt; thus by shifting emphasis in this manner he gets around many resistances in therapy. I believe this to be an extremely important clinical point because the therapist who proceeds in this manner, such as some of us have proposed, tells the patient in effect: "This is your illness. These are the things that made you ill. This is not the real you." Thus the patient is relieved of further guilt, self-reproach, and anxiety. In certain other therapeutic systems there is often an unfortunate emphasis upon the implication: "This is you. That is what you are like," which sometimes becomes the source of new anxiety, new defenses, and further guilt reactions. The author, in line with my own favored therapeutic approach, tells the patient explicitly and implicitly: "This is not the real you. This is something that makes you sick; this is your illness. You will free yourself from it and I will help you to do so." This formulation is, I believe, both realistically and scientifically valid, as well as clinically sound and practically helpful.

When Doctor Syz then proceeds to point out to the patient that all his conscious and unconscious attempts to uphold his artificial self-image have not protected him from the destructive effects of his self-centered trends and competitiveness the patient can accept such interpretations—which are so important in arousing a will to change—without resentment; and therapy proceeds unimpeded. I think that the author has made a great contribution by pointing this out in such a lucid manner.

I am very much impressed with the examples he gives and the skill with which he helps his patients. Take the case of the over-protective mother when he helps her to understand that what she has considered "self-sacrificing love, thoughtfulness, and moral superiority"—albeit mixed with reactions of irritation—is actually possessive self-interestedness. I think a particularly fortunate formulation in terms of what the patient could accept was to call all such domineering attitudes "trespassing" and "misappropriation" of the rights of others. These were the very misdemeanors which this patient so thoroughly resented, and when once she saw the connection she wanted to dissociate herself from them. I believe this interpretation of the mother's overprotectiveness as actual trespassing made it possible for her to give it up, while as long as she believed her behavior to be an expression of love and protection it fitted in with the socially conditioned self-image she was trying to maintain.

In other words, the pivotal issue was resolved by insight-therapy without recourse to tracing back to earlier events, which were not necessarily germane to the acute problem.

I believe that in the past we have placed too much emphasis on early genetic events. Since many of these earlier genetic events are so common to all human beings they certainly do not adequately discriminate between well and sick people. I therefore believe they are merely the common mainsprings of all human behavior, not the pivotal points at which these patients become sick. The pivotal point, according to my understanding of Doctor Syz, is the personality distortion arising from efforts to enhance an unrealistic self-image without realizing that much of one's behavior is based on egocentric and socially nonacceptable motives.

In the case just mentioned the patient was surprised at her own altered attitude which permitted her to disregard issues which previously had upset her greatly. I believe that these latter issues were ancillary to the central issue of possessiveness which was here so ingeniously resolved. I think possessiveness is frequently a very important issue, particularly in child-parent relationships, and I am glad that here the author for the first time in this paper mentioned the word "issue," which is a clinically practical concept. Irving Rosen and I[8] have been able to distinguish a good many similar issues, such as envy, perfectionism, acceptance, physical integrity, and others which, in the light of the author's very lucid presentation, have to do with difficulties arising from unrealistic self-images.

Doctor Syz proposes the name "inclusive revaluation" for this therapeutic technique. I do not know whether this term is the happiest that might be chosen because it is so hard to visualize what the author means before one has actually studied his paper. I would favor the simpler term "resolution of issues."

And again, I would like to commend Doctor Syz for the ingenious way in which he does not insist on going further than he needs to go. In other words, I believe he has resolved the issue of perfectionism concerning his own method of therapy by his recognition of the existence of inherent constructive forces that are released in the patient by the resolution of these issues. The author has thus been able to carry out brief psychotherapy in a truly ingenious way. He has recognized that once an issue of the illness is resolved and the anxiety so relieved, varying degrees of psychodynamic reorganization will occur, and the forces toward health will help many other things fall in place.

I believe therefore that Doctor Syz has contributed an important, workable, theoretically and clinically sound method which is eminently suitable for brief psychotherapy and which will contribute further toward freeing psychotherapy from the rigid mold of orthodox perfectionism in which it has tended to be cast so often in the past. The perceptive recognition of the issues that need to be "inclusively re-valuated" in the therapeutic work by the doctor and his patient is presented here in a clearcut, didactic context.

I hope that Doctor Syz' valuable method will be accepted and utilized. Its succinctness will make it possible to be appreciated and applied also by physicians not primarily trained in psychotherapy, for at the general practice level I believe much useful therapeutic work can and must be done.

An important ingredient in his therapy is his firm belief in the innate, healthy propensities, the "biological, integrative, and socially cohesive assets" of the individual.

Doctor Hinkle and his collaborators' interesting study corroborates Doctor Syz' views in many respects. Their conclusions can be summarized as follows: among their Chinese subjects unable to return to their own country, periods of illness correlate most closely with periods of disruption of or conflict arising in significant interpersonal relationships while the geographic change in physical environment and the resulting adaptive problems appear to be much less frequent causes of periods of illness. The authors are aware that their sample represented a particularly mobile social segment of the population, for whom coming to the United States represented not a sudden and dramatic break with a stable cultural and social background, but merely another episode in the rapid and continuous social change which they had known throughout their lifetime. Moreover, it is evident from the authors' data that their subjects were actually bilingual and bicultural. Furthermore, they were members of a sociocultural and intellectual stratum which is not limited by vertical boundaries but cuts horizontally across them; in this sense they suffered less ecologic dislocation in being transplanted from Peking to Princeton than had they been banished from Peking to Yenan in their own country.

The authors' study thus highlights the factors that make for successful adaptation. There was capacity to communicate by language and shared socio-cultural values. Furthermore, the socio-intellectual stratum of society in which these subjects were transplanted was hospitable, helpful, and supportive, possibly as a result of reaction formation against repressed xenophobia, but with the definite result that these subjects suffered no significant loss of status or self-respect.

This is the traditional helpful and supportive welcome that this stratum of this country's society has always extended to political and religious refugees, including those of the Nazi era. When some of these same originally welcome exiles later re-entered this country as veterans of the United States Army, they met—some of them for the first time—a hostile, competitive stand-offishness which they had not experienced when they had been exiles; obviously a sign that they had now become truly integrated into the life of the country, including its internal tensions and family squabbles.

In other words, this stratum of society repressed its xenophobia, but not its fear of its own returning soldiers. I wonder in which way the acceptance of these Chinese refugees differs from the acceptance accorded by this same stratum of society to the young generation of American-born Chinese.

In contrast to the individuals described by the authors are those groups of migrants and immigrants who encounter total language barrier and profound change of status, such as the Polish farmers who used to come to work in West German mines. Among these men rather characteristic severe stuporous anxiety psychoses developed, with which I became familiar during my psychiatric training in Frankfurt on Main. In spite of the best care then possible some of these men died much in the manner elucidated by Doctor Richter's recent studies on trapped animals. I saw such a case recently: a former sergeant of police from Palermo, Italy, who came to this country at his wife's insistence, only to meet a total language barrier and total loss of status. I believe that electroshock in this case was a life-saving measure. His eventual rehabilitation will depend on his capacity for mastering the English language and on his again achieving status and suitable acculturation.

The authors' perceptive study is of great practical importance in these days of dislocations of populations and belies Kipling's "East is East and West is West"; apparently our artificial iron curtains are more divisive than oceans or continents.

REFERENCES

1. HORNEY, K.: The Neurotic Personality of our Time. New York, Norton, 1937.
2. HEIDEGGER, M.: Existence and Being. Introd. by W. Brock, Chicago, Regnery, 1949.
3. PLESNER, H.: Uber die Menschenverachtung. In Offener Horizont. Munich, Piper, 1953.
4. BINSWANGER, L.: Grundformen und Erkenntnis menschlichen Daseins. Zurich, Niehans, 1942.
5. SONNEMANN, U.: Existence and Therapy. New York, Grune & Stratton, 1954.
6. ALEXANDER, L.: Treatment of Mental Disorder. Philadelphia, W. B. Saunders Co., 1953, I-XI, 1-507.
7. GURJIEFF, G.: All and Everything. New York, Harcourt, Brace & Co., 1950, pp. 14-15.
8. ALEXANDER, L. AND ROSEN, I. M.: Management of psychological issues in conjunction with physical treatment, Dis. Nerv. Syst., 16: 232-236, 1955.
9. FRANK, J. D. Psychotherapeutic aspects of symptomatic treatment. Am. J. Psychiat., 103: 21-25, 1946.
10. FENICHEL, O.: The Psychoanalytic Theory of Neurosis. New York, W. W. Norton & Co., 1945, I-X, 1-703.
11. ALEXANDER, L.: Treatment of Mental Disorder, pp. 407-415.
12. STAINBROOK, E.: A Cross-Cultural Evaluation of Depressive Reactions. In Depression, Hoch, P. H., and Zubin, J. New York, Grune & Stratton, 1954.

12

Samuel W. Hamilton Award
AWARENESS, ATTENTION & PHYSIOLOGY
OF THE BRAIN STEM

By STANLEY COBB, M.D., D.Sc.*

D R. HAMILTON was 10 years my senior, so I remember meeting him with some awe at the various conventions when we came together. With his wide view of psychiatry and his great interest in making the mental hospital a factor in public health, as well as making psychiatry a part of general medicine, I am sure he would have approved of your program this year with its emphasis on experimental psychopathology. And I appreciate deeply the honor of being asked to give the Samuel W. Hamilton Memorial Lecture.

It is obvious that in my title I am trying to avoid the term "consciousness." It is a word so often misused and so variously used that it can hardly be considered a scientific term. Many psychologists, psychiatrists and neurologists use the term as practically synonymous with "mind";[1,2] others accent the variety of uses and insist on defining the word anew for each use.[3]

In a paper appearing in May, 1955, Rioch[4] has at last defined "consciousness" in an operational way. He describes certain characteristics of the patterns of interaction observed. These patterns of interaction (or "transactions") are then correlated with the anatomy and physiology of the brain. This is an important paper and can be read and re-read with profit by all psychiatrists, especially as it gives a definite idea of what is meant by "the unconscious" as used by psychoanalysts. He mentions much important new work, and says there is evidence for connections from particular cortical areas to particular structures in the sub-thalamus and midbrain. But he also agrees that work on alertness and sleep indicates that certain mechanisms modify

* Bullard Professor of Neuropathology, Harvard University, Emeritus; Consultant, Massachusetts General Hospital, Boston; Consulting Neurologist, Boston City Hospital and Children's Hospital, Boston.

the functions of the whole brain. He makes an interesting comparison of alertness to anxiety.

My data apply only to part of what Rioch calls "consciousness"—to that part related to the general integration of the brain to which one may attribute changes in awareness, alertness, attention, and wakefulness. My own experience in this field is not experimental. I have only observed the "experiments of nature" as Adolf Meyer used to call clinical phenomena.

With the cooperation of Dr. Fuller Albright's endocrine study group at the Massachusetts General Hospital and Dr. J. C. White's neurosurgical service, Dr. Bruce Sloane and I were able to study 116 cases with disease of the pituitary gland or its neighborhood. This group of patients was chosen because we had formerly studied the mental reactions of patients with other endocrine disorders,[5,6] so the patients showing panhypopituitarism seemed especially worthy of psychiatric scrutiny.

The 116 cases, when classified according to endocrine status (as determined by clinical observation and from laboratory data supplied by Dr. Albright's group) fell into three categories:

> Panhypopituitarism 48
> Other endocrine syndromes 43
> No endocrine dysfunction 25

When classified etiologically the causes were as follows:

> Tumor 88
> Necrosis and atrophy 22
> Unknown 6

When divided in relation to the presence or absence of mental symptoms the data show the following:

> Mental symptoms 51
> No mental symptoms 65

Forty-four of the 51 disorders with mental symptoms were caused by tumors; 22 showed the panhypopituitary syndrome. Of the 65 cases without mental symptoms, 44 were caused by tumor and 26 showed the syndrome of panhypopituitarism. In other words, 43% of the cases were mentally disturbed. Under this heading are not included personality traits such as the passivity, immaturity and shyness seen in the patients with gonad deficiency, nor the lack of drive and "flat affect" of the patients with Sheehan's syndrome developing post-partum. "Mentally disturbed" in these patients meant some degree of intellectual deterioration, somnolence, apathy, disinhibition, and memory loss.

Five patients from the neurosurgical service illustrate this especially well. They have been used by Doctor White[7] to illustrate the need for early operation, before mental symptoms occur in a patient with pituitary tumor. It is then already too late for operation, and radiation therapy is usually only palliative.

Case I

Forty-six, male, faulty vision for nine years; retired from Navy to live in China because of restricted temporal visual fields, did nothing about it until return to America when his mother noticed personality changes consisting of increasing apathy with irritable outbursts of profanity. Then he had three epileptic seizures and was hospitalized. Under observation he was found to be generally dull with periods of irritable restlessness during which he was belligerent, profane and showed poor judgment. His behavior strongly reminded one of a patient after lobotomy. He had the characteristic findings of a mild hypopituitarism. X-ray showed great erosion of the sella. At operation (undertaken reluctantly but deemed necessary because of the fits and subsequent stupor) the tumor was found extending into the frontal lobes, and was partly removed. He died 18 hours after operation. The tumor was found to have extended not only frontally but posteriorly and laterally into the temporal lobes. It was a chromophobe adenoma.

Case II

A housewife of 43 complained of visual failure for 16 months; with amenorrhaea, lactorrhaea, and obesity. She had been treated by X-ray of the pituitary region. Then headaches came on and vision again failed. Operation revealed a large suprasellar cyst, which was evacuated. It was found to be a chromophobe adenoma. Vision again improved. But six months later loss of vision necessitated another operation, with removal of more tumor and visual improvement for only six weeks this time. An operation for transnasal drainage was performed, with improvement in vision for nine months. Then mental symptoms appeared; she became drowsy, confused, and showed a marked memory defect with confabulation. In two months she deteriorated from an ambitious and conscientious housewife to a slothful and slovenly woman. Mental examination showed poor memory, loss of retention and attention, and inability to understand similarities. She confabulated freely. Another operation was performed and the tumor was found to extend upward into the third ventricle. Two weeks later she was still confabulating, attention was somewhat improved, but she was disoriented for time and place. Memory and retention were still very poor. Because of increasing internal hydrocephalus a ventriculomastoidostomy was performed. This relieved pressure, but she became increasingly stuporous and died a month later. A large, partly cystic tumor was found at the base of the brain completely filling the third ventricle and compressing the diencephalon. Diagnosis: chromophobe adenoma.

Case III

A housewife of 52 who had had signs of acromegaly for 15 years had concomitant glaucoma which led to failure to diagnose the cause of the gradual loss of vision. She had persistent headaches, large nose, hands, feet, and sinuses; diabetes mellitus. The sella was enlarged. She was drowsy by day and restless at night, her mental processes were slow, and she had difficulty remembering and in concentrating her attention. There were many paranoid ideas. A transnasal operation was performed with the removal of 10 cc. of fluid, leaving a small cavity. Headaches abated but vision remained at little more than light perception. The mental state became more disturbed during the next six months. Pneumo-encephalography showed a large tumor with extension upward. Another transnasal operation was performed with little relief; specimens taken at operation proved it to be a chromophil adenoma in which the eosinophilic cells were no longer secreting.

Case IV

A 60-year-old negro began losing vision four years before admission, until he could see only to count fingers; and that was restricted to the upper nasal quadrants of the fields. Endocrinologically he showed the symptoms and chemical changes of a mild hypopituitarism. X-ray showed marked destruction of the sella and of the sphenoids; pneumo-encephalography indicated extensive forward and upward growth. He was dull a good deal of the time, but when aroused was restless and suspicious; paranoid delusions were conspicuous at times. Operation disclosed a large suprasellar tumor, part of which was removed. He had post-operative hyponatremia which responded poorly to salt and cortisone therapy. Later his delusions increased and he was confused, belligerent, profane and seemed to be having hallucinations. Radiation therapy was of no avail. Three months after operation he was sent to a mental hospital where he died about a month later. Diagnosis: chromophobe adenoma.

Case V

A 46-year-old man had headaches for two years with visual difficulty for three months; and had the endocrine picture of a mild panhypopituitarism. Visual field examination showed a typical bitemporal hemianopsia; X-ray showed an enlarged and eroded sella; Pneumo-encephalography revealed a displacement of the floor of the third ventricle upward and backward. At operation a large suprasellar cyst was evacuated. At a second operation two months later a large solid tumor was removed. After operation there was polydipsia and polyuria and a shock-like picture, but he was soon stabilized and returned home. A year later vision showed no improvement; he had one convulsion, was apathetic, but when aroused showed emotional outbursts of weeping and anger. His memory was poor; with an effort he could concentrate his attention on a problem but his responses were slow, circumstantial, and labored. His perceptions were dulled. He had no delusions. His general information was greatly restricted. Diagnosis: Craniopharyngioma.

DISCUSSION

From the clinical standpoint these cases indicate that there are two types of change of personality found in disease of the pituitary region. The first is the less conspicuous, being minor and chronic and causing behavioral disturbances often considered within normal limits; probably due to endocrine dysfunction. The second is more acute and causes mental deterioration; probably due to pressure on the brain. These five cases illustrate the latter.

Personality changes are common in patients with endocrine disturbances. Panhypopituitarism, especially if the gonads are much affected, often makes a person immature, shy, and passive. This picture was common in our survey of 116 cases. The sudden onset of Sheehan's syndrome may be like a sudden castration, causing a lack of initiative and drive, a "flat affect" and much anxiety. Replacement therapy in some patients caused a return of libido after years of impotence. Such events change social relations radically and upset the patient's interpersonal adjustments. Clinical pictures of this kind might be considered as the endocrine aspect of the personality problem. They are often severe but can usually be treated by a physician who not only understands the endocrine situation but has a knowledge of psychiatric reactions.

When symptoms of damage to the brain appear the approach must be quite different. The symptoms, as they were shown in the five severe cases, are tabulated in Table 1:

TABLE 1. *Distribution of Psychological Symptoms*

Case	1	2	3	4	5
Convulsions	+				+
Irritable, Restless	+	+			
Belligerent or Profane	+			+	
Poor Judgment	+	+		+	+
Delusions or Hallucinations		+	+	+	?
Paranoid or Suspicious			+	+	
Loss of Memory		+	+	+	+
Confabulation		+		+	
Concentration and Attention Loss		+		+	+
Dull, Slow, or Apathetic	+	+	+	+	+

Such mental symptoms are familiar to physicians who deal with diseases of the brain: tumor, trauma, or inflammation. Case I presented a picture remarkably similar to that of a person shortly after he has had an extensive bilateral leucotomy. This was the patient whose frontal lobes were most extensively invaded by tumor. The other four patients were rather similar to each other, but their symptoms varied greatly in severity. All were dull, slow, and apathetic most of the time, but they could be aroused and caused to react, sometimes violently. At such times they showed lack of inhibition and could be emotional or belligerent. Poor judgment was obvious; three of them showed paranoid delusions and two had hallucinations. All four had disturbances of memory; in two this was accompanied by confabulation. The examiners remarked on the similarity of the symptoms to those seen in Korsakow's psychosis. Difficulty in concentration on a task was especially noticeable in four patients. They could not keep their attention centered on a problem for long enough to do a continuous job. For example, the subtraction of "serial-sevens" was slowly done with much effort and many inaccuracies. Their perceptions were dull, and they were often said to be disoriented, but this seemed to be due more to apathy than to confusion. When aroused to good cooperation for a few minutes their responses were surprisingly accurate and showed that they were still capable of abstraction.

These four are the patients whose tumors largely spread upward, or upward and backward, causing pressure on the diencephalon. The lesions are too gross to allow for accurate localization of symptoms, but the general location certainly suggests, as French[8] has pointed out, that such symptoms in human patients are analagous to the behavioral changes observed in the recent experimental work on monkeys and cats.

In 1906 Sherrington published his epoch-making work "The Integrative Action of the Nervous System."[9] For the next twenty-five years he studied mammalian reflexes in great detail and gave to medicine a concept of reflexology that was new and illuminating; he described and explained a great number of reflexes and combinations of reflexes and their integration by such mechanisms as facilitation and inhibition. In a summarizing lecture in 1933[10] he says concerning the cerebral neocortex:

> Contrasting this with the predictability of simple reflex action he [the observer] may judge that here the reflex principle is departed from. But under pure reflex

action the same entrant signal may do now one act, at another time another. Nodal points over which the signaling runs are internally switched this way or that. The issue depends on the amounts of inhibition and of excitement obtaining at the time. A reflex offering alternative results is still a reflex. Such flexible mechanisms combined in numbers collaterally and serially, nerve-net upon nerve-net, into one huge compound total mechanism introduce no new principle into the mechanism, though the upshot on any given occasion may well be unpredictable.

He looked on the cortex as "one of several bridges from input to output, though it is of them all the longest way around and the most complex."

Sherrington did not conceive of a special system of neurons with the function of general integration. The description of such a system was not made until after his death; in fact, it was not made by any one physiologist but by the accumulative and combined work of several. The origin of the concept and its present status is well described in a book published in late 1954[11] entitled, "Brain Mechanisms and Consciousness,' edited by Delafresnaye, Adrian, Bremer, and Jasper. It reports a symposium organized by the Council for International Organizations of Medical Science, under the auspices of UNESCO and WHO. The symposium brought together a small group of eminent investigators competent in this difficult field.

The history of this concept may be traced to Dempsey and Morison's work (1942) on recruitment mechanisms in the thalamus of the cat; Magoun's experimental work (1949-1954) on the ascending, activating mechanism in the reticular formation of the upper brainstem of monkeys: Penfield's concept (1948-1954) of a centrencephalic system developed from evidence gathered at the operating table; and Jasper's (1949-1954) careful delineation of the unspecific, internuncial neuronal system of the thalamus and cortex. All of this was made possible by the basic work of Hess (1929) and Ranson (1939).

Adrian, at the symposium, made a masterful speculation. He suggested the hypothesis that an "editing" or "selecting" function takes place in the reticular formation and that this may result in what we call "attention." This area is the meeting ground of signals from all receptor organs; the reticular mechanism might reinforce or withhold impulses and thus suppress specific afferents. Lashley favored a cortical origin for the mechanism of attention and considered that the brainstem centers had a general awakening function. Jasper agreed with

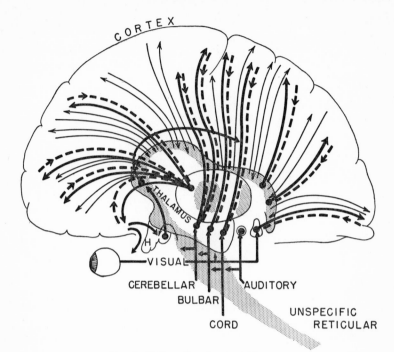

FIG. 1. Diffuse Intralaminar System.

Adrian, emphasizing that the convergence of collateral fibers from the various sensory tracts upon the reticular formation is an important consideration. Hess (son of the Swiss professor who did the original work) argued that sleep was an active process, not merely the lack of wakefulness and attention. Gastaut gave evidence from lesions in human brains that there are subcortical regulators of cortical activity.

Penfield discussed these various points of view in relation to his hypothesis of "centrencephalic integration." He believes that "an area of final functional integration must exist—a ganglionic area in which that stream of nervous impulses must arise that produces voluntary activity." He quotes Jackson as considering "the neural substratum of consciousness" to be the highest level of functional integration. Penfield locates this in the diencephalon or upper brain stem. Here are to be found those mechanisms which "are prerequisite to the existence of intellectual activity and prerequisite to the initiation of the patterned stream of efferent impulses that produce the planned action of the conscious man." He believes that the most important part of this integration does not take place in the cerebral cortex because: "Any portion of the cerebral cortex can be removed without producing unconsciousness. On the other hand, injury to the brain stem does result in unconsciousness."

Fessard reviewed philosophically the arguments against the concept of a center of consciousness, but he felt that there must be a neuronal basis and hence some location. He believes that it makes our understanding clearer if we attach consciousness to a center than if we look on it as the result of a distributed activity. He considers the mass of neurones with short axones in the reticular formation of the brainstem to be the best mechanism for bringing together present and past experience to form a whole. He thinks it is an ideal integrating mechanism, where impulses can be brought together spatially and coordinated temporally.

In my review[2] of January, 1955, only the short texts read at the symposium were available to me. The book gives more detailed papers in which definition and explanation are much more clear. Although some of the authors seem to confuse the concepts of "mind" and "consciousness," Fessard seems to agree with me that "consciousness" is but one attribute of "mind." I would say *that part which has to do with awareness of self and of environment*. It varies in degree from moment to moment in man, and from fish to man in phylogeny. It may be that invertebrates and even plants have a rudimentary form of awareness of self.

Schiller says,[12] "Consciousness can have no seat, any more than terms like circulation or contractility." It is a function that we cannot quantify, because it is subjective, but we can deduce much about it from an organism's behavior. It is a function distinctly on the sensory or input side of the integrating mechanism. Fessard's synonym for it, "experienced integration," is most helpful. He was good enough to quote my opinion[13] that "mind" is the integration itself. When this integration, through phylogeny and ontogeny becomes complex, it is experienced. Consciousness is an attribute of mind that seems to become more prominent as the brain becomes more and more complex in the ascent of the phylogenetic scale. It can only be proved to be present in man, and then only by personal experience and introspection. It can, however, be inferred to be present from behavioral evidence in other men and other animals.

Of course there is some localization of such functions. They are integrated more in some parts of the central nervous system than in others—certainly more in brainstem and cerebral cortex than in cerebellum and cord. But if, as I believe, "mind" is a function of the living brain in action—the integration itself, the relationship of one functioning part of the brain to another—it cannot be relegated to a center, or even to a level. If we seriously believe in the recent advances in neurophysiology which indicate that the brain is equipped with extensive feed-back mechanisms and reverberating circuits of neurones, we should expand our concept of a "center." Even "levels" become too restricting, because sequences of impulses in time have to be taken as major considerations. These circuits are now proved by anatomical and physiological observations. They range all the way from the recurrent collaterals of axones to polysynaptic fields of the reticular system and the complex thalamocorticostriatal circuits discussed by Olszewski, Nauta, and Whitlock.[11]

When dealing with such concepts, one must modify his thinking about "higher and lower" or "higher levels." A circle has no top. Certainly there are differences in complexity and in the number of neurone circuits that impinge on certain cerebral areas. In this sense the reticular formation of the brainstem stands out as one of the most likely locations for the most complex functions. But I do not believe that any one "area for final functional integration" exists. Integration, by its very nature, cannot be "final," and one part of an integrated whole is not more important than another. To my mind the discriminative function of the cortex is just as essential as the coordinating and selecting function of the diffuse reticular system of the diencephalon— neither could function without the other.

I agree that the "planned action of the conscious man" is the essence of civilized behavior, but I do not consider that one should think in terms of "conscious" or "unconscious," "planned" or "involuntary." These parts of mental activity are not to be taken as either *present* or *absent*. They are matters of degree. Penfield says that "any portion of the cerebral cortex can be removed without producing unconsciousness." I would say that *no considerable portion of the cerebral cortex can be removed without reducing consciousness.* Small lesions in certain parts of the brain stem only produce somnolence or other partial losses of consciousness. Here, too, it is a matter of degree. Awareness, attention, alertness, wakefulness, and their opposites are attributes of "consciousness," as it is an attribute of "mind."

But the simpler, constituent attributes are easier to define, easier to work with, and therefore better objects of scientific observation. In animal experiments their presence can only be deduced by observation of behavior. For all the subjective side of the picture, the more directly reported and therefore the more accurate part, one must rely on reports from human subjects. It is here that the "experiments of nature," like the five cases reported, are invaluable. If and when neurosurgery advances to the point where it is justifiable to change personality by cerebral operation, much can be learned quickly from human experiments. Animal experimentation can point the way, but in the field of human psychopathology it can never give definite answers.

REFERENCES

1. ABRAMSON, H. A., ed.: Problems of Consciousness. New York, Macy, 1954.
2. COBB, S.: Review of neuropsychiatry. Arch. Int. Med., *95:* 129, 1955.
3. MILLER, J. G.: Unconsciousness. New York, Wiley & Son, 1941.
4. RIOCH, D. M.: Certain aspects of "conscious" phenomena and their neural correlates, Am. J. Psychiat., *111:* 810, 1955.
5. TRETHOWEN, W. H. AND COBB, S.: Neuropsychiatric aspects of Cushing's syndrome, Arch. Neurol. & Psychiat., *67:* 283, 1952.
6. CLARK, L. D., QUARTON, G. C., COBB, S. AND BAUER, W.: Further observations on mental disturbance associated with cortisone and ACTH therapy, New Eng. J. Med., *249:* 178, 1953.
7. WHITE, J. C. AND COBB, S.: Psychological changes associated with giant pituitary neoplasms, Arch. Neurol. & Psychiat. *74:* 383, 1955.
9. FRENCH, J. D.: Brain lesions associated with prolonged unconsciousness. Arch. Neurol. & Psychiat., *68:* 727, 1952.
9. SHERRINGTON, C. S.: The Integrative Action of the Nervous System, New Haven, Yale Univ. Press, 1906.
10. SHERRINGTON, C. S.: The Brain and its Mechanisms. Cambridge Univ. Press, 1933.
11. DELAFRESNAYE, J. F., ed.: Brain Mechanisms and Consciousness, Blackwell, Oxford, 1954.
12. SCHILLER, F.: Consciousness reconsidered. Arch. Neurol. & Psych. *67:* 199, 1952.
13. COBB, S.: On the nature and locus of mind. Arch. Neurol. & Psych. *67:* 172, 1952.

INTRODUCTION

The investigations reported in this session (IV) are the result of teamwork utilizing the approach to which this volume is dedicated—experimentation. This teamwork tries to fuse, as is demonstrated in the papers, the experimental with the clinical, the theoretical with the practical, and the physiodynamic with the psychodynamic. We are aware of the fact that a full integration of the aforementioned elements in psychiatry is not yet attainable, but we believe that an attempt in this direction is worthwhile.

P.H.H.

13

THE PROBLEM OF SCHIZOPHRENIA IN THE LIGHT OF EXPERIMENTAL PSYCHIATRY

By PAUL H. HOCH, M.D.

ONLY IN COMPARATIVELY RECENT TIMES have attempts been made to attack the problem of schizophrenia experimentally. This became possible when chemical compounds were available that produced schizophrenia-like symptoms in normal individuals and also influenced persons already suffering from schizophrenia. Some of these drugs, like mescaline, were experimented with in the 1920's, but most of the experimentation at that time confined itself to the study of alterations in perception which were then in the foreground of interest. These studies were later reactivated but more from the point of view of studying the whole clinical picture, and to use this so-called model psychosis for a better understanding of the clinical, neurophysiological, and biochemical changes which occurred. Later other drugs were introduced like d-LSD$_{25}$, harmine, n-allymorphine, and bufotomine, and most likely others still to come with which psychotic manifestations can be produced.

205

As in any new investigative process when certain questions are answered, simultaneously many new ones are raised. We should like to discuss some of the questions which came up in connection with the study of experimental psychosis.

First, there is a certain amount of confusion as to how to clarify these experimental psychotic states from a clinical point of view. Some psychiatrists believe these are states of intoxication and therefore belong in the group of organic psychoses. They argue that a similarity exists between intoxication with mescaline, D-LSD$_{25}$, marihuana, hashish, cocaine, alcohol, etc. Some of the publications—for instance that of Stoll—speak about d-LSD$_{25}$ as a 'Rauschgift' which translated into English means intoxicant. Many of those mental manifestations seen were described from the point of view of intoxication. Here the visual hallucinations, illusions, and other perceptive alterations are stressed similarly to those seen in organic states of intoxication. Others deny that a mescaline or d-LSD$_{25}$ psychosis is an intoxication. We feel it cannot be denied that these compounds produce a state of intoxication because any substance introduced into the body which has properties like these drugs must be listed among the intoxicants. On the other hand it is correct to state that they fall into a special group. In their action they are not identical to intoxicants like alcohol, hashish, etc. The differentiation of the intoxication states with alcohol, hashish, etc. from mescaline and d-LSD$_{25}$ will hinge on interpretations as to how far consciousness is altered. In all intoxicants which produce an organic-like psychosis one of the main features is the alteration of consciousness. Consciousness becomes blurred, hazy; orientation functions become disorganized, and all the other mental and emotional manifestations occur in the framework of a disorientative, amnesic, hallucinatory syndrome.

Mescaline and d-LSD$_{25}$ most likely also alter consciousness. However, this alteration is much more subtle, at least in the doses we used to produce this psychosis, than those seen in the organic states. The preservation of consciousness and the ability to report what is going on during such a state of intoxication sets them apart from the common intoxicants. What is particularly schizophrenic-like in the experimental psychosis is the ability to be aware of happenings in the outside world and at the same time aware of happenings in the inside world. This double registration of consciousness has to be emphasized. It is a phenomenon to which we shall return later in our discussion. Therefore, we think that those drugs which produce these abnormal mental states are intoxicants, but they are not a 'Rauschgift' in that they do not produce a 'Rausch' in an organic sense.

The second question discussed in this connection is how far the states produced by these drugs can be called psychoses. This, of course, depends entirely on one's definition of a psychosis. We feel that here certain questions enter which have nothing to do with the basic assessment of the symptoms observed in such individuals. Some say they will not consider a mental state a psychosis which is temporary in a sense that it lasts only a few hours. However, we do not think that the time element is a valid objection. Others differentiate between psychoses and mental changes which occur in brain diseases which they treat separately, establishing practically a synonymity between psychosis and schizophrenia. Still others would like to reserve the designation psychosis for conditions which are psychogenically produced and therefore not applicable to states which are produced by a chemical compound.

For the sake of clarity we believe we have to leave out all these secondary questions when we define a condition which rests essentially on clinical phenomenological observations. Descriptively speaking, a patient who is under the influence of one of these aforementioned drugs shows all the signs of a psychosis, namely the impairment of ego function, impairment of reality appraisal, and inability to integrate different mental processes. In many patients other manifestations characteristic for a psychotic picture appear such as hallucinations, delusions, and regression phenomena. A full psychotic picture is not produced in all patients with average doses; it is possible to produce this psychotic picture in most individuals with high doses. These psychiatric pictures are schizophrenia-like because of the many special characteristics which they show. They are not identical with schizophrenia and we agree with those who call them schizophrenia-like. On the other hand, we do not agree with those who think this condition is only psychosis-like because we cannot visualize something which is only psychosis-like, but not a psychosis. As far as we are concerned, the difference of opinion could be only to call these conditions organic psychoses or schizophrenia-like states. We feel any other interpretation evades the essential observations made in these patients and introduces unnecessary confusion.

Another moot question is if alterations in behavior produced by these drugs in animals can be called psychosis or even schizophrenia; mescaline and d-LSD$_{25}$ produce alterations in behavior in dogs, cats, mice, and other animals. The alterations of behavior in some of these animals could be interpreted as hallucinations or catatonic responses. On the other hand, not being able to receive information from them exactly as to what their experiences are during such a period, it is difficult to interpret them. We believe the best position to take here is that which is expressed by Julian Huxley in the foreword to Konrad Z. Lorenz' book, *King Solomon's Ring*, that it would be unfair to assume that brains of higher organisms are "really nothing but reflex machines, like a bit of special cord magnified and supplied with special sense organs." Lorenz equally repudiates "the uncritical and often wishful thinking of the sentimental anthropomorphizers, who not merely refuse to take the trouble to understand the radically different nature of animals' minds and behaviour from our own, but in fact are satisfy-ing some repressed urge of their unconscious by projecting human attributes into bird and beast."

We feel that it may be possible to speak about a psychosis in a higher animal. On the other hand, it is not permissible to speak about schizophrenia because the understanding of schizophrenia, even in a human, necessitates a knowledge of some of the thinking and feeling processes going on in that particular person. If and when schizophrenia can be diagnosed biochemically or neurophysiologically this requisite probably can be dropped. The different organizations of the nervous system in animals will probably always be a barrier in expressing mental disorders in terms valid outside the human species. This does not mean that experimentation in altering the function of the nervous system should not go on in animals and conclusions should not be reached by analogy, but it would be important to know where to stop in this analogizing. Otherwise concepts could be so diluted they would become meaningless. It could be claimed that in altering a certain behavior pattern of a fish that it is schizophrenia. I do not know whether we would gain anything by this type of approach.

One of the questions that arise is whether the psychotic states pro-duced in human beings are cases of schizophrenia or not. We think that, phenomenologically speaking, the states which are produced are states of a psychosis because the reality control of these individuals is altered. They are dominated by symptoms such as visual and auditory hallucinations; alterations of somatic sensations; paranoid, grandiose, or hypochondriacal delusions; depersonalization experiences; disturbances of thought, incoherence, flight of ideas; and blocking. In addition, marked emotional alterations like euphoria, depression, and anxiety are present. The change of reality, the impairment of integration of psychic functions like alteration of perception, the changes in feeling and thinking to a degree that the person is dominated by them fulfill the criteria of a psychosis. Of course, the question is, what kind of psychosis? Some workers in the field like Meyer-Gross interpret the psychotic manifestations to be of organic origin. Others feel that they are schizophrenia-like or even schizophrenia. The main difference between the clinical pictures produced by mescaline and d-LSD$_{25}$ and the usual organic psychotic pictures is in the sphere of consciousness. In the organic psychoses consciousness is invariably altered to a noticeable degree leading to disorientation, memory impairment, and amnesia. In the psychotic states produced by the above-mentioned drugs consciousness is interfered with but in a very much more subtle way than seen in the organic states. The alteration of consciousness closely resembles the changes seen in schizophrenia.

Persons under the influence of the experimental drugs are not able to associate or think quite clearly. They are preoccupied with the alteration of what is going on inside of them, and at the same time they are fully aware of what is going on around them. There is a kind of "double" orientation present—directed inward and outward. This slight interference in the function of consciousness makes these drugs so valuable for investigative purposes. If normal subjects and schizophrenia patients are under the influence of these drugs they show both similarities and dissimilarities in their reactions. The vegetative changes like pupillary dilation, nausea, and vomiting occur in normals and psychotics. The visual hallucinations, illusions, and distortions of body image occur in both. The content of perceptual change is roughly comparable in both groups. The alteration of time sense, unreality feelings are also similar. In the emotional sphere, depression and frequent paranoid manifestations are seen in both. The hebephrenic and catatonic pictures produced in normals are physiologically similar to those seen in schizophrenics. Nevertheless, there are differences between the reactions of normal and schizophrenic individuals to mescaline. For instance, euphoria occurring in normals is stressed by all investigators. Euphoric manifestations are occasionally observed in schizophrenics, but generally speaking they are rare.

Sexual content and behavior are frequently encountered in schizophrenics under the drug; this is rare among normals. The reactions of schizophrenic patients to the drug are much more intense. Anxiety is much more marked, and disorganization of thought and emotional pattern is much more intense than in normals.

We could speak generally and say that a normal individual retains a better reality control and remains more of an observer of the various perceptual changes rather than being completely dominated by them. The disorganization of schizophrenics is more marked than that of normal people. It is our impression that even though many symptoms produced by the drug in normals resemble those of schizophrenia they are not exactly the same. Nevertheless there are some partial symptoms produced by mescaline and d-LSD$_{25}$ so similar to those seen in schizophrenics that the resemblance is striking.

There is no great difficulty in seeing the similarities between the fullblown experimentally produced schizophrenia-like psychosis and the cases occurring spontaneously. However, the situation becomes much more difficult when we investigate the more subtle symptoms of schizophrenia. Here a great many questions will have to be clarified. Of course, the questions which arise in the experimentally-produced mental states are also present in schizophrenia proper. The relationship of the subtle schizophrenic or schizophrenic-like manifestations to the fullblown psychosis is not fully clear. In the following we would like to illustrate some of the issues involved. We wish to show a table of symptoms observed in patients suffering from the pseudoneurotic form of schizophrenia. This is a form of schizophrenia in which the clinical symptoms are subtle; gross psychotic manifestations occur at times or only with the last phase of the disorder, and in which most of these persons show only clinical manifestations, characterized by the absence of gross psychotic symptoms like delusions, hallucinations, and marked regressive phenomena.

PSEUDONEUROTIC SCHIZOPHRENIA

I. *Primary symptoms of schizophrenia:*
> Autism, dereism, intrapsychic ataxia, ambivalence, associative changes, and affective changes.

II. *Symptoms of pseudoneurotic schizophrenia: One symptom is not pathognomonic; several must be present.*

    A. Impairment of emotional regulation.

       1. Underdevelopment of emotional regulation.

2. Volatility of emotional responses, insufficient modulation of emotional responses or no modulation and absence of emotional response.
3. Inability to regulate aggression (obedient submission versus defiant negativism). Gross ambivalence in all realms of behavior.
4. Desire for protection versus rejection of protection. Marked dependency craving (archaic oral longing), need for ego support, narcissism.
5. Craving for reality contact versus repudiation of it.
6. Impairment of empathy.
7. Great sensitivity, feeling easily hurt. Ego referential: everything has meaning as related to the ego.
8. Impairment of self-assertion, lack of self-confidence and self-esteem. Sense of inferiority and failure in all spheres of functioning.
9. Anhedonia, lack of feeling tone. Inclined to emulate behavior of others in effort to achieve emotional feeling. This produces a caricature of normal behavior. Continuous search for experience which will bring emotional feeling.
10. Intolerance to tension. Inability to cope with stimulation. Low threshold to frustration. Striving for quick, magical gratification. Intolerant of sustained activity toward future goal.

B. Impairment of thinking processes.
1. Paralogic thinking. Catathymic thinking. Categorical impairment.
2. Disorders of concept formation and of ability to think abstractly. Concretizations.
3. Loosening of associations: relating ideas to one another which have no logical relationship. Literal use of symbolic connections. Unconscious thinking processes on surface.
4. Feelings of unreality, depersonalization, being hazy, doped, dazed. Fantasy-reality border is shaky.
5. Complex-bound associations.
6. Pseudo-philosophizing with confused, esoteric debates about love-hate, life-death, male-female, etc.
7. Inflexible, stereotyped concepts about self-authority, man, woman, various institutions, etc. Formulates universal concepts on basis of limited experiences.
8. Inclination to handle situations with intellect as substitute for emotional responses. Repudiation of emotion as "weak."
9. Dominating fantasy life which cannot be turned off at will or repudiation of fantasy life.
10. Confusion of aims and purposes, of means and goals.
11. Urge to function according to formulas.

C. Impairment of action processes.
1. Symptoms
   a. Pan-anxiety
   b. Pan-neurosis
   c. Pan-sexuality. (Chaotic sexuality with anhedonia in action and fantasy).

2. Energy regulation
   a. Dysregulation of energy output
   b. Difficulty in initiating activity, sustaining activity and/ or stopping activity.

3. Autonomic dysfunction
   a. Low threshold to organ or system dysfunction in association with anxiety (skin, GI, GU, respiratory, cardio-vascular, etc.).
   b. Lack of vegetative homeostasis.

We feel our present knowledge about the primary symptoms of schizophrenia is very limited. Primary symptoms like autism, association changes, etc. which have been described in the past are valid, but they do not explain the whole disorder. Today we can state that schizophrenia is a disconnection of mental integration and an inability to cope in an integrative and regulated way with stimulation coming from within and without. However, this dysregulation of mental integration is valid only in humans and we do not know much about the psychic organization of animals. The details of this inability to regulate and integrate have not been worked out. In our opinion the symptoms of schizophrenia can be grouped as follows: Primary symptoms unknown consisting essentially of an integrative and regulative deficiency (1). The more subtle symptoms which could be called microscopic as a direct sequence or compensatory reaction to the primary cause (2a). The more macroscopic symptomatology consisting of a marked disorganization and disintegration expressing itself in gross psychotic symptoms like delusions, hallucinations, regressive phenomena which are quantitative exaggerations or modifications of the symptoms described under the 2a heading (2b).

The relationship between the primary symptoms listed under No. 1 and the secondary symptoms listed under Nos. 2a and 2b is most likely a quantitative one. How far qualitative differences also appear is not quite clear. However, the quantitative relationship can be fairly conclusively demonstrated by using mescaline or d-LSD$_{25}$ in producing gross schizophrenic reactions in individuals who only have a subtle symptomatology. It was possible to magnify and underscore the symptoms present. With drugs like sodium amytal, pervitin, and thorazine it is possible to abolish the gross psychotic manifestations produced by mescaline and d-LSD$_{25}$, returning the person to the level of organization which prevailed prior to the injection of the drug. Here again it can be demonstrated that the intensity of symptoms can be reduced and that a quantitative relationship exists. It should be mentioned, in passing, that actually treatment methods at our disposal in schizophrenia today like psychotherapy, shock treatment, lobotomy, and also the new drugs like Thorazine and resperine are able only to reduce quantitatively the symptoms of the disorder. All these methods do not affect primary symptoms. At times the quantitative reduction of symptoms is so marked that the obvious manifestations of schizophrenia are eliminated, but none of these treatment methods as far as we know affects the primary symptoms of the disorder per se.

The next questions are how far individual differences can be demonstrated in the use of these psychosis-producing drugs and how consistent is the response of the individual exposed at different times to these drugs. Individual differences were observed already by early workers in this field. For instance, Stockings and Bensheim felt that schizothymic and cyclothymic individuals reacted differently to mescaline. Beringer, however, found no correlation between the previous personality and the reaction to the drug in normals. This aspect of the problem was not sufficiently investigated. We feel that schizoid individuals are more susceptible to the effects of these drugs than others. But not enough material has been gathered on the reactions of cyclothymic individuals. It is also possible that the differences in reaction are not alone determined by the basic temperamental makeup of the individual but also by psychodynamic factors, and even constellative factors, at the time of the experiment. This too will have to be further investigated.

In addition to the very important psychological factors which operate there are also biochemical metabolic differences among individuals which have to be stressed. This, of course, is not new. The susceptibility to drugs, the allergy to them, the response or non-response are known to play an important role in assessing drug actions. Nevertheless there is a constant tendency to ignore these individual metabolic differences and treat all persons alike or in a standardized fashion.

The dosages used are also of importance and sometimes findings differ with different investigators because various dosages were used. In chronic deteriorated schizophrenic individuals, for instance, average doses of mescaline and d-LSD_{25} often produce vegetative manifestations, but do not intensify the schizophrenic symptoms. An activation of the psychosis can be achieved when high doses are used.

With regard to the consistency of response it has been assumed by some that in many patients the response to the drug would be different from time to time and that the patient would adapt himself to the experiences under the drug and become less responsive to it. Cholden's experiments show that if you give mescaline or d-LSD$_{25}$ several days in succession it loses its potency and an adaptation to the drug is developed. If a person does not receive the drug for several days and it is applied again it regains its potency. It is also interesting to note that a cross-adaptation exists between mescaline and d-LSD$_{25}$.

If the drug is used repeatedly the basic pattern of response often remains the same in the same individual. If a paranoid attitude was displayed it appears again and again, but the content of the paranoid ideation changes from session to session. Again, some patients show new clinical symptoms not previously displayed. Further research will have to elucidate why in some individuals some patterns are kept and why deviation from this established pattern occurs in some with these psychosis-producing drugs.

At this point we wish to mention the connection between the changes brought about in the vegetative nervous system by the psychosis-producing drugs and the psychic alterations. Mescaline and d-LSD$_{25}$ invariably alter the function of the vegetative nervous system even though quantitatively these charges are not always the same; nausea, malaise, dizziness, palpitations, dilated pupils, sweating, diuresis, and changes in blood pressure are present. Usually these vegetative nervous system changes appear first after injection, and the alterations of perception and the other psychic phenomena follow later. Some relationship exists between the vegetative changes and the psychic changes, but this relationship is not an absolute one in the sense that one can be measured as a function of the other. Sometimes marked vegetative changes can be observed without any pronounced psychic alterations. The reverse is also seen even though far less often. If drugs are used to abolish the effect of mescaline and d-LSD$_{25}$, the psychic manifestations are eliminated first and the vegetative manifestations last. The interaction or correlation between the vegetative changes and the psychic changes will have to be an important research goal. On the basis of our present knowledge, attempts to link the two are fully justified. On the other hand, we feel that research based on the premises of an absolute relationship between these two systems is premature. A similar relative relationship exists between EEG findings and the affect of mescaline and d-LSD$_{25}$. The EEG sometimes is changed under the effect of these drugs. But often marked psychic alterations can be seen; for instance hallucinations with a normal EEG.

The structure of the psychosis produced by these drugs is of great interest and will be the source of much future research. Some of this material which we obtained will be taken up in detail in the papers of Doctor Cattell and Doctor Pennes. I only wish to mention here a few general observations.

We have pointed out that the alteration of the vegetative nervous system appeared first under the influences of mescaline and d-LSD$_{25}$. This is usually followed by alterations of perception, body sensations, and changes of body image. In many patients it appears as if the perceptual alterations and the proprioceptive changes produce anxiety, uncertainty, and at times rage. In turn, this leads to a lowering of reality control which is then followed by depressive, aggressive, and paranoid manifestations. Further investigations showed that in the majority of the subjects the appearance of anxiety was concomitant with the onset of perceptual abnormalities. Both the form and content of these perceptual abnormalities generated anxiety but apart from this general relationship little appeared that could be correlated in a more specific way. For example, different subjects had different emotional reactions (anxiety, depression, hostility, etc.) despite perceptual experiences of the same form. There was often no evident correlation between the apparent intensity of the perceptual and concomitant emotional experiences in different subjects. Finally the same individual, upon repeated administration of the drug, could experience the same type and intensity of perceptual change with a decreasing intensity of emotional reaction. It is yet unclear whether the emotional alterations seen in these patients are due to an action of the drug per se, or due to the experiencing of an alteration of reality which comes about by changes in the perceptive and proprioceptive apparatus. This important issue is still unclear. We can only say in general that the drugs produce a disturbance of homeostasis, physically and emotionally, which leads to a lowering of mental integration that in turn produces the different psychiatric syndromes. It is also unclear whether anxiety is a secondary mechanism due to the alteration of perception and proprioception or emotional integration and is an indicator of an impaired psychic homeostasis, or whether anxiety is the primary factor involved.

The evolution of complicated psychiatric symptoms like depressive, aggressive, and paranoid manifestations and the elimination of these symptoms with counteracting drugs will elucidate in the future their true nature. We feel that it will be demonstrated that these symptoms are not primary or secondary to emotional processes like anxiety, with which the individual is not able to cope.

Finally we would like to make a few remarks about production and elimination of this experimentally produced psychoses. Due to lack of time we can only mention a few observations. We are able to produce psychosis experimentally with different substances like mescaline, d-LSD$_{25}$, harmine, n-allymorphine, and a number of others. The number of compounds is increasing which have psychosis-producing propensities. Some of these chemical compounds are perhaps chemically related; others, however, are not. A search is going on to find a common denominator to explain the action of these drugs. At present no such common denominator exists and we shall have to assume that different chemical substances are able to produce similar psychiatric pictures. This is not surprising, because in the realm of the organic psychoses we see every day that different noxae produce similar clinical pictures. There are now several known substances which counteract the action of mescaline and d-LSD$_{25}$. For instance Sodium Amytal, methamphetamine, chlorpromazine, frenquel, and others. Because these antidotal drugs have different chemical constructions it was not possible to evolve a common denominator explaining their action. It is even unclear whether they act on the same part of the brain (cortex or sub-cortex), affect synaptic conduction, or influence enzyme systems in the same way. It is important to emphasize that they are as unspecific in their action as the psychosis-producing drugs themselves.

The great question remains: Is the disorder seen in experimental psychosis due to a local impairment of brain function, to a diffuse chemical alteration affecting the higher nervous system, or to a combination of both in the sense that certain chemical substances have a special affinity to certain parts of the nervous system like the brainstem and are able to produce a functional alteration there? The counteracting substances, of course, do the same in the reverse. Most of the clinical and experimental evidence indicates that what we call schizophrenia today is a special form of integrative disorganization. This disorganization pattern is as widespread and characteristic as the so-called chronic reaction type. We could speculate that the organic psychoses are due to preeminently cortical impairment where the preeminently subcortical impairment is what we observe in the schizo-phrenic reaction pattern. Evidence is accumulating, which we cannot enlarge upon here, that if we excite the subcortical gray, psychotic manifestations appear. If you clamp down on it—the subcortical gray, for instance with drugs like thorazine or serpasil, psychotic manifesta-tions do not occur or occur only in a much milder form. The same applies if we disconnect the cortex from the subcortical gray by different methods of frontal lobotomy.

In this paper we have indicated only some of the questions and in a very cursory fashion. Our understanding of schizophrenia will depend on further biochemical, neurophysiological, and psychodynamic investi-gations performed in an integrated fashion.

14

USE OF DRUGS IN PSYCHODYNAMIC INVESTIGATIONS

By JAMES P. CATTELL, M.D.*

THE INVESTIGATION of psychoanalytic or psychodynamic concepts is attracting attention from certain psychoanalysts, psychiatrists, and workers in allied fields. The need for research studies has long been evident but has been slow in developing, partly in association with certain unique aspects of the theory and practice of psychoanalysis. There is a growing demand for experimental validation of those conceptual and technical aspects which can be investigated by techniques available at the present time. The literature on these issues deals with the methodological approaches to the problems and reports of some of the studies that have been completed.[9,13,15,25,36] One such approach is the investigation of the effects of various drugs on patients with different types of emotional disorder as well as on normal subjects. There are a number of papers dealing with the psychopathological, psychodynamic, and psychotherapeutic changes associated with the acute introduction of several different drugs.[4,16,18,19,23,26,28,29,31,32,33,34,38,39,47] There is a variable emphasis on these three aspects of the effects of drugs and in some instances an inclination to ignore their interrelatedness, especially with regard to psychopathological and psychodynamic material. It would seem that some investigators take for granted concepts most in need of validation and use the research tool, the drugs, as a valid and established adjunct to psychotherapy. In some reports, symptomatic improvement and relief of anxiety are attributed to the manipulation of the content of the patient's productions in drug-intoxicated and subsequent drug-free interviews, overlooking the possibility that the change may have been associated with many other factors. Somewhat analogous conclusions are often stated or implied concerning psychodynamic material and mechanisms, with emphasis on content or productions and with little regard for the

* Assistant Clinical Professor of Psychiatry, College of Physicians and Surgeons, Columbia University; Associate Psychiatrist, New York State Psychiatric Institute.

clinical status of the patient or for other factors which might influence the reaction.

The acute administration of such drugs as mescaline, d-LSD$_{25}$, amobarbital, methamphetamine and chlorpromazine may produce a disturbance in the equilibrium, both physiological and psychological, of the human organism. In response to this disturbance, there are reactions in many areas of functioning toward maintaining or regaining homeostasis. The changes and experiences in the psychic realm are often described and explained in psychodynamic or psychoanalytic terminology with particular emphasis on alterations of ego integration and alterations of repression-resistance with release of repressed material, including affect, early memories, conflicts, and overt transference manifestations.[7,10,14,26,30,33,41,43,45,47] Primary needs are said to be gratified by certain drugs and others facilitate gratification of secondary needs which are listed as narcissism, exhibitionism, and sadism.[47] Other investigators ascribe reduction in basic drives to certain drugs as well as reduction in secondary drives, which they designate as anxiety, depression, and self-punishment.[33] There are differences of opinion concerning drug-specific and personality-specific reactions to administration of various drugs. Several studies have reported more striking evidence of personality-specific reactions than drug-specific responses.[3,8,22,34,37,48] One group[49] found no specific relationship between the noxious agent and the form and content of the disturbance. Another team[39] emphasized a predominantly personality-specific reaction to multiple drug administration. It has been noted repeatedly in animal studies that the same behavioral effect can be produced by diverse noxious stimuli and that a given stimulus can be dealt with by different actions or behavior.[24] This equivalent response to heterogeneous stimuli and heterogeneous response to the same stimulus may have some relation to our discussion of drug reactions in man.

It would be useful to be able to define the "normal" response to drug administration at all levels of behavior, but this is not possible. The basic neurophysiological action is known for some of the drugs used in psychodynamic investigations. Mescaline and d-LSD$_{25}$ induce transient changes in autonomic, sensorimotor, emotional, ideational, perceptual, and behavioral spheres in a relatively clear state of consciousness.[10,18,34,44] Amobarbital, a barbiturate, produces signs of central depression in the form of sedation and hypnosis.[30,37,46] Methamphetamine, a cephalotropic, sympathomimetic amine usually creates signs of central stimulation.[21,28] Chlorpromazine, a phenothiazine derivative, has a selective depressant effect on the central nervous system producing inhibition of drive without impairment of consciousness or responsiveness.[17,27] From the standpoint of psychodynamic research, such information is of little assistance in regard to the "normal" reaction to drugs.

Another approach entails the administration of a drug to a group of volunteer subjects, so-called normal controls.[1,12,43,48] Evidence can usually be found in support of the fundamental neurophysiological effects with some exceptions. The more dramatic superstructure of the reaction appears in a wide range of varying responses when a given drug is administered to a group of subjects, whether patients or normal controls, or on successive occasions to the same subject.

The material and methodology of these observations have been published elsewhere.[3,34] A group of normal control subjects, including graduate psychology students, medical students, and nurses, was also used in these investigations. Important aspects of the methodology and the psychopathological features of the drug reactions are presented in a companion paper by Dr. Harry H. Pennes.[35] It is pertinent to re-emphasize the importance of the baseline or drug-free evaluation of the patient. This includes a careful investigation of psychopathological status, behavior, associational patterns in therapy or serial interviews, and a psychodynamic formulation. In addition, one should assess the meaning of the drug administration to the patient (and to the investigator), the relationship between patient and therapist, the alterations of this relationship with drug administration, and the pattern and content of associative material and affective reaction in the drug-intoxicated state.

Psychodynamic Features in Response to Drug Administration

From a psychodynamic point of view the introduction of a drug disturbs the homeostasis of the total organism, bringing about a mobilization, and probably a regrouping of forces and defenses, to maintain or regain equilibrium at the pre-drug level or to achieve a more expedient equilibrium with less domination by emotional problems. The administration of mescaline or d-LSD$_{25}$ to some normal control subjects produces the characteristic autonomic and perceptual experiences with a reaction of mild, diffuse anxiety, episodic and mild euphoria which the subject associates with contemplation of the perceptual phenomena and feelings *suggestive* of depersonalization in relation to time-space-body-image distortions. The latter are often reported *as if* things are unreal. Depersonalization may be the reaction to perceptual distortions but is not synonymous with them. There may be some irritability about conversing with the investigator inasmuch as the reverie is interrupted, but the subject may voice concern about being left unattended. Some anxiety is often expressed about the difficulties in concentrating and reporting, though such subjects are usually quite productive and one gains the impression of having as complete an account as possible. Hallucinations may be limited to the colored, shifting geometric patterns and a few simple images such as eyes and oriental dragons, which are of common occurrence. One important feature is the reaction to the visual phenomena as a *parade* rather than as an *attack,* just as the other distortions often are not regarded as jeopardizing body integrity and reality control. Repetition of the drug experience in these subjects produces a comparable reaction but there may be less anxiety and some differences in the relative dominance of various perceptual phenomena.

Other normal control subjects, about whose emotional stability there was some question, developed frank paranoid or catatonic syndromes. They had not sought psychiatric treatment before the drug experience and were reluctant to participate fully in interviews necessary for a comprehensive psychodynamic formulation.

A number of patients with pseudoneurotic schizophrenia[20] and overt schizophrenia had repeated studies with several of the drugs under consideration. Time and space preclude the detailed presentation of the baseline and drug-associated material but certain points can be illustrated.

Case 1

This 34-year-old man had an eight-year history of phobias, diffuse anxiety, and depression, as well as bizarre ideas about the horrible appearance of the right side of his face. Feelings of genital inferiority, fears of sexuality with women, and fascination with homosexuality were also obtained. He had lived with an alcoholic, ne'er-do-well father who showed some affection, and with a carping, increasingly psychotic mother until the age of five, when both parents were institutionalized and he was sent to an orphans' home. Childhood and early adolescence were spent in such institutions or in foster homes and he received beatings and harsh treatment for trivial offenses.

During adolescence he felt inferior and unwanted, not without justification, and was guilty about masturbation. At 19, he visited his married sister for the first time in many years and had difficulty in suppressing sexual interest in her. From age 20 to age 33, he spent most of his time at sea in the Navy or Merchant Marine and was aboard a ship that was torpedoed during the war. Though uninjured, he was terrified and drank heavily while ashore. Heterosexual relationships were carried on with prostitutes for the most part and gave him little pleasure. He had some homosexual experiences at sea "out of curiosity," and lived in the home of an overt homosexual while ashore, though he declined his host's invitation to sexual play. He was studied in our series during his second hospitalization at Psychiatric Institute. The diagnosis was pseudoneurotic schizophrenia.

With the first administration of mescaline he had severe anxiety, agitation and weeping with a variable paranoid reaction, thinking disorder, inappropriateness, and hallucinations in all spheres. During much of the time he was attending the circus with his father, seeing crocodiles, elephants, and other animals and alternately enjoying himself and being frightened. Most of his productions were verbalized in a childish voice and there was some unintelligible babbling. He carried on a conversation with his father, expressing much enthusiasm about the circus, alarm at seeing snakes about to attack him, and fearful concern that the monkeys were laughing at him. In the midst of all this, he said: "Oh God, I have to go to the bathroom. I wet the bed. I'm sorry, Dad." He made several references to having the breasts of a girl and being genitally inferior as a man. At one point he mentioned that the nurse resembled his sister. Later he spoke of an evil-looking bird with one eye, perhaps a duck, sitting on his right. This or someone set fire to the right side of his hair. After he had received an antidotal drug later in the day, he stated that he used to go to the circus with his father though this had never been mentioned during a long period of psychotherapy. Most of the drug-free memories of his father he had reported were condemnatory and disdainful. He made no reference to mother, orphanage, foster homes, or war-time experiences and mentioned the nurse's resemblance to his sister only in passing.

He had spontaneously anticipated the mescaline experience with much optimism, hoping it would cure him. Afterward, he said that he had relived his childhood from three to five and that his condition was improved as a result. He no longer felt that the right side of his face was horrible and associated this change in attitude with the strange bird and the fire in his hair on that side.

There was a dream-like quality to the circus experience with oscillations between frightening elements and fairly simple, wish-fulfillment scenes. His retrospective comment that he had relived his life from ages three to five is an exaggeration. The mescaline productions might be regarded as a condensation of his personality problems with particular reference to his concept of himself, body image, ambivalent relationship to father and men, and his fearful, rejecting attitude toward women, who were seen as threatening, ridiculing, dangerous animals, prototypically the mother. It is questionable that all of this dynamic material was included and a number of the other aspects of his personality structure were not evident. Some of this crystallization of content under the influence of mescaline was new, though the dynamics were reasonably clear before the drug was administered. The patient's impression of psychodynamic insight and clinical improvement with the drug experience is a not infrequently observed manifestation in schizophrenic patients. In particular, he related the strange bird and the fire in his hair on the right side to diminished concern about the horrible appearance of the right side of his face. This is a simple illustration of the facility in shifting emphasis which such patients have. This type of alteration is sometimes recognized as a psychotherapeutic or psychodynamic gain or improvement and is attributed to a variety of psychotherapeutic, pharmacologic, or other maneuvers.

The patient had mescaline experiences of variable severity on four subsequent occasions but with less anxiety than in the first, and the story-like quality was absent. There were remarks about the circus on each occasion with frightening and pleasurable reactions to various animals, dragons, skeletons, fish, dead pheasants; children in red, white, and blue clothing; a woman's breasts, perhaps his mother's; a girl with candy, perhaps his sister; and a hamburger with onion. In addition there were many other random visual perceptions such as a Walt Disney movie with Mae West and Alice Faye, a Mobilgas station, and an eye staring at him. His father was not mentioned in any of these subsequent drug experiences. During the second mescaline test there was marked depression for a few hours, and during the third he reported feeling better than he had ever felt in his life. He refused the antidotal drug, preferring to enjoy the visual experiences. Following the fourth mescaline administration he was depressed, tense, and blocked for a few days as he had been after the first and second. During the fifth test he was more withdrawn than previously but without giving evidence of pleasurable contemplation of the experiences. Subsequently, he volunteered that he no longer felt that the mescaline cleared up problems and regarded the administration as just an experiment.

The intravenous injection of amobarbital was associated with a relaxing, euphorizing effect, and there was a brief hallucination of a sexually inviting blonde girl beside him. He identified her tentatively as his sister. Otherwise the interview was characterized by discussion of drug-free material less gloomily and he referred to the therapist-investigator as his best buddy. The second amytal experience differed from this in the absence of hallucinatory phenomena and in the unusual presence of humor and facetiousness in his productions with a variable persistence of hostility toward another male patient. The administration of amphetamine produced a dysphoria with increased tension and depression, and there was no difference in the mental content or in the associative pattern.

In this series of drug reactions, one can see a general pattern of personality-specific responses which are more evident than drug-specific reactions. There is an emphasis on various aspects of the psychodynamic material at different times but there is never a complete view of the personality structure. One can observe some of the vicissitudes of ego integration and the defense mechanisms under the influence of these special stimuli with particular reference to repression and regressive phenomena. The important family figures in the patient's life are present in some of the experiences or there is partial misidentification of someone other than the therapist. Thus, the concept of transference is not applicable in the usual sense. To the extent that one of the drugs facilitates relaxation, positive feelings may be enhanced and likewise, unpleasant experiences with drugs may revive attitudes and feelings about harsh treatment with a reaction of hostility and resentment which may be expressed or evidenced by depression. Positive or negative feelings in this context may or may not be sexualized. These drug experiences did not have any significant influence on the behavior and progress in psychotherapy from a long-range point of view, nor did they affect the clinical course.

Case 2

A 44-year-old married woman had a 20-year history of weakness, hypochondriacal complaints, temper tantrums, anxiety, and depression and a 13-year history of increasingly frequent sexual relations with men whom she met casually. Initially there was intercourse but this soon failed to interest her, and mouth-genital relationships became preferred with subsequent predilection for seeing the man ejaculate, following which she would go off and urinate. Productions in drug-free psychotherapeutic sessions were characterized by her usual complaints with some material about her sexual activities, her ability to have orgasm by thinking of sexual play, and the importance of the relation between urination and orgasm. In addition, there were some expressions of guilt about her sexual practices.

Domination by anxiety and other symptoms interfered with her working effectually in psychotherapy and it was not possible to obtain as clear a picture of her personality structure as might be wished. Nevertheless, the clinical picture and psychodynamics could be formulated with reasonable accuracy. Following the administration of d-LSD 25 once and mescaline on two occasions, she experienced an apparent sexual ecstasy mixed with irritability, paranoid trends, hallucinations in all spheres, and tremendous productivity. There was an experiencing and some dramatization of masturbation, intercourse, fellatio, cunnilingus, with evidence of excruciating pain and pleasure as well as voyeurism and exhibitionism. The objects were father, mother, sister, other women and men from the past, the therapist, and herself. She spoke of needing a penis in her vagina night and day, of wanting to be male, of seeing the therapist as a penis; and she recounted a masturbatory fantasy since age 13 of cunnilingus performed by her father. She saw many people of both sexes nude. There was a great deal of rhythmic pelvic movement and manual stimulation of her genital area, often accompanied by sucking movement of her lips. On several occasions she began to undress, wishing or assuming that the therapist was about to have intercourse with her. Gross ambivalence toward family members was verbalized and she spoke of killing each of them at one time or another. She acknowledged responsibility for the death of a sister of cancer at 21 because the latter had come between the patient and her father.

In response to injections of methamphetamine on two occasions, she verbalized much shame and guilt about sexual practices, was depressed, spoke in passing of observing parental intercourse at 12 and of having continuous obsessive thoughts about sexual play in all positions. With the first injection of amobarbital she was very anxious and tense; she complained of somatic symptoms and had a gross body tremor. The reaction to the second injection resembled her response to mescaline with a mixture of sexual rapture and sobbing about the pain. It was evident that she experienced the intravenous injection as intercourse with one of her lovers.

Two fairly stereotyped reactions are seen here in response to quite different drugs, and again they are more personality-specific than drug-specific. The patient revealed much which had not been mentioned in the drug-free state, but one cannot arbitrarily assume that this was all repressed material. Almost all of the combinations and permutations of infantile sexuality are in evidence here but in a chaotic, patternless form. One can speculate that she is ill because of conflicts, repressions, fixations, and regressions represented here. However, it can also be postulated that this chaotic content and behavior are symptomatic, that the personality is relatively amorphous without sufficient integration to warrant discussion in terms of fixation and regression. At another hospital she was given a diagnosis of psychopathic personality with pathologic sexuality. Our studies revealed definite evidence of the primary symptoms of schizophrenia with a superstructure of many neurotic symptoms and mechanisms. A diagnosis of pseudoneurotic schizophrenia was made. No change was noted in psychotherapy or in the clinical status in association with the drugs.

A woman with a severe obsessive-phobic-hypochondriacal syndrome was studied under the influence of barbiturates of various types on eight occasions; methamphetamine and d-LSD 25 were each given twice and she received mescaline, morphine, and tridione once. There was variable relaxation with the barbiturates and tridione and a dysphoric response to the other drugs, characterized by elaboration of obsessional ideas and phobias. There was a minimal perceptual response to the hallucinogenic drugs, though she did report seeing her baby's face and hearing it cry while she was resting in bed two hours after receiving one of the barbiturates. Another woman with the same symptom constellation reacted to mescaline as a little child. She wanted to be held in the nurse's arms, to kiss her hand and would scream if left alone for a moment. She pled utter helplessness and terror though she had only minimal perceptual phenomena.

These excerpts from a large number of extensive and intensive studies may serve to demonstrate certain aspects of the range and variety of reactions to drug administration. The psychodynamic features of the drug reaction are consistent with the personality structure of the patient, but the particular material which the patient will "select" in a given drug experiment is not predictable in our experience.

DISCUSSION

A number of the psychodynamic changes after drug administration, which have been attributed to various drugs, appear to be more closely related to a specific personality reaction to an equilibrium-disturbing stimulus. The subject is rendered more vulnerable by the effects of the drug in distortion of autonomic functioning, perception, thinking, and emotional regulation. His reaction can be seen as consistent with his personality structure though his psychological response to a particular drug, or to subsequent administration of the same drug may vary. He may react with little anxiety, regard the experience as ego-alien, and maintain personality organization or ego integration with only a minimum need to mobilize special defenses. It is not clear how this is accomplished; it might be attributed to ego-strength, predominance of the conscious over the unconscious mechanisms or systems, a lack of unconscious conflicts, or to other factors. One can say that this kind of reaction is consistent with mental health but one is reluctant to conclude that such responses are diagnostic or prognostic tests of mental health. A more extensive and intensive study of normal control subjects is indicated.

Most subjects experience much anxiety in the mescaline and d-LSD 25 experiments. It is not clear whether some of this is primary anxiety, a direct effect of the drug on the central nervous system, or whether it is all reactive anxiety, in response to other apparently direct effects of the drug. There may be marked disorganization of functioning in all spheres and again it is not understood to what extent this is a direct drug effect or a response to anxiety. The disorganizing effects of anxiety are well known and certainly play an important role in these reactions. The other phenomena like frightening or gratifying hallucinations, depersonalization, and regression may be viewed as defensive reactions to anxiety, as products of disorganization or both. There have been statements that the personality is laid bare or that one obtains a true picture of the personality through the administration of some of these drugs.[5,14,43] It would seem more accurate to say that one obtains *another* view of the personality. This might be illustrated by the analogy of stripping layers of an onion, but unevenly and to different depths. It is unlikely one gains a view of the personality barren of defenses, but rather the second and third lines of defenses or fragments of these are revealed. These are more primitive, archaic, and gross. There seems to be a general assumption which has never been adequately validated, that the concepts of ego organization and defense mechanisms are applicable in a similar way to the understanding of normal, neurotic, schizophrenic, and organic psychotic behavior as well as to behavior following administration of various drugs.[25] Much of the emotional feeling and the colorful content produced under the influence of drugs is designated as repressed material which has been released and which is equivalent in meaningfulness to the content of psychoanalysis with attendant therapeutic value. Depending on the content and the investigator's point of view, the material has been regarded as an unadulterated product of the unconscious; a screen memory or a compromise formation comparable to the manifest content of a dream, from which the latent content can be analyzed.

Is it a valid assumption that all such content was necessarily repressed prior to drug administration? An adequate pre-drug study should reveal the important material which is conscious, and survey the preconscious content and the subject's ability and willingness to communicate these. Then according to the assumption, any new material would represent a release of repressed content. Is it possible that the drug-induced productions are a more primitive conscious or preconscious representation of those reported in the drug-free state or that still other explanations may obtain?

The relationships between anxiety, repression, and productivity are quite complex in drug-free investigations. It has long been accepted that repression is caused by anxiety and is the primary technique of defense against anxiety.[11] There is a strong resistance to conscious recognition of repressed material and the work of psychoanalysis deals with this resistance and with the transference. Conscious anxiety and domination by symptoms often interfere with productivity and the treatment process. Amobarbital and other narcotizing drugs may have a relaxing effect with decrease or elimination of anxiety or other symptoms. With the drug effect many patients are more productive, sometimes of new material or an elaboration of drug-free material. This is said to be release of repressed material. But what happened to the resistance? We can observe the relaxation, the diminution of social inhibition, and the increased productivity. But is the productivity directly associated with the relief of anxiety, is the resistance diminished or eliminated through the relief of anxiety, or is the drug affecting the unconscious resistance directly, neutralizing it and releasing the repressed material? With amobarbital all the possible combinations of relaxation or dysphoria, increased or unaltered productivity and new or drug-free material are seen, nor is a given patient's response necessarily consistent on repetition of drug administration. Methamphetamine in moderate doses often produces a feeling of well-being with temporary loss of symptoms and increased productivity and may have the same effect as amobarbital. Thus the application of a sedative *or* a stimulant may be attended by relaxation and increased productivity. The relation of this to repression-resistance is not clear.

There is a reasonable correlation between the quantity of emotional disturbance and the productivity of personality-specific material following administration of mescaline and d-LSD$_{25}$. In such subjects anxiety is often increased and symptoms are intensified or produced. Productivity may be enhanced qualitatively or quantitatively. Again the content is often called repressed material.[2,6,7] Thus the administration of pharmacologically *different drugs which have different physiological and psychopathological effects* may be associated with the release of material which has been designated as repressed by many investigators.

It is also stated that the reaction to drug administration may be regressive.[3,25,26,37,47] In psychoanalytic terms, regression may be said to have a phylogenetic connotation and an ontogenetic connotation. In discussing sleep and dream formation, Freud[11] notes that older and more primitive forms of activity are manifested such as primitive symbolic representations, which we may call a phylogenetically lower order of functioning than in the waking state. The return to an ontogenetically earlier pattern of satisfying behavior on being confronted with frustrations in the present is the more usual connotation of regression. Though these two types or aspects of regression occur together they may possibly occur separately at times, or one is markedly predominant. Phylogenetic regression induced by drugs may influence production of ontogenetically regressive material. Whether regression in the phylogenetic sense is always psychodynamically defensive is not entirely clear. Under the influence of drugs some of the behavior and content often termed regressive may be phylogenetically more primitive, i.e., release phenomena in the neurological sense, rather than return to an earlier level of satisfaction. Hilgard[15] discusses the possibility of differentiating regression from primitivization; a turning away to less mature patterns of responding which are not necessarily related to the personal biography.

How does phylogenetic regression affect repression? Freud, in discussing dream formation,[11] has stated: "It is as much the result of the archaic regression in the mental apparatus as of the demands of the censorship that so much use is made of the representation of certain objects and processes by means of symbols which have become strange to conscious thought." Little attention has been given to the influence of regression in this sense on the censorship or to the effects of the relative strength of the one on the other. In dream formation repression-resistance is decreased, permitting repressed content to be expressed through the dream work in the manifest dream. Reactions to drug administration may include experiencing apparently repressed childhood or more contemporary scenes; childhood or more recent phantasies or apparent compromise formations comparable to the usual dream. In other reactions there may be little content and a dramatization of infantile helplessness, as noted in the woman who wanted to be held and kissed by the nurse. Despite reasonable control of the variable factors, some patients respond in a more or less stereotyped pattern to repeated administration of the same or different drugs. Others follow a pattern in a more general sense but there are notable differences in the regressive and resistance phenomena which may or may not be related to release of repressed material.

One can point to certain theoretical differences between disorganization of thinking, feeling, and action on the one hand and the phylogenetic and ontogenetic aspects of regression on the other. Regression may be characterized as having a certain organization and harmoniousness as can be noted in sleep and dreaming and in some patients who have emotional illness with regressive phenomena. There is integrated functioning on a given level or among several levels. Content and affect have some meaningfulness if they can be adequately understood. Disorganization would be a relative lack of integrated functioning; a random, disharmonious discharge of content, feeling, and motor behavior which is essentially meaningless. Both types of phenomena are probably seen in certain deteriorated schizophrenic patients and can be observed in some patients after drug administration. Though such a differentiation can be made theoretically it is probably not possible clinically to see the disorganization in pure form, but rather a mixture of this and regression. Some discrimination would then be necessary in evaluating the subject's clinical state and the quantity and quality of his behavior in drug-free and drug-intoxicated states.

Clinical and psychodynamic observations suggest that the human organism has only a limited range of reactivity. In all probability a given subject has a fairly definite threshold to stimuli precipitating anxiety,[1] disorganization, regression, and various other defensive maneuvers. Evidences of this are seen in everyday practice and in responses to drug administration. Some of the interrelationships of these phenomena have been noted. Other aspects of this reactivity may be noted in considering the vicissitudes of some of the other defensive mechanisms of the ego under the influence of drugs. The investigation of these more observable mechanisms is pertinent in evaluating the effects of drugs on repression—the most important defense mechanism which is least available to direct study.

There is some question as to whether the concept of transference and methods of dealing with it in psychoanalysis are equivalently applicable in drug-intoxicated subjects. Under the influence of a drug emotionally important figures in the subject's life may be perceived in hallucinations; someone in the room other than the therapist may be misidentified as an emotionally important person or the therapist may be. In psychoanalysis one can say that transference is a misidentification, but it is more than that. Transference may be termed a *pars pro toto* identification of the analyst with some member of the patient's original family constellation. Attitudes, affects, and reactions are displaced; the therapist becomes their object and can observe the situation at first hand as well as analyze those aspects which impair the progress of treatment. Transference phenomena in psychoanalysis usually take place on a conceptual level rather than a perceptual level and the differentiation should be noted in discussing productions of subjects who have received drugs. Some concept of the emotionally charged object must underlie the false perception or the perceptual misidentification but the whole process strikes one as being much more simple and primitive than that which obtains in analysis. The necessity or even the possibility of transference to the therapist may be said to be obviated to the extent that the important family member appears in the hallucinatory experience or a random person is selected as the object of displacement. If there is a well established therapeutic relationship the drug experience is a notable interruption in the usual procedure and may temporarily jeopardize the positive transference, while underlining the negative transference. In anticipation, during the drug experience or retrospectively, the experience may be viewed as either a wished-for or dreaded sexual attack, a further proof of the magical or malignant power of the therapist. This can facilitate a nurturing or a release of hostile feelings toward the treatment, the therapeutic value of which would need to be demonstrated. The relationships between transference and regression in psychoanalysis and in drug-intoxicated states warrants attention, but space limitations precludes such considerations here.

Is it possible to validate psychoanalytic or psychodynamic concepts through the use of drug studies of this type? Kubie,[25] who has written extensively on this subject, remarks that "states of induced and controlled dissociation" offer a good approach to the study of relationships between conscious and unconscious processes. Various techniques of inducing such states are used, including hypnosis and drugs, some of which produce definite alterations in the sensorium and delirioid states. Relationships between conscious and unconscious levels of behavior are said to be self-translating, and complicated transference phenomena become transparent. The induction of drug-intoxicated states, with or without gross impairment of consciousness, is a simple procedure but the control of such states is a very complex issue. One can modify drug dosage for a given patient and antidotal drugs may be used. This is the extent of our ability to control the situation aside from efforts at psychological manipulation. As has already been noted, the reactions of a given patient are variable, unpredictable, may include a great deal of colorful material, or be quite comparable to drug-free interviews.

The use of drugs in psychodynamic investigations shows promising possibilities. However, this approach is more on the order of a new frontier than a familiar and developed territory. With psychoanalytic technique, one can observe many of the aspects of the relationships between conscious and unconscious processes and the defensive maneuvers of the ego. The administration of drugs may reveal these aspects as well as other aspects of these relationships and maneuvers. It is doubtful that they render the unconscious, the repression, or the transference transparent. In some patients there are productions which resemble repressed material and dramatizations of the classical issues of conflict. However it must be emphasized that drugs may be useful tools for the validation of psychoanalytic theory, in contrast to utilizing psychoanalytic theory to validate the reactions to drugs.

The great value of drug administration as a research tool lies in the fact that drugs induce phenomena which often bear a close resemblance to those we observe in clinical and therapeutic work. For most of the acutely produced reactions, there are antidotal drugs which attenuate or eliminate them rapidly. Affect, mood, content, perception, and behavior can be affected in various ways and then the baseline condition can be approximately reinstated in minutes. The hallucinogenic drugs may produce a reaction resembling schizophrenia or there may be dream-like states. In any event rapport can be maintained with the patient and the reaction can be scrutinized. Certain aspects of our concepts of symptom formation, dream formation, depersonalization phenomena, conscious-preconscious-unconscious relationships, repression, regression, and some of the other mechanisms of defense can be tested, better understood and modified as indicated. Some light may also be thrown on our means of dealing with resistance and transference in psychoanalysis. However, the basic rule pertaining to free association may not be applicable in the strict sense in drug-intoxicated states. One can ask the patient to report everything that comes to mind but there are difficulties in terms of thinking disturbances, perceptions shifting too rapidly to be fully reported, inability to find adequate vocabulary for experiences, domination by emotion, and suppression or conscious withholding. Most of these difficulties resemble those which obtain in psychoanalysis and we have techniques of obviating them. Are the same techniques useful in drug-intoxicated states or must new ones be devised? Resistance and transference are altered with drug administration and again technical modifications may need to be developed in order to facilitate our investigating them adequately.

The therapeutic value of these drugs is a highly controversial issue except for a few specific and established uses of the barbiturates. There are reports of remarkable results with methamphetamine, amobarbital, mescaline with chlorpromazine, and d-LSD$_{25}$ used once or in serial administration.[7,26,40] Other investigators have been less optimistic. [1,3,8,42] The positive results are usually attributed to psychotherapy facilitated by the drug or to psychodynamic change in association with the drug experience. The description of the patient material, the procedure and the method of evaluating results are not entirely clear in many reports. Usually there is a relatively short follow-up period and the long term results are not known.

The evaluation of the effects of psychoanalysis and psychotherapy is a difficult problem. An appraisal of the mechanisms which bring about positive results is even more complex. To assess the therapeutic efficacy of drug-expedited psychotherapy, one must account for all the other variables introduced by drug administration. It may be that some of the questions as to the psychodynamic effects of drug administration must be answered before the therapeutic value can be determined and well understood.

REFERENCES

1. ANDERSON, E. W. AND RAWNSLEY, K.: Clinical studies of lysergic acid diethylamide. Monatsschr. Psychiat. u. Neurol., *128:* 38-55, 1954; Abstract in Dig. Neurol. & Psychiat., *22:* 403 1954.

2. BUSCH, A. K. AND JOHNSON, W. C.: LSD 25 as an aid in psychotherapy. Dis. Nerv. Syst., *11:* 241, 1950.

3. CATTELL, J. P.: The influence of mescaline on psychodynamic material. J. Nerv. & Ment. Dis., *119:* 233-244, 1954.

4. DELAY, J.: Pharmacological exploration of personality: Narco-analysis and methedrine shock. Proc. Roy. Soc. Med., *42:* 491-496, 1949.

5. ———, PICHOT, P., LAINE, B. AND PERSE, J.: Less Modifications de la personnalité produites par la diethylamide de l'acide lysergique (LSD 25). Ann. Med. Psychol., *2:* 1-13, 1954; Abstract in Dig. Neurol. & Psychiat., *22:* 355, 1954.

6. DENBER, H. C. B., MERLIS, S., HINTON, H.: Action of mescaline on the clinical and brain wave patterns of schizophrenic patients before and after ECT. Abstract, 3rd Int. EEG Congress, 1953, p. 30.

7. ——— AND MERLIS, S.: A note on some therapeutic implications of the mescaline induced state. Psychiat. Quart. *28:* 635, 1954.

8. DeShon, J. Rinkel, M., and Solomon, N. C.: Mental changes experimentally produced by LSD. Psychiat. Quart., 26: 33-53, 1952.
9. Escalona, S,: Problems in psycho-analytic research. Internat. J. Psycho-Analysis, 33: 11, 1952.
10. Forrer, G. R. and Goldner, R. D.: Experimental physiological studies with lysergic acid diethylamide (LSD 25). Arch. Neurol. & Psychiat., 65: 581-588, 1950.
11. Freud, S.: Revision of the theory of dreams, Lecture XXIX. New Introductory Lectures on Psychoanalysis. New York, W. W. Norton & Co., 1933.
12. Gastaut, H., Ferrer, S., et al: Action of lysergic acid diethylamide on the psychic functions and EEG. Confinia Neurol., 13: 102, 1953.
13. Glover, E.: Research methods in psycho-analysis. Internat. J. Psycho-Analysis, 33: 403, 1952.
14. Guttman, E.: Artificial psychoses produced by mescaline. J. Ment. Sci., 82: 203-221, 1936.
15. Hilgard, E. R.: Experimental approaches to psychoanalysis. In Psychoanalysis as Science, Pumpian-Mindlin, E., ed. Stanford, Stanford Univ. Press, 1952, p. 3.
16. Hoch, P. H.: Experimentally-produced psychoses. Am. J. Psychiat., 107: 607-611, 1951.
17. ——: Experimental psychiatry. Am. J. Psychiat., 111: 787-790, 1955.
18. ——, Cattell, J. P., Pennes, H. H.: Effects of mescaline and lysergic acid (d-LSD 25). Am. J. Psychiat., 108: 579-584, 1952.
19. ——: Effect of drugs: Theoretical considerations from a psychological viewpoint. Am. J. Psychiat., 108: 58-589, 1952.
20. —— and Polatin, P.: Pseudoneurotic form of schizophrenia. Psychiat. Quart., 23: 248-276, 1949.
21. Hope, J. M., Callaway, E., and Sands, S. L.: Intravenous pervitin and the psychopathology of schizophrenia. Dis. Nerv. Syst., 12: 67-72, 1951.
22. Katzenelbogen, S. and Ai Ding Fang: Narcosynthesis effects of sodium amytal, methedrine and LSD 25. Dis. Nerv. Syst., 14: 85, 1953.
23. Klüver, H.: Mechanisms of Hallucinations in Studies of Personality. New York, McGraw-Hill, 1942.
24. ——: Functional differences between the occipital and temporal lobes with special reference to the interrelations of behavior and extracerebral mechanisms. In Hixon Symposium: Cerebral Mechanisms in Behavior. New York, John Wiley & Sons, 1951. pp. 147-199.
25. Kubie, L. S.: Problems and techniques of psychoanalytic validation and progress. In Psychoanalysis as Science, Pumpian-Mindlin, E. ed. Stanford, Stanford Univ. Press, 1952. p. 46.
26. —— and Margolin, S.: The therapeutic role of drugs in the process of repression, dissociation and synthesis. Psychosom. Med., 7: 147, 1945.
27. Lehmann, H. E., and Hanrahan, G. E.: Chlorpromazine: New inhibiting agent for psychomotor excitement and manic states. Arch. Neurol. & Psychiat., 71: 227-237, 1954.
28. Levine, J., Rinkel, M. and Greenblatt, M.: Psychological and physiological effects of intravenous pervitin. Am. J. Psychiat., 105: 429-434, 1948.

29. LIDDELL, D. W. AND WEIL-MALHERBE, H.: The effects of methedrine and LSD on mental processes and on blood adrenaline level. J. Neurol. *16:* 7, 1953.

30. LINDEMANN, E.: Psychological changes in normal and abnormal individuals under the influence of sodium amytal. Am. J. Psychiat., *11:* 1083-1091, 1932.

31. ———: The neurophysiological effects of intoxicating drugs. Am. J. Psychiat., *90:* 1007, 1934.

32. ——— AND MALAMUD, W.: Analysis of psychopathological effects of intoxicating drugs. Am. J. Psychiat., *13:* 853-881, 1934.

33. ——— AND CLARKE, L. D.: Modification in ego structure and personality reactions under the influence of the effects of drugs. Am. J. Psychiat., *108:* 561, February, 1952.

34. PENNES, H. H.: Clinical reactions of schizophrenics to sodium amytal, pervitin hydrochloride, mescaline sulfate, and d-lysergic acid diethylamide. J. Nerv. & Ment. Dis., *119:* 95-112, 1954.

35. ———: Effects of various drugs on clinical psychopathology. In Experimental Psychopathology, Hoch, P. H., and Zubin, J., eds. New York, Grune & Stratton, 1957, chap. 15.

36. PUMPIAN-MINDLIN, E. ed.: Psychoanalysis as Science: The Hixon Lectures on the Scientific Status of Psychoanalysis. Stanford, Stanford Univ. Press, 1952.

37. REDLICH, F. C., et al.: Narcoanalysis and truth. Am. J. Psychiat., *107:* 586, 1951.

38. RINKEL, M., DeSHON, H. J. AND HYDE, R. W.: Experimental schizophrenia-like symptoms. Am. J. Psychiat., *108:* 572-577, 1952.

39. RUBIN, M. A., MALAMUD, W. AND HOPE, J. M.: Electroencephalographic and psychopathological manifestations in schizophrenia as influenced by drugs. Psychosom. Med., *4:* 309-318, 1942.

40. SANDISON, R. A., SPENCER, A. M. AND WHITELAW, J. D. A.: The therapeutic value of lysergic acid diethylamide in mental illness. J. Ment. Sci., *100:* 491-507, 1954.

41. ———: Psychological aspects of the LSD treatment of the neuroses. J. Ment. Sci., *100:* 508-518, 1954.

42. SAVAGE, C.: Lysergic acid diethylamide, a clinical psychological study. Am. J. Psychiat. *108:* 896, 1952.

43. STOCKINGS, G. T.: A clinical study of the mescaline psychosis, with special references to the mechanism of the genesis of schizophrenia and other psychotic states. J. Ment. Sci., *86:* 29-47, 1940.

44. STOLL, W. A.: Lysergsäure-diäthylamid, ein phantastikum aus der mutterkorngruppe. Schweiz, Arch. f. Neurol. u. Psychiat., *60:* 1-45, 1947.

45. STOLL, W. A.: Rorschach tests under LSD. Rorschachiana, *1:* 249, 1952; abstract in Excerpta Med., *7:* 689 (3119), 1954.

46. SULLIVAN, D. J.: Psychiatric uses of intravenous sodium amytal. Am. J. Psychiat., *108:* 411-418, 1942.

47. WIKLER, A.: Mechanism of action of drugs that modify personality function. Am. J. Psychiat., *108:* 590-599, 1952.

48. WOLF, S. AND RIPLEY, H. S.: Studies on the action of intravenously administered sodium amytal. Am. J. M. Sci., *215:* 56-62, 1948.

49. WOLFF, H. G. AND CURRAN, D.: The nature of delirium and allied states. Arch. Neurol. & Psychiat., *33:* 1175-1215, 1935.

15

EFFECTS OF VARIOUS DRUGS ON CLINICAL PSYCHOPATHOLOGY

By HARRY H. PENNES, M.D.*

A PREVIOUS REPORT has described the clinical effects of a series of four drugs each of which was given independently to a group of schizophrenics.[1] The drugs were Sodium Amytal, Pervitin hydrochloride (methamphetamine, desoxyephedrine, etc.), mescaline sulfate, and d-lysergic acid diethylamide. The general findings were as follows: (1) each drug produced relatively specific effects on mental symptomatology and (2) some subjects experienced exacerbation of symptoms with each drug. This paper deals principally with certain aspects of symptom intensification.

MATERIALS AND METHODS

The earlier report gives descriptive data on the 55 hospitalized schizophrenic subjects, with dosages and routes of drug administration.[1] Group I patients were pseudoneurotic schizophrenics; Groups II and III, classical schizophrenics. Group II patients had slight or no deterioration; Group III, moderately severe or severe deterioration. The drugs will be referred to hereafter briefly as Amytal, Pervitin, mescaline, and LSD.

Subjective reports and objective examinations were used in evaluating the results. The overall reaction to each drug was placed in one of the three following categories: normalization, intensification, and diphasic. These descriptive, phenomenological terms refer to the directional effect of the drug administration on the pre-drug clinical symptomatology. Normalization means the reduction or elimination of one or more of the baseline clinical symptoms. Intensification consists of exacerbation of one or more baseline clinical symptoms.

* Director of Clinical Research, Eastern Pennsylvania Psychiatric Institute, Philadelphia, Penna. The actual study was done at the New York State Psychiatric Institute, Department of Experimental Psychiatry.

The diphasic reaction consists of a combination of normalization and intensification responses in the same subject. The diphasic responses had a fairly high incidence of occurrence, particularly after pervitin; their inclusion complicates the analysis but avoids undesirable distortion of the data.

The following types of response were included in the diphasic category: 1. Reduction in some symptoms and increase in others; most examples of this type of response were definite by both subjective and objective criteria. However, an important methodological consideration needs description. When a subject had a number of different psychopathological manifestations in the pre-drug state, some were intensified but others were often not manifested at all during a given drug reaction of relatively short duration. For example, pre-drug obsessive-compulsive activity might not be manifested and a phobic component might be accentuated during the drug reaction. In the general case an attempt was made to distinguish between passive disappearance and active reduction of the previous symptom which did not appear under drug. The only criterion available was the subjective account. If combined normalization and intensification were reported, the reaction was considered diphasic; if no normalization were reported, the reaction was classified as pure intensification. 2. Alternating increase and decrease of the same symptom over a period of time. 3. A marked disparity between the subjective report and apparent objective effects of the drug, occurring in relatively few instances.

The specific pharmacological effects of the drugs were handled as follows: If, in spite of the central depression and stimulation produced by Amytal and Pervitin, sufficient symptom reduction occurred so that the subject reported only improvement after these drugs, the response was rated as normalization. However, if the patient reported that his status was unfavorably altered (Amytal drowsiness, incoordination, Pervitin overactivity, etc.) the response was rated as either diphasic or intensification according to the rest of the clinical reaction. Mescaline and LSD were rated as intensifiers on the basis of increase in baseline symptoms (in consistency with the definition of intensification used here) and not on the basis of the primary effects these drugs produce in normals as well as in mental patients (perceptual and intellectual disturbances, etc.)

TABLE 1.—*Symptom Exacerbation Following Administration of Sodium Amytal* and Pervitin Hydrochloride.†*

	Amytal	Pervitin
	10 patients	20 patients
1. Emotional discharges including anxiety depression, self-depreciation, hostility, guilt, and suspicion.	1	8
2. Phobic or hysterical manifestations.		
3. Catatonic withdrawal, excitement, rigidity, or cerea flexibilitas.	1	8
4. Paranoid reactions: persecutory or grandiose.	5	3
5. Hebephrenic reactions: inappropriateness, grimacing, mannerisms, sterotypies, etc.	3	5
6. Schizophrenic thinking disorder.	2	6
7. Auditory and visual hallucinations.	1	2
8. Obsessive-compulsive urges.	0	1

NOTE: Each drug was given independently to the sample of 55 patients (Groups I, II, and III). Above major symptoms were distributed throughout the sample. The symptom exacerbations occurred as part of diphasic or pure intensification reactions. Figures for a given drug overlap since a single subject often exhibited exacerbation of several different types of symptoms.

Mescaline sulfate (0.4-0.6 Gm. I.V.) and LSD (0.010-0.120 mgm., oral) also intensified the above range of symptoms in the material as a whole.

* 0.25-0.50 Gm., I.V.
† 20.0-40.0 mgm., I.V.

The dosages used (Table 1.) were sufficient to permit classification of each response in one of the categories, with the exception of one subject after pervitin. Interview technique was non-directive and open-ended in order to minimize psychological manipulation of the subjects.

RESULTS

I. *Individual Drugs*

Drug effects were classified as follows for the group as a whole: Amytal was preponderantly a normalizer (65.4%); Pervitin showed all three effects without undue preponderance (normalization, 37.0%; intensification, 20.4%; diphasic, 42.6%); mescaline was a regular intensifier (100.0%); and LSD was usually an intensifier (64.0%) with 24.0% diphasic reactions. The magnitude of these figures reflects the composition of the total patient sample because the frequency of type of response with Amytal and Pervitin varied with the diagnosis and degree of deterioration. Thus, Amytal produced the highest incidence (75.0%) of normalization responses in Group I, intermediate (64.0%) in Group II, and lowest incidence (50.0%) in Group III. Pervitin also displayed a clearer trend in this direction, with 55.0% normalization in Group I, 29.2% in Group II, and 20.0% in Group III. Pervitin, therefore, produced a higher incidence of intensification and diphasic reactions than Amytal both for the entire series and for the three sub-groups. This higher incidence was reflected mainly in emotional discharges, phobic, hysterical, and catatonic manifestations (Table 1).

Two types of effect on degree of wakefulness were noted with pervitin and were most apparent in Group I patients. The first, which usually began immediately after injection, consisted of intense relaxation which often progressed to the point of subjective drowsiness; facial expression became more relaxed and motor activity was reduced. After about 5 to 30 minutes, drowsiness began to disappear and a sense of mild stimulation appeared. This was a state of relaxation with increased alertness, self-confidence, energy and drives, assertiveness, and overall ability to function optimally. A minority of subjects reported only the stimulant effect from the beginning, rather than the sedative-stimulant sequence. Most subjects with the preliminary sedative phase reported normalization during this period, which increased in intensity during the period of mild stimulation. Some patients spontaneously likened the normalization during the preliminary phase to that occurring with a "sedative." The sedative phase of Pervitin action was not included in the previous report on these subjects.[1]

II. Symptom Intensification

Symptom exacerbation by drugs may be analyzed according to mechanism and type of intensified symptoms.

A. Mechanisms may be regarded broadly as of direct drug origin (primary pharmacological actions) or of individual, personality- determined origin. At the clinical level of observation, the specific pharmacological activity of amytal will be taken as depression of level of consciousness (drowsiness, etc.) plus "release" or "disinhibition"; the corresponding activity of pervitin will be taken as the stimulation phase previously described (sedative phase disregarded because principally associated with normalization). Symptom intensification with these two drugs occurred during these phases of action, particularly the "disinhibition" or "release" phase of amytal and the excessive stimulation phase of pervitin activity. These are only correlations and further presumptive evidence is required that these pharmacological actions generated intensification per se. This evidence is provided by the subject's verbal data and behavior; typically, no concern was expressed about the fact of drug administration or the associated pharmacological effects of the drugs. The patients could give only vague surmises for their more disturbed state. Mental contents dealt usually with past and present preoccupations and conflicts. However, secondary psychological reactions are obviously not excluded by these facts since some subjects may not have expressed the pertinent considerations.

Amytal initially reduced symptoms in diphasic reactors with the onset of the central depressant action. This was manifested most often by decrease in anxiety, tension, and other psychopathology. This phase then typically progressed into an intensification phase: emotional discharges with production of affectively-loaded material, etc. (Table 1). The usual diphasic sequence with Pervitin was as follows: initial normalization occurred during a preliminary sedative-mild stimulant sequence, as described (Results, I). As drug action continued, the stimulation appeared to increase and became subjectively unpleasant; symptom intensification concomitantly appeared (Table 1). In subjects with pure intensification with Pervitin the stimulant phase usually appeared to be excessive and unpleasant from the beginning.

With mescaline and LSD, the basic effects—motor, perceptual, intellectual alterations, etc.—were undoubtedly drug-induced on an acute toxic basis. In most cases these basic effects were not present in the drug-free state. Increase of pre-drug manifestations could have been and probably were partly of drug origin, but personality factors will be considered below. The clinical pharmacology of mescaline and LSD does not offer so ready a basis for primary drug intensification as the well-recognized concepts of Amytal "release" and Pervitin over-stimulation.

There are various reasons, not given here, for concluding that intensification reactions were not exclusively of primary "placebo" origin; however, an effect must probably be assigned to this factor. There was much evidence on the other hand for a secondary type of psychological reaction to the drugs. Specific examples were: withdrawal and paranoid reactions following the "drugged" feeling produced by Amytal; anxiety over the surge of Pervitin stimulation; varied reactions to the bizarre and disturbing perceptual and other changes elicited by mescaline and LSD. The pharmacological changes elicited by the drugs may be interpreted by these patients as threatening, ego-alien, or unfavorable and reacted to by increased defensive measures or disorganization characteristic of the drug-free state. Secondary personality reactions may also conceivably include unfavorable responses to drug-induced normalization or intensification of symptoms. Detailed psychodynamic explanations may also be offered. It has already been mentioned that the subject's verbal data and behavior provide only presumptive evidence for direct drug action. The same limitations exist for the importance of personality factors, since an apparently secondary psychological reaction may well be of direct drug origin. For example, a subject under mescaline may express anxiety over bizarre perceptual disturbances; it is not thereby excluded that part or all of the anxiety may be of direct origin.

With the present methodology, exclusive significance cannot be ascribed therefore to either direct drug or individual personality effects as the basis for the occurrence of symptom intensification. In most cases, there was probably a merging of the two factors in the same patient.

B. Type of Intensified Symptoms. Many different symptoms were exacerbated after a given drug in different subjects; all four drugs also intensified the same wide range of symptoms (itemized for Amytal and Pervitin, Table 1). These findings indicate non-specificity of intensification both for type of symptom and for type of drug. This relative non-selectivity is consistent with either mechanism of intensification discussed above under II, A. If direct drug action were responsible, then the non-selectivity may be expressed by the following statement: the form of the output (intensified symptom) depends on the nature of the input (drug) and on the condition of the system as expressed in pre-drug symptomatology. The same statement applies to personality-induced intensifications insofar as they are relatable to specific actions of the drug. Although non-selectivity was evident for symptom intensification in general some specificity occurred as to particular symptoms. Emotional changes of various types were the most frequent form of symptom intensification with all four drugs in this patient material. The earlier report has indicated how the patients' pre-drug psychopathological status merged with and influenced intensification reactions.[1]

DISCUSSION

Some previous studies[2,3,4,5] of the mental effects of drugs have been qualitatively analyzed in terms of the relative contributions of drug and individual (particular personality, specific content of psychosis, psychodynamics, nature of perceptual processes, etc.). The present point of departure from these studies has consisted of the analysis of the data in terms of normalization and intensification. The conclusions reached by previous workers have generally been confirmed in this framework. The incidence of occurrence of symptom intensification was different for each drug (Results, I). The mechanisms appeared to be a combination of direct drug and individual psychological factors; subject's pre-drug symptom status merged with the intensification responses.

Valuable studies have recently been reported by Lasagna, von Felsinger, and Beecher in which subjects of various types received a series of four drugs and the mental effects were correlated with personality.[6,7] A minority group of reactors occurred who displayed atypical effects with each drug. In their series, amphetamine (closely related in structure and action to Pervitin) atypically produced dysphoria and sedation rather than euphoria and stimulation; Nembutal (related to Amytal) atypically produced dysphoria. These minority responses in their normal group tended to occur in subjects with the most severe personality maladjustments. The authors interpreted the correlation between atypical drug reaction and maladjusted personality in terms of secondary psychological reactions to the basic pharmacological actions of the drugs.

This interpretation applies in part to the reactions observed with the schizophrenics of this study. Some patients did appear to develop alarm reactions to the intense stimulation associated with Pervitin and the depression of consciousness characteristic of Amytal. However, another group showed symptom intensification under the same pharmacological conditions without evidence of secondary psychological reactions. The validity of these statements is of course subject to the usual limitations inherent in mechanism from verbal and behavioral data.

Lasagna, et al., interpreted the apparently paradoxical sedative effect of amphetamine as a defensive withdrawal to a threatening surge of stimulation. If this explanation were to apply also to the mental patients in this study it might be expected that the sedative effect of pervitin would be associated with intensification features. However, when relaxation and drowsiness did occur these features were usually associated with moderate normalization aspects (Results, I). The succeeding phase of early mild stimulation often eliminated symptomatology completely. It could be assumed then that the sedative effect was of primary drug origin which directly reduced symptomatology. An alternative explanation is that Pervitin somehow reduced anxiety, tension, and other symptoms exclusively by its mild stimulant action. If anxiety and tension are viewed as states of hyper-awareness or hyper-vigilance, abrupt reduction of these states by this action might secondarily produce the subjective misimpression of drowsiness whereas, in fact, the subject has only moved from a hyper-aware to a normally aware level of consciousness.

In the earlier report on the present subjects, a minority group was designated "intensification reactors." Comparison of this group with the minority group of Lasagna, et al., is limited by methodological differences in the two studies. "Intensification reactors" showed some type of symptom exacerbation with each of the four drugs which have already been itemized in detail.[1] These subjects showed diphasic and/or intensification response with both Amytal and

Pervitin; all subjects had intensification and/or diphasic responses to mescaline and LSD. The occurrence of this minority group points to the fact that some cases normalized with Amytal and Pervitin, while others of grossly similar clinical description showed symptom exacerbation. This may be explained by postulating a difference in basic drug action, a tendency to secondary psychological reactions of unfavorable type, or a combination of these two mechanisms. Major differences were not present, however, between the intensification reactors and the remainder of the material with respect to gross clinical variables, overall pre-drug psychological status, and hypothetical latent disintegration tendency. Possible differences in the central actions of the drugs were of course not excluded by the clinical methodology.

Symptom intensification in general probably originates in response to the environmental constellation of administration and continues on a direct drug basis, plus secondary personality disorganization or defensive maladaptation to the primary drug actions. The relative contribution of these various mechanisms probably varies for the different drugs and with different subjects. The preferred explanation also bears a relationship to theoretical ideas on the mechanism of symptom formation. If symptoms are taken as personality-determined, defensive modes of maladjustment to external and internal reality, then symptom intensification under drugs may be viewed as quantitative extension of such maladjustments to handle the drug experience. If symptoms are taken as direct evidence of disorganization at a somatic level and without defense or restitutive value, then the drugs increase such disorganization by further disruption of somatic mechanisms. Either explanation would fit the observed intensification responses in this study, but a multifactoral mechanism is probably closer to the actual state of affairs.

SUMMARY

1. Symptom intensification by drugs in schizophrenics is described and analyzed. The drugs employed are Amytal, Pervitin, mescaline, and LSD.

2. Mescaline and LSD produced symptom intensification more regularly than did Amytal and Pervitin at the dosage levels used.

3. The mechanisms of symptom intensification appear to include both direct drug action and secondary, personality-determined factors.

4. Many different symptoms were intensified in different subjects

after a given drug was administered; all four drugs intensified the same wide range of symptoms.

REFERENCES

1. PENNES, H. H.: Clinical reactions of schizophrenics to Sodium Amytal, Pervitin hydrochloride, mescaline sulfate, and d-lysergic acid diethylamide (LSD 25) J. Nerv. Ment. Dis., *119:* 95-112, 1954.
2. LINDEMANN, E., AND MALAMUD, W.: Experimental analysis of the psychopathological effects of intoxicating drugs. Am. J. Psychiat., *13:* 853-881, 1934.
3. RUBIN, M. A., MALAMUD, W. AND HOPE, J. M.: Electroencephalogram and psychopathological manifestations in schizophrenia as influenced by drugs. Psychosom. Med., *4:* 355-361, 1942.
4. WIKLER, A.: Mechanisms of action of drugs that modify personality function. Am. J. Psychiat., *108:* 590-599, 1952.
5. LINDEMANN, E., AND CLARK, L. D.: Modification in ego structure and personality reactions under the influence of the effects of drugs. Am. J. Psychiat., *108:* 561-567, 1952.
6. LASAGNA, L., VON FELSINGER, J. M., AND BEECHER, H. K.: Drug-induced mood changes in man. 1. Observations in healthy subjects, chronically ill patients and "post-addicts." J.A.M.A., *157:* 1006-1020, 1955.
7. VON FELSINGER, J. M., LASAGNA, L., AND BEECHER, H.K.: Drug-induced mood changes in man. 2. personality and reactions to drugs. J.A.M.A. *157:* 1113-1119, 1955.

16

EXPERIMENTAL INVESTIGATIONS ON PSYCHOSURGICAL PATIENTS

By STANLEY LESSE, M.D.*

I N SPITE OF THE FACT that many thousands of psychosurgical procedures of various types have been performed during the past 20 years, very little is known as to what happens during and immediately following the lobotomy proper. Also, there are large gaps in our knowledge as to what occurs when various areas of the brain are stimulated in schizophrenic patients. There are many reasons for performing these operations under general anesthesia, not the least being that most patients requiring psychosurgery are unpredictable and cannot tolerate the usual stresses of life, let alone an intracranial operation. Unfortunately, though, the opportunity to collect valuable psychological and psychophysiological data is lost when the patient is unconscious.

METHODOLOGY

Between October 1952 and November 1954 we performed 42 large frontal craniotomies, under procaine or nuprocaine anesthesia, through which bilateral pre-frontal leukotomies were performed under direct observation. Forty-one of the patients had schizophrenia of various subtypes while one patient suffered from intractable pain. The details of our methods of preoperative evaluation and the preparation and observation of schizophrenic patients during a three to five hour psychosurgical procedure performed under local anesthesia, will be presented in another publication.

The general aim of the pre-operative preparation was to make the patient extremely dependent on the neuropsychiatrist who would be in attendance at the operation. This was accomplished by means of daily repetitive explanations during which time various aspects of the

---

* Neurological Institute of the Presbyterian Hospital of New York and Department of Neurology, College of Physicians and Surgeons, Columbia University. Formerly Senior Research Psychiatrist, New York State Psychiatric Institute.

operation were discussed. General descriptions of the theory behind the operation, the techniques used, and sensations that would be experienced were given. This technique tended to minimize the "anticipation of the unknown" that builds tremendous tension in most operative patients, particularly in those who are mentally ill. In spite of the fact that all of our patients had experienced psychotic manifestations for many years and had many years of therapy both in and out of mental institutions, only nine of the 42 patients required that the local anesthesia be terminated with pentothal sodium prior to the completion of the lobotomy proper.

Stimulation of the Temporal Lobe Cortex

In 1952 Penfield[1] reported that he was able to produce what he called "evoked memories" or "evoked recollections" by stimulating the temporal lobe cortex in patients operated upon for various organic brain processes. We attempted to reproduce these "evoked" phenomena by stimulating the temporal lobes in 13 schizophrenic patients who had no evidence of organic brain disease. Some of these patients had been actively hallucinating before and during the early phases of the operations.

The general techniques of stimulation that were followed were based on work previously performed by others in the operative team.[2,3] Square wave pulses were used and a stimulation frequency of 100 per second was utilized in all instances, while the pulse width was kept at 5.0 millisecond. The voltages were gradually increased to the point where an electrical after-discharge was produced (in a few instances seizures occurred) or to the point beyond which there was danger of tissue damage. The superior and middle temporal gyri were stimulated repeatedly at many points, from the temporal pole as far posterior as the general location of the anastomotic vein of Labbé. All these points were anterior to the transverse gyrus of Heschl (areas 41 and 42 Brodmann). In one patient the angular gyrus was stimulated; the right uncus was stimulated in another.

In none of these patients were we able to produce anything that simulated the "evoked memories" described by Penfield. Not one of them demonstrated any mental aberrations. Even those who were actively hallucinating during the operation gave no evidence that the hallucinations could be "fired" off or in any way affected by electrical stimulation of the areas of the temporal lobes that we investigated.

Observations During Lobotomy

Thirty-three of the original 42 patients had pre-frontal leukotomies performed while they were fully conscious. Immediately preceding each leukotomy a repeat evaluation of each patient's psychic status was made. We reviewed the: (1) state of consciousness; (2) level of cooperation; (3) degree of anxiety (motor, affectual, and verbal components; and (4) memory and orientation. We attempted to quantify the first three points and most of our patients were very cooperative. Only four showed any significant degree of depression of consciousness and all of these were slight. Only one patient showed any deficit in recent memory or orientation and this was slight also. All of the patients demonstrated moderate to marked anxiety. Chart No. 1 summarizes the evaluation of the 33 patients immediately prior to lobotomy.

For consistency we divided each frontal lobe into approximate halves, a medial half and a lateral half. This made four quadrants in all that had to be cut. Various patterns of quadrant cutting were used, for we were attempting to investigate the frequently expressed concept of dominance of one hemisphere over the other in intellectual and emotional functioning. As recently as 1953, Greenblatt and Solomon stated "the right sided cases obtained greater benefit than the left."[4]

A review of our material revealed some very interesting data. It was found that the various components of anxiety (motor, affectual, and verbal) were not relieved by the same degree of frontal lobe sectioning. There appeared to be a possible quantitative relationship between the amount of frontal lobe cut and the degree of amelioration of anxiety.

We found that more than 80 percent of patients lobotomized under local anesthesia demonstrated definite symptoms and signs of lessened tension. (This figure might be even higher but we were unable to evaluate the level of anxiety in six patients because they developed acute organic mental reactions during the lobotomy). It was noted that all of the patients in the group in which anxiety was significantly reduced had a definite decrease in the motor component of anxiety. The affectual component was not ameliorated as often and the verbal aspect was changed even less frequently.

It was found that cutting the first quadrant decreased the motor component to a slight or moderate degree in more than half of the patients. There were some, however, who showed no decrease in the motor aspect until the second quadrant was cut; two patients showed no change until the entire lobotomy had been completed. It should be noted that as more brain was sectioned the degree of muscle relaxation increased.

With regard to the affectual component only two patients showed any definite change after just one quadrant had been changed. This was in striking contrast to the alterations in the motor aspect already described. The sectioning of the second and third quadrants saw a definite decrease in affect. Again, it appeared that the more brain that was sectioned the greater the decrease in the affectual expression of anxiety.

In contrast to both the motor and affectual aspects of anxiety no changes in verbal content occurred until three or even all four quadrants were sectioned; an exception, one patient in whom the verbal content changed after the cutting of the second quadrant. It should be noted also that even after the completion of the leukotomy, only six of every ten patients who demonstrated significant amelioration of the motor and affectual components demonstrated a significant change in verbal content.

To summarize, it appeared that a greater amount of frontal lobe white matter had to be sectioned to cause a change in affect than was required to cause a decrease in muscle tension or motor activity. Similarly it appeared that an even larger leukotomy was necessary to produce a change in verbal content. I gained the impression as I observed these reactions in one patient after the other that there was a certain lower threshold, unique for each given patient, below which each patient's tension had to pass before the verbal content was altered. These observations were often very dramatic. It was most impressive to witness the change, within a span of one-half to five minutes, from marked restlessness, muscle tension, and obvious fear to a state in which the patient was calm and said in response to questioning, "I feel good" or "Nothing bothers me."

In the majority of patients in whom the overt expression of anxiety was marked, the secondary defense mechanisms such as obsessive-compulsive phenomena, phobias, hypochondriacal complaints, delusional thinking, illusionary mechanisms, and even hallucinations either completely disappeared or were greatly reduced in degree, all in a matter of minutes. On the other hand, if the overt expression of anxiety to begin with was not great, the degree of amelioration of these symptoms was noticeably less or there was no improvement at all. There were no significant differences in the degree of amelioration of anxiety, rage, and depression. If one affectual pattern was reduced, all the rest were.

We could observe no difference in the degree of improvement when the right lobe or left lobe was cut first, which was what we anticipated before we began our studies. In a few instances there was an initial increase in anxiety after the first quadrant was cut. However, as more brain was sectioned this quickly subsided.

DISCUSSIONS AND CONCLUSIONS

The patients in this series were particularly suited for this type of study. In general they were in much better condition mentally and physically than those reported upon from the large state hospitals. In fact, only a few of our patients demonstrated any evidence of affectual or intellectual deterioration, and in those it was only slight. With the exception of one patient who had epileptic seizures secondary to a previous topectomy, nobody in the group had clinical or laboratory evidences of organic disease. Although the level of anxiety was high in most cases prior to the operation, the vast majority of patients could be prepared so that they were cooperative during the procedures. Our case material included schizophrenic patients of all subtypes but had a higher percentage of pseudoneurotic schizophrenics than had series reported from other institutions. This type of patient has been shown to respond particularly well to psychosurgery.[5]

In 1952, when Penfield[1] reported upon his observations of "evoked memories" or "evoked recollections" which he had produced by stimulating the temporal lobe cortex, it caused a great deal of comment among neurologists and psychiatrists alike. These phenomena in many ways resembled hallucinations. In a subsequent report[6] it was more clearly stated that these observations appeared to be re-enactments of recent or past events in the patients' lives and that they could appear in visual or auditory spheres or both. These same recollections could be reproduced at times by successive stimulations in the same spot or in adjacent areas. On other occasions stimulation at the same area might produce a different recollection or no response at all might be noted. It was difficult to evaluate, from the articles, whether the patients were dominated by these electrically produced experiences in the same manner that the schizophrenic patients are dominated by hallucinations. Penfield postulated that electrical stimulation of the temporal cortex caused these aberrations by activating the same pattern of brain elements as were activated when the original experiences occurred. He stated that only specific psychic phenomena could be reactivated and not generalizations.

To help account for these phenomena, he postulated a "centrencephalic system" which consisted of those parts of the brain stem, including the thalamus, which have symmetrical connections with both hemispheres. He conceived of the "system" as being a ganglionic region where sensory impulses of all types were received, where information with regard to past experiences was made available; an area where mechanisms that were prerequisite to the existence of intellectual activity and to the initiation of efferent impulses that produce consciously planned action were to be found. He further stated that consciousness was made possible by an interaction of the cerebral cortex and centrencephalic system, that there was a two-way passage of impulses between them. The explanation was proposed that those experiences of which the individual was "aware" were recorded in the temporal lobes. When the temporal lobes were stimulated experimentally "evoked memory" was possible, if a ganglionic pattern which originally recorded that experience was again activated, setting off an interaction between the temporal cortex and the centrencephalic system.

All the patients studied by Penfield had organic brain deficits, and this immediately raised questions as to whether these same phenomena could be produced in schizophrenic patients who, as far as we could tell by our present diagnostic techniques, had no organic brain impairment. As mentioned previously, we were unable to produce any response by stimulating the anterior or middle portions of the superior or middle gyri of the temporal lobe that in any way simulated "evoked recollections." Nor did the electrical stimulations affect any hallucinatory pattern already present. It is true that our series of temporal lobe explorations included only 13 cases and that many of the points from which Penfield produced his findings[1,6,7] were posterior to the areas that we were safely able to reach through our exposures. However, we repeatedly stimulated areas from which he reported producing his psychic responses; our parameters were in the range that he used. Penfield's findings may have great theoretical importance in explaining some of the phenomena seen in psychomotor epilepsy, but as yet it is questionable whether these theories can be generalized to be valid for an understanding of the hallucinations that occur in schizophrenia. Further studies along these lines are planned.

From our studies it appeared that symptomatic improvement during a prefrontal leukotomy did not occur until the patient's anxiety was reduced below a certain threshold that was unique for each individual. It was noted too that these symptoms were not significantly altered when the leukotomy had proceeded just far enough to relieve the motor component of anxiety, but not far enough to alter the affectual or verbal components; it was usually not until one half or more of the brain had been sectioned. It should be noted that there was no significant improvement in the clinical picture if there was very little overt expression of anxiety at the start.

Our studies demonstrated that more frontal lobe white matter had to be sectioned to produce a change in affect than was necessary to reduce the muscle tension or motor activity, and that an even greater section had to be made to alter the verbal content. There is still the question, however, of whether these different changes were due to the sectioning of specific fiber groups or whether the frontal lobe areas are equipotential and the psychic changes purely reflections of the quantity of brain cut. The literature contains evidence for both sides of the question.

With regards to the quantitative aspect of the problem, Meyer and Back[8] correlated the neuroanatomical findings in a large number of cases with the post-leukotomy clinical results. These patients had died months or years following psychosurgery, the deaths being unrelated to the operations. They pointed out the general relationship between quantitatively insufficient leukotomies and poor clinical results on the one hand, and better clinical results with adequate cuts on the other. Greenblatt and Solomon[4] also felt that one of the factors contributing to psychosurgical failures was an inadequacy in the degree of frontal lobe sectioning. In spite of a few papers giving reports of improvement with unilateral lobotomy,[4,9,10] other investigators consider it an inadequate procedure.[11,12,13] Freeman and Watts[14] suggest that in the "rare instances" in which unilateral operations are successful, the neurosurgeon has penetrated the genu of the corpus callosum producing lesions in the opposite hemisphere. Against the pure quantum theory are the observations by McLardy and Davis,[15] who, after a study of the brains of psychosurgical patients who had shown clinical relapse, found that relapse occurred in some in whom there was almost complete isolation of the prefrontal cortex. Meyer and Beck[8] found that the amount of brain cut in relapsing cases was only slightly less than in non-relapsing cases.

Recent stereotaxic studies, regional undercuttings, and more restricted lobotomies have presented evidence suggesting that cutting the dorsolateral white matter and particularly the dorsolateral cortex is associated with more undesirable post-lobotomy sequelae than if these areas are spared.[8,16,17,18,19]

It is my feeling, from information gathered from these studies and from the literature, that all areas of the frontal lobe are not equipotential but that the amount of brain cut in specific regions is also an important factor in the clinical results. Specific quantitative sectionings with stereotaxic methods will have to be performed to further the information relative to this problem.

REFERENCES

1. PENFIELD, W.: Memory mechanisms. Arch, Neurol. & Psychiat., *67:* 178, 1952.
2. GLUSMAN, M., RANSOHOFF, J., POOL, J. L., GRUNDFEST, H. AND METTLER, F. A.: Electrical excitability of the human motor cortex. I. The parameters of the electrical stimulus. J. Neurosurg., *9:* 461, 1952.
3. ——, ——, —— AND SLOAN, N.: Electrical excitability of the human uncus. J. Neurophysiol., *16:* 528, 1953.
4. GREENBLATT, M. AND SOLOMON, H. C.: Frontal Lobes and Schizophrenia. New York, Springer, 1953.
5. HOCH, P. H., POOL, J. L., RANSOHOFF, J., CATTELL, J. P. AND PENNES, H. H.: The psychosurgical treatment of pseudoneurotic schizophrenia. Am. J. Psychiat., *111:* 653, 1955.
6. PENFIELD, W.: Studies of the cerebral cortex of man. Brain Mechanisms and Consciousness, Springfield, Thomas, 1954, pp. 284-304.
7. ——AND JASPER, H.: Epilepsy and the Function of Anatomy of the Human Brain. Boston, Little, Brown, 1954.
8. MEYER, A. AND BECK, E.: Prefrontal Leukotomy and Related Operations. Springfield, C. C. Thomas, 1954.
9. GREENBLATT, M., ARNOT, R. AND SOLOMON, H. C.: Studies in Lobotomy. New York, Grune & Stratton, 1950.
10. WATTS, J. W. AND FREEMAN, W.: Prefrontal lobotomy: six years experience, comment by Lyerly, J. G. South. M. J. *36:* 478, 1954.
11. GAYLE, R. F. AND NEALE, C. L.: The treatment of certain mental disorders by psychosurgery. Virginia M. Monthly *71:* 36, 1945.
12. SIMONS, A., MARGOLIS, L. H., ADAMS, J. E. AND BOWMAN, K. M.: Unilateral and bilateral lobotomy: a controlled evaluation. Arch. Neurol. & Psychiat. *66:* 494, 1951.

13. Freeman, W. and Watts, J. W.: Psychosurgery, 1st ed. Springfield, C. C. Thomas, 1945.

14. —— and ——: Progress in Neurology and Psychiatry, Spiegel, ed. 1952, Ch. 21.

15. McLardy, T. and Davies, D. L.: Clinical and pathological observations on relapse after successful lobotomy. J. Neurol., Neurosurg. & Psychiat. *12:* 231, 1949.

16. Rylander, G.: Personality Changes After Operations on the Frontal Lobe. A Study of 32 Cases. Copenhagen, E. Munksgaard, 1939.

17. ——: Relief of symptoms and personality changes after superior convexity and orbital undercutting. V. Internat. Neurol. Cong. *2:* 213, 1953.

18. Sargent, W.: Ten years' clinical experience with modified leukotomy operations. Brit. M. J. *2:* 800, 1953.

19. Scoville, W. B. ,Wilk, E. K. and Pepe, A.: Selective cortical undercutting. Results in a new method of fractional lobotomy. Am. J. Psychiat. *107:* 730, 1951.

Discussion of Chapters 13-16

By DAVID McK. RIOCH, M.D.*

THE PAPERS PRESENTED TODAY are concerned with the general problem of the brain and behavior; in particular the brain and psychotic behavior. This is an area of psychiatry which has been in a confused state since the early days of the phrenologist. There has been too great a tendency to assume "functions" and then to find "centers" which perform these functions. The resulting mosaic of hypothetical centers performing a mass of preconceived functions has never been found satisfactory or useful. It seems to me that an analogy from general medicine is of value in this context.

At one time physicians treated a variety of illnesses as "fever." Only after years spent studying both the body and noxious agents did it become clear that certain symptoms had to be considered primarily as responses of the host to a wide variety of etiologic agents. Other symptoms had to be considered more specific, and procedures required for identifying the etiologic agents were often not at all the same as those used to measure the body's responses. Thus "fever" was studied by a variety of physiological techniques, none of which gave any clue to the etiologic agent. It is to be noted however that the old *treatment* of fever was often sufficiently successful to permit the survival of a medical profession. Of greater significance for psychiatric research is the fact that the host's response, (e.g., fever) may itself become an etiologic agent resulting in further damage and at times must be "treated" per se regardless of its primary basis.

In psychiatry we need to differentiate the phenomena representing the responses of the host from concepts of etiologic agents. The papers this afternoon have brought this problem into sharp focus and represent an important contribution in analyzing it and in indicating specific areas requiring study before an operationally useful solution may be developed.

In the first paper Doctor Hoch summarized in a clear, concise form the data from a large series of studies and formulated the application

* Director, Division of Neuropsychiatry, Walter Reed Army Institute of Research, Washington.

of the results to current psychiatric theory. His careful comparison of the symptoms which are at times evoked by such drugs as mescaline and lysergic acid with the symptoms of schizophrenia led logically to his conclusion that the drug effects must be regarded as organic psychoses. As he points out, the differentiation between these conditions is subtle, and better understanding of the relationships between symptoms in the total economy of the subjects' transactions is needed.

A number of studies are in progress in several laboratories on modifications of function of certain parts of the nervous system by drugs. Some of these are concerned with whole sub-systems such as neocortex, reticular formation, etc.; a few are concerned with single neurones in particular nuclei. Data from all these areas will be necessary to answer many of the problems Doctor Hoch has raised, just as in anatomy we have proceeded from the form of the body in movement by the early artists to gross, microscopic and now sub-microscopic observations. The addition of new tools, such as particular pharmacologic agents, is one of the more important steps in our progress.

Doctor Cattell and Doctor Pennes have provided convincing evidence of the importance not only of personal factors, but also of the transaction in which the person is engaged for determining the psychological responses to a wide variety of drugs. Their findings suggest that it would be valuable to conduct experiments in which the drugs were introduced during the course of a variety of "real life" situations in addition to the controlled laboratory tests, in order further to investigate current and immediately anticipated environmental factors in structuring behavior.

The interpretation of so-called conscious phenomena, either in the form of verbal behavior or in the form of feelings, moods, delusions, or hallucinations, is extremely difficult. It seems to me that these all belong to the class of *anticipatory* behavior and are related to the problem of maintaining spatial and temporal stability of the transaction between the subject and the environment—the latter of which, for man, is almost entirely interpersonally defined. I should like to call attention here to the analysis of symbolic behavior in patients with brain injury by Doctor Edwin Weinstein for its bearing on these problems. Following brain injury many patients show symptoms analogous to those which have been described this afternoon. The changes in symbolic behavior, including most of what is frequently dismissed as amnesia, confusion, confabulation, etc., are organized in integrated patterns related to earlier value systems of communication and to current problems.

Doctor Lesse's observations on stimulation of the temporal lobes add further evidence to the conclusion that Penfield's "memory phenomenon" is related to the conditions which result in epileptic seizures in the temporal areas. His observation that symptomatic changes observed during frontal leucotomy are delayed for as long as five minutes following the section of the connections to the frontal cortex raises a number of interesting speculations. It would at least indicate that the fibers sectioned are not a necessary part of the anatomical substrata mediating the functions which were observed, like anxiety or tension, but that they only secondarily affected these symptoms.

It seems clear that in the study of behavior we are leaving the era of mythologically and philosophically derived functions and are entering the period of biological description and operational definition. With the change in methods of investigation certain aspects of the attitudes of investigators to the subject matter will have to change. The problem of learning to trust tools and artifactual indicators is not an easy one with our tendency to over- or under-estimate their potency and significance. The experimental approach to psychiatric problems represented by the careful and critical studies presented here promises much for the future. Not of less value is their further emphasis that psychopathology is a natural phenomenon and not a "sacred disease."

By SIDNEY MALITZ, M.D.*

THE PAPERS PRESENTED HERE encompass a dynamic and exciting phase of present day psychiatric research. Through the use of appropriate tools in the form of selected drugs and psychosurgical procedures in the waking state, we are now able to produce model psychoses and alter behavior in the crucible of the present so that reactions to stress can be readily induced, intensified, or ameliorated and then carefully studied over the time span of their development. This has obvious advantages over the perusal of static anamnestic

* Department of Experimental Psychiatry, New York State Psychiatric Institute and Department of Psychiatry, Columbia University.

data in an attempt to reconstruct the dynamics of the past although the value of the latter remains unquestioned.

We must be very careful, however, to familiarize ourselves with the limitations and eccentricities of our tools and techniques and with the extent of our goals. Doctor Hoch has pointed out that the toxic states produced by drugs like mescaline and d-LSD$_{25}$, while actually "psychoses" by definition (as a result of their impairment of ego functioning, reality appraisal, and mental integration) still only *approximate* schizophrenia—as all models only approximate the original items they attempt to copy. Just as we learn from other models and eventually replace them with newer and truer models, so can we benefit from the production and study of schizophrenia-like states.

Doctor Hoch has pointed out a number of clear-cut similarities and differences between the model and the original in drug-induced schizophrenia-like states. He has also focussed on the fuzzy, nebulous area of shaded over-lap between schizophrenia and experimental psychosis; the subtle similarities from which our greatest knowledge may yet be obtained if we sharpen and refine our instruments of investigation. The whole problem of quantitative and qualitative differences between schizophrenia and drug-induced psychotic states discussed by Doctor Hoch should also be made clearer by more sensitive refinements in biochemical, neurophysiological, psychodynamic, and biometric techniques.

Discrepancies in the work of various investigators, as Doctor Hoch points out, may be due to psychological or metabolic differences in individuals being tested, to variations produced by administering differing quantities of drug, or more likely to the interaction of all of these together.

Touching on the problems of drug experiments with animals, he points out the differences in structure between the human and animal nervous systems, the difficulty in assessing so-called "emotional response" in animals, and the impossibility of obtaining the confirmatory evidence of subjective homeostatic disturbances usually communicated through speech.

Doctor Cattell has stressed the dangers inherent in using a research tool as an accepted technique of psychotherapy. In our enthusiasm for new means to alleviate emotional anguish we may delude ourselves into thinking that the investigative instrument is also the cure. As he has further pointed out, taking for granted concepts most in need of validation may contribute to this error.

Doctor Pennes and Doctor Cattell have both carefully delineated some of the more important problems in assessing any drug action. Three major factors always to be considered are the following:

1. The direct toxic and metabolic action of the drug.

2. The personality pattern of the patient, which will determine his individual reaction to stress.

3. The influence of the experimental milieu, which includes the physical setting of the experiment, the interaction between the patient and investigator, and the expectation and unintentional bias of the experimenter.

Many other variables are involved, some of which we are aware of but many of which we are not. One of the problems of future research will be to ferret out and limit these variables as much as possible.

Doctor Pennes, by examining his data in terms of normalization and intensification of symptoms, has utilized yet another tool in the multifaceted approach to effects of drugs on the psyche. Since his results tend to corroborate data collected by other investigators using different methods of handling and treatment—in terms of content of productions, the psychic structure, or individual drug effects, for example—another rubric of cross-validation has been added to our knowledge.

Doctor Lesse, in his paper, has succinctly delineated for us the opposing theories that attempt to explain the action of psychosurgery in alleviating anxiety. One assumes that the more cortical tissue cut the greater the relief. The other states that there are selective fiber groups in the frontal lobes more significant than others.

At the present time, owing to our lack of knowledge of the neurophysiologic and psychodynamic significance of some of these tracts and even of their location in some instances, we are still governed in our clinical judgment by equating in a direct ratio the amount of cortex to be cut with the degree of anxiety. Thus if a patient is considered severely anxious, a more extensive surgical procedure is usually performed than if he were less anxious. Continued neurophysiologic and psychiatric investigation through stimulation of the cortex in the waking state during psychosurgery may someday reward us with a long sought-after goal: maximal control of anxiety with minimal destruction of brain tissue.

Doctor Lesse has chosen to divide manifestations of anxiety seen during lobotomy into motor, affectual, and verbal components. He has noted that they disappear in that same order when the frontal lobes are cut. We might speculate that the reason for this sequence could be a lack of conscious awareness of the lessened anxiety until the motor and affective components have been first relieved and that this quantitative summation was sufficient to penetrate awareness. This would then account for verbalization, which is the loudspeaker of conscious awareness, coming last. But the explanation may even be more complex than that or more directly dependent on the total amount of brain cut, as Doctor Lesse seems to imply.

In regard to the alleviation of hallucinations following surgery reported by Doctor Lesse, we do not feel there are specific localized centers for these phenomena in the brain although at least one investigator has theorized about the temporal lobe being the center for auditory hallucinations.

It is our hypothesis that the phenomena of hallucinations are highly complex and involve still unknown neurophysiological and biochemical changes occurring diffusely throughout the brain. Therefore when diminution of hallucinatory phenomenon has occurred following lobotomy, we do not consider it the direct result of cutting a specific center or fiber bundle, but rather an indirect phenomena secondary to the primary reduction of anxiety accomplished by the surgery which then sets in motion the reversal or neutralization of the undiscovered neurophysiologic or biochemical processes that originally produced the hallucinations.

Doctor Lesse cites the mounting body of evidence from the literature that cutting the dorsolateral cortex is one of the major causes of personality change following pre-frontal lobotomy. This may well prove true, but it is important to keep in mind that the whole subject of personality change following psychosurgery is still controversial. In many instances what appears to be personality change after operation may actually be an uninterrupted progression of the patient's underlying mental illness which continues despite operation. This is often overlooked. The patients we have seen operated on in recent years have been very well preserved and no gross evidence of personality change could be detected in any of them a year after operation.

There is no doubt that in the near future concerted attempts will be made to consolidate the methods of drug research with those of psychosurgical investigation. It is entirely feasible to administer substances such as mescaline and d-LSD$_{25}$ to a lobotomy candidate preoperatively and then to study the effect of cutting various cortical and subcortical pathways on the development and alteration of an experimental psychosis. Such research may bring us one step closer to our ultimate understanding of mental illness.

APPENDIX

OFFICIAL MEMBERSHIP LIST OF THE AMERICAN PSYCHOPATHOLOGICAL ASSOCIATION

E. Stanley Abbot, M.D.*
P.O. Box 119
Wayland, Massachusetts

Theodora M. Abel, Ph.D.
815 Park Avenue
New York, New York

David Abrahamsen, M.D.
1035 Fifth Avenue
New York 28, New York

Nathan Ackerman, M.D.
42 East 78th Street
New York 21, New York

Alexandra Adler, M.D.
32 East 39th Street
New York 16, New York

Leo Alexander, M.D.
433 Marlboro Street
Boston, Massachusetts

Edward B. Allen, M.D.
P.O. Box 561
Brunswick, Maine

George S. Amsden, M.D.*
Acworth, New Hampshire

Victor V. Anderson, M.D.*
Anderson School
Staatsburg, New York

Lesile R. Angus, M.D.
138 Greenwood Avenue
Jenkintown, Pennsylvania

Irma Bache, M.D.
1 East 368
The Pentagon
Washington, D.C.

Lauretta Bender, M.D.
140 W. 16th Street
New York 11, New York

Daniel Blain, M.D.
American Psychiatric Association
3126 Woodley Road, N.W.
Washington 8, D.C.

Albert N. Browne-Mayers, M.D.
55 E. 86th Street
New York 28, New York

A. Louise Brush, M.D.
55 East 86th Street
New York, New York

Dexter M. Bullard, M.D.
Chestnut Lodge Sanitarium
Rockville, Maryland

Ernest W. Burgess, Ph.D.
University of Chicago
1126 East 59th Street
Chicago 37, Illinois

Asterisk indicates Associate Member.

263

Donald Ewen Cameron, M.D.
1025 Pine Avenue, W.
Montreal 2, Canada

Norman Cameron, M.D.
Northford, Connecticut

Carl D. Camp, M.D.*
304 South State Street
Ann Arbor, Michigan

Douglas G. Campbell, M.D.
490 Post Street
San Francisco, California

G. Colket Caner, M.D.
63 Marlboro Street
Boston, Massachusetts

Edward J. Carroll, M.D.
121 University Place
Pittsburgh, Pennsylvania

Brock Chisholm, M.D.†
World Health Organization
Geneva, Switzerland

Robert Clark, M.D.
Friends Hospital,
Roosevelt Blvd. & Adams Avenue
Philadelphia 24, Pennsylvania

Hollis E. Clow, M.D.
121 Westchester Avenue
White Plains, New York

Eugene Davidoff, M.D.
1101 Nott Street
Schenectady 8, New York

Oskar Diethelm, M.D.
525 East 68th Street
New York 21, New York

John M. Dorsey, M.D.
1401 Rivard Street
Detroit 7, Michigan

Roy M. Dorcus, Ph.D.
University of California
Los Angeles 24, California

Franklin Smith DuBois, M.D.
Silver Hill Foundation
Valley Road
New Canaan, Connecticut

H. Flanders Dunbar, M.D.
1 East 69th Street
New York, New York

William W. Elgin, M.D.
Sheppard and Enoch Pratt Hospital
Towson 4, Maryland

Milton H. Erickson, M.D.
32 West Cypress
Phoenix, Arizona

Robert H. Felix, M.D.
National Institute of Mental Health
U.S. Public Health Service
Bethesda 14, Maryland

Arthur N. Foxe, M.D.
25 West 54th Street
New York 19, New York

Jerome D. Frank, M.D.
Johns Hopkins Hospital
School of Medicine
Baltimore 5, Maryland

Richard L. Frank, M.D.
745 Fifth Avenue
New York, New York

† *Dagger indicates Honorary Member*

Fritz A. Freyhan, M.D.
Farnhurst, Delaware

Frieda Fromm-Reichmann, M.D.
Chestnut Lodge Sanitarium
Rockville, Maryland

Daniel H. Funkenstein, M.D.
74 Fenwood Road
Boston 14, Massachusetts

William Goldfarb, M.D.
Ittleson Center for Child Research
5050 Iselin Avenue
Riverdale 71, New York

William Horsley Gantt, M.D.
Johns Hopkins Hospital
Baltimore 5, Maryland

Francis J. Gerty, M.D.
University of Illinois
College of Medicine
912 South Wood Street
Chicago, Illinois

Arnold Gesell, M.D., Ph.D.
185 Edwards Street
New Haven, Connecticut

Bernard Glueck, M.D.
7 Parkway Road
Briarcliff, New York

Bernard Glueck, Jr., M.D.
Department of Psychiatry
University Hospitals
Minneapolis, Minnesota

Jacques Gottlieb, M.D.
Lafayette Clinic
951 E. Lafayette Street
Detroit 7, Michigan

Ernest M. Gruenberg, M.D.
746 Irving Avenue
Syracuse 10, New York

Roscoe W. Hall, M.D.
St. Elizabeth's Hospital
Washington, D.C.

Volta R. Hall, M.D.
422 Beacon Street
Boston, Massachusetts

A. Irving Hallowell, Ph.D.
Box 14, Bennet Hall
University of Pennsylvania
Philadelphia, Pennsylvania

Donald M. Hamilton, M.D.
121 Westchester Avenue
White Plains, New York

Irving B. Harrison, M.D.
142 Garth Rd.
Scarsdale, New York

Harry H. Harter, M.D.
82-42 Kew Gardens Road
Kew Gardens 15, New York

Lynwood Heaver, M.D.
61 Irving Place
New York 3, New York

Morris Herman, M.D.
30 East 40th Street
New York, New York

Paul H. Hoch, M.D.
1165 Park Avenue
New York, New York

Leslie B. Hohman, M.D.
Duke Medical School
Durham, North Carolina

Justin Morrill Hope, M.D.
New England Center Hospital
Boston, Massachusetts

William A. Horwitz, M.D.
722 West 168th Street
New York 32, New York

Joseph Hughes, M.D.
111 North Forty-Ninth Street
Philadelphia 39, Pennsylvania

William A. Hunt, Ph.D.
Northwestern University
Evanston, Illinois

George A. Jervis, M.D., Ph.D.
Letchworth Village
Research Department
Thiells, Rockland County, New York

Ernest Jones, M.D.†
The Plat, Elsted,
N. Midhurst,
Sussex, England

Lothar B. Kalinowsky, M.D.
115 East 82nd Street
New York, New York

Franz J. Kallmann, M.D.
722 West 168th Street
New York, New York

Abram Kardiner, M.D.
1100 Park Avenue
New York, New York

Solomon Katzenelbogen, M.D.
The Woodner
16th Street, Spring Road, N.W.
Washington, D.C.

Edward J. Kempf, M.D.
Wading River, New York

Isabelle V. Kendig, Ph.D.
Ashton, Maryland

Richard D. Kepner, M.D.
P.O. Box 3119
Honolulu 2, Hawaii

Lawrence Kolb, M.D.
6645 32nd N.W.
Washington 15, D.C.

David M. Levy, M.D.
15 East 91st Street
New York, New York

Nolan D. C. Lewis, M. D.
Neuropsychiatric Institute
Princeton, New Jersey

William T. Lhamon, M.D.
1 Blalock Circle
Houston, Texas

Vladimir Theodore Liberson, M.D.
62 Roslyn Street
Hartford, Connecticut

Howard S. Liddell, Ph.D.
Department of Psychology
Cornell University
Ithaca, New York

Reginald S. Lourie, M.D.
Children's Hospital
Washington 9, D.C.

Lawson Lowrey, M.D.
25 West 54th Street
New York 19, New York
also
2 Topland Road
Hartsdale, New York

John G. Lynn, M.D.
305 Royal Hawaiian Ave.
Honolulu 15, Hawaii

Charles A. McDonald, M.D.*
106 Waterman Street
Providence 6, Rhode Island

Edwin E. McNiel, M.D.*
3875 Wilshire Boulevard
Los Angeles 5, California

Donald J. MacPherson, M.D.
270 Commonwealth Avenue
Boston 16, Massachusetts

Benjamin Malzberg, Ph.D.
New York State Department of
  Mental Hygiene
Albany, New York

Edward E. Mayer, M.D.*
5601 Forbes Street
Pittsburgh 17, Pennsylvania

William C. Menninger, M.D.
Menninger Foundation
Topeka, Kansas

Joseph S. A. Miller, M.D.
Hillside Hospital
Glen Oaks, Long Island, New York

John A. P. Millet, M.D.
25 East 92nd Street
New York 28, New York

J. Allison Montague, Ph.D.
25 East 10th Street
New York 3, New York

Merrill Moore, M.D.
382 Commonwealth Avenue
Boston 15, Massachusetts

Thomas Verner Moore, M.D., Ph.D.†
Carthusian Foundation in America, Inc.
Sky Farm
Whitingham, Vermont

Harry Merrill Murdock, M.D.
Sheppard and Enoch Pratt Hospital
Towson 4, Maryland

Henry A. Murray, M.D., Ph.D.*
48 Mount Auburn Street
Cambridge, Massachusetts

Leo P. O'Donnell, M.D.
Harlam Valley Hospital
Wingdale, New York

Raymond L. Osborne, M.D.
140 East 54th Street
New York 22, New York

Winfred Overholser, M.D.
St. Elizabeth's Hospital
Washington 20, D.C.

Grosvenor B. Pearson, M.D.
5555 Forbes Street
Pittsburgh 19, Pennsylvania

Harris B. Peck, M.D.
135 East 22nd St.
New York, New York

Zygmunt A. Piotrowski, Ph.D.
New Jersey Neuropsychiatric Institute
Skillman, New Jersey

Phillip Polatin, M.D.
722 West 168th Street
New York 32, New York

Hyman L. Rachlin, M.D.
33 East 39th Street
New York, New York

Sandor Rado, M.D.
50 East 78th Street
New York, New York

George N. Raines, Captain (MC) USN
U. S. Naval Hospital
Portsmouth, Virginia

John L. Smalldon, M.D.
Norwich State Hospital
Norwich, Connecticut

Evelyn B. Reichenbach, M.D.
St. Elizabeth's Hospital
Washington, D.C.

George W. Smeltz, M.D.
Chalfonte Hotel
Atlantic City, New Jersey

David McK. Rioch, M.D.
Neuropsychiatric Division
Walter Reed Medical Center
Washington 12, D.C.

Lauren H. Smith, M.D.
111 North 49th Street
Philadelphia, Pennsylvania

Margaret Rioch, M.D.
4607 Dorset Avenue
Chevy Chase 15, Maryland

Harry C. Solomon, M.D.
74 Fenwood Road
Boston, Massachusetts

Fred V. Rockwell, M.D.
Grasslands Hospital
Valhalla, New York

Rene A. Spitz, M.D.
1150 Fifth Avenue
New York 28, New York

Howard P. Rome, M.D.
Mayo Clinic
Rochester, Minnesota

Edward J. Stainbrook, M.D., Ph.D.
University Hospital
150 Marshall Street
Syracuse, New York

Theodore Rothman, M.D.
444 North Bedford Drive
Beverly Hills, California

Charles W. Stephenson, M.D.
South Hero, Vermont

William S. Sadler, M.D.*
533 Diversey Parkway
Chicago, Illinois

Gregory Stragnell, M.D.
2314 La Mesa Drive
Santa Monica, California

G. Wilson Schaffer, Ph.D.
Johns Hopkins University
Baltimore, Maryland

Joseph G. Sutton, M.D.
Essex County Overbrook Hospital
Cedar Grove, New Jersey

David Shakow, Ph.D.*
National Institute of Mental Health
U. S. Public Health Service
Bethesda, Maryland

Hans C. Syz, M.D.
The Lifwynn Foundation
Westport, Connecticut

Alexander Simon, M.D.*
Langley Porter Clinic
San Francisco, California

William S. Taylor, Ph.D.
55 Dryads Green
Northampton, Massachusetts

Harry A. Teitelbaum, M.D.
1801 Eutaw Place
Baltimore, Maryland

William B. Terhune, M.D.
Box D
New Canaan, Connecticut

Charles B. Thompson, M.D.
The Lifwynn Foundation
Westport, Connecticut

Clara Thompson, M.D.
12 East 86th Street
New York, New York

Kenneth J. Tillotson, M.D.*
1265 Beacon Street
Brookline, Massachusetts

Vladimir G. Urse, M.D.*
1447 Keystone Avenue
River Forest, Illinois

Roy McL. Van Wart, M.D.*
10431 Bellagio Road
Los Angeles 24, California

Heinrich B. Waelsch, M.D., Sc.D.
722 West 168th Street
New York 32, New York

Raymond W. Waggoner, M.D.
University Hospital
1313 East Ann Street
Ann Arbor, Michigan

James Hardin Wall, M.D.
121 Westchester Avenue
White Plains, New York

George A. Waterman, M.D.*
200 Beacon Street
Boston, Massachusetts

David Wechsler, Ph.D.
Bellevue Hospital
New York, New York

Livingston Welch, Ph.D.
Hunter College
Park Avenue & 68th Street
New York, New York

Frederic Lyman Wells, Ph.D.*
19 Bowdoin Street
Newton Highlands 61, Massachusetts

Louis Wender, M.D.
59 East 79th Street
New York, New York

Frederick L. Weniger, M.D.
3811 O'Hara Street
Pittsburgh 13, Pennsylvania

Mary Alice White, Ph.D.
121 Westchester Avenue
White Plains, New York

Robert W. White, Ph.D.
Department of Social Relations
Harvard University
Cambridge, Massachusetts

John C. Whitehorn, M.D.
Johns Hopkins Hospital
Baltimore 5, Maryland

Cornelius C. Wholey, M.D.*
121 University Place
Pittsburgh, Pennsylvania

Robert S. Wigton, M.D.*
105 S. 49th Street
Omaha 3, Nebraska

George B. Wilbur, M.D.*
South Dennis, Massachusetts

Emanuel Windholz, M.D.
2235 Post Street
San Francisco 15, California

Lawrence Woolley, M.D.
490 Peachtree Street
Atlanta, Georgia

Cecil L. Wittson, M.D.
415 North 61st Street
Omaha 5, Nebraska

S. Bernard Wortis, M.D.
410 East 57th Street
New York, New York

Lewis R. Wolberg, M.D.
55 East 86th Street
New York, New York

Joseph Zubin, Ph.D.
722 West 168th Street
New York 32, New York

PAST AND PRESENT OFFICERS OF THE AMERICAN PSYCHOPATHOLOGICAL ASSOCIATION

Presidents

1912	Adolf Meyer	1936	Nolan D. C. Lewis
1913	James T. Putnam	1937	Nolan D. C. Lewis
1914	Alfred R. Allen	1938	Samuel W. Hamilton
1915	Alfred R. Allen	1939	Abraham Myerson
1916	Adolf Meyer	1940	Douglas A. Thom
1917	Adolf Meyer	1941	Roscoe W. Hall
1918	Smith Ely Jelliffe	1942	Roscoe W. Hall
1921	William A. White	1943	Frederick L. Wells
1922	John T. MacCurdy	1944	Frederick L. Wells
1923	L. Pierce Clark	1945	Bernard Glueck
1924	L. Pierce Clark	1946	Robert P. Knight
1925	Albert M. Barrett	1947	Frederick L. Wells
1927	Sanger Brown, II	1948	Donald J. MacPherson
1928	Ross McC. Chapman	1949	Paul Hoch
1929	Ross McC. Chapman	1950	William B. Terhune
1930	William Healy	1951	Lauren H. Smith
1931	William Healy	1952	Joseph Zubin
1932	J. Ramsay Hunt	1953	Clarence P. Oberndorf
1933	Edward J. Kempf	1954	David McK. Rioch
1934	Edward J. Kempf	1955	Merrill Moore
1935	Nolan D. C. Lewis		

Vice Presidents

1924	William Healy	1928	Edward J. Kempf
	George H. Kirby		E. Stanley Abbot
1925	J. Ramsay Hunt	1929	Edward J. Kempf
	Sidney I. Schwab		E. Stanley Abbot
1927	Ross McC. Chapman	1930	J. Ramsay Hunt
	Edward J. Kempf		Herman N. Adler

1931 J. Ramsay Hunt
     Herman N. Adler
1933 Albert M. Barrett
     Trigant Burrow
1934 Albert M. Barrett
     Trigant Burrow
1935 J. Ramsay Hunt
     Smith Ely Jelliffe
1936 J. Ramsay Hunt
     Smith Ely Jelliffe
1937 Samuel W. Hamilton
     Ray G. Hoskins
1938 Lydiard H. Horton
     Hans Syz
1939 Roscoe W. Hall
     Douglas A. Thom
1940 George S. Sprague
     Bernard Glueck
1941 Frederick L. Wells
     Lowell S. Selling
1942 Frederick L. Wells
     Lowell S. Selling
1943 Lowell S. Selling
     Flanders Dunbar

1944 Lowell S. Selling
     Flanders Dunbar
1945 Thomas V. Moore
     Robert P. Knight
1946 Paul H. Hoch
     Thos. A. C. Rennie
1947 William C. Menninger
     Ruth Benedict
1948 Ruth Benedict
     Lauren H. Smith
1949 Arthur N. Foxe
     Norman Cameron
1950 Harry M. Murdock
     William S. Taylor
1951 Harry M. Murdock
     Lauretta Bender
1952 William Horwitz
     S. Bernard Wortis
1953 David McK. Rioch
     Merrill Moore
1954 Merrill Moore
     Howard S. Liddell
1955 Oskar Diethelm
     Howard S. Liddell

Secretaries

1921 H. W. Frink
1922 Sanger Brown, II
1923 Sanger Brown, II
1924 Sanger Brown, II
1925 Sanger Brown, II
1926 Sanger Brown, II
1927 Martin W. Peck
1928 Martin W. Peck
1929 Martin W. Peck
1930 L. Eugene Emerson
1931 L. Eugene Emerson
1932 L. Eugene Emerson
1933 L. Eugene Emerson
1934 L. Eugene Emerson
1935 L. Eugene Emerson
1936 L. Eugene Emerson
1937 L. Eugene Emerson
1938 L. Eugene Emerson

1939 L. Eugene Emerson
1940 Merrill Moore
1941 Merrill Moore
1942 Merrill Moore
1943 Merrill Moore
1944 Samuel W. Hamilton
1945 Samuel W. Hamilton
1946 Samuel W. Hamilton
1947 Samuel W. Hamilton
1948 Samuel W. Hamilton
1949 Samuel W. Hamilton
1950 Samuel W. Hamilton
1951 Samuel W. Hamilton
1952 Donald M. Hamilton
1953 Donald M. Hamilton
1954 Donald M. Hamilton
1955 Donald M. Hamilton

Treasurers

1924	William C. Garvin		1940	William C. Garvin
1925	William C. Garvin		1941	William C. Garvin
1926	William C. Garvin		1942	William C. Garvin
1927	William C. Garvin		1943	Joseph Zubin
1928	William C. Garvin		1944	Joseph Zubin
1929	William C. Garvin		1945	Joseph Zubin
1930	William C. Garvin		1946	Joseph Zubin
1931	William C. Garvin		1947	Joseph Zubin
1932	William C. Garvin		1948	Joseph Zubin
1933	William C. Garvin		1949	Joseph Zubin
1934	William C. Garvin		1950	Joseph Zubin
1935	William C. Garvin		1951	Joseph Zubin
1936	William C. Garvin		1952	Bernard Glueck, Jr.
1937	William C. Garvin		1953	Bernard Glueck, Jr.
1938	William C. Garvin		1954	Bernard Glueck, Jr.
1939	William C. Garvin		1955	Bernard Glueck, Jr.

INDEX